Walking in Portugal

2nd edition

Bethan Davies
&
Ben Cole

Pili
Pala
Press

Walking in Portugal
2nd edition 2000

Published by
Pili Pala Press
7a Athenaeum Street, The Hoe, Plymouth PL1 2RQ
www.pilipalapress.com

First edition 1994 published by Footprint Guides

Printed in Great Britain by
MPG Books Ltd
Victoria Square
Bodmin
Cornwall
PL31 1EB

British Library Cataloguing in Publication Data
A catalogue record for this book is available at the British Library

ISBN 0 9522668 1 4

We've tried to make the information in this guide as accurate as possible,
but the authors and Pili Pala Press accept no responsibility for any loss,
injury or inconvenience sustained by any person using this book.

Walking in Portugal

2nd edition

Thank you

Thanks to everyone who helped put *Walking in Portugal* together.

Kerry Davies & Sharon King for additional research and great company. Staff in all the tourist offices throughout Portugal, particularly in Ponte de Lima, who answered our questions and humoured our bad Portuguese. The drivers of Portugal who didn't hit us as we cycled along. Maria and Jorge Afonso who drove us to the nearest bike shop from the middle of nowhere, and Carlos Pereira, who made himself late for lunch by fixing the bike. João Isabel for pointing out the defensive frailties of Braga FC. Cristina Gonçalves at Gouveia who let us sleep in the shed when the campsite flooded. Kathrin Klemm for the lowdown on Portugal's natural park system. Amy and Amber at Eagle Creek for the free travel gadgets.

ICN in Portugal for letting us use their park symbols. Carmen Mills & Terry Sunderland for putting up with endless design questions. Shirley Lew, Graham Giles, Derek Anderson, Marc Stewart and especially Michael Harling for proofreading: all the mistakes are their fault. Jason Addy, Vanessa DiCicco, Johan Groebner, Edwin Luciano, Alison Roy, Cudrah & Clive. Tony McCurdy for encouragement, proofreading & forgiving our absence.

And to our parents, for love, support, storage and banking.

About Pili Pala Press

Pili Pala Press emerged from the chrysalis of Footprint Guides in time for a new millenium. (Pili pala, for the uninitiated, is Welsh for butterfly.) We try to cover walking destinations that are overlooked and forgotten, and hope that you'll use our guides to discover, enjoy and respect the outdoors. For each book sold, we donate 50p to enviromental organizations in Portugal.

Trails become overgrown, quiet lanes become main roads, and pensões close down. Drop us a line if you find something new or different, and check out our website for updates.
www.pilipalapress.com
7A Athenaeum Street, The Hoe, Plymouth PL1 2RQ

Contents

How This Guide Works

Glimpse of Portugal (p 2)

Background information about walking, geography, food & drink, history and the arts.

Flora (p 13) & Fauna (p 16)

English, Portuguese and Latin names of birds, mammals, reptiles, amphibians and trees. Includes detailed identification tips, quirky facts and illustrations.

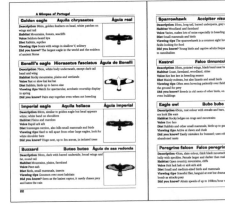

Area chapters (p 32)

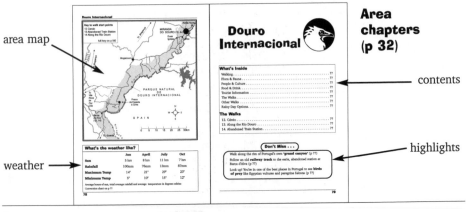

area map

Douro Internacional

What's Inside

contents

What's the weather like?

weather

Don't Miss . . .

highlights

Area chapters (p 32)

area symbol

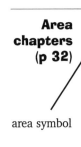

regional flora & fauna, people & culture, food & drink & tourist information

---

fast facts

walk highlights

walk description

Area chapters (p 32) walk descriptions

Walking maps (centre pages)
Full-colour maps with contours, rivers, roads, tracks & places of interest

key to walking routes, cross-referenced to walk description pages

Map of Portugal

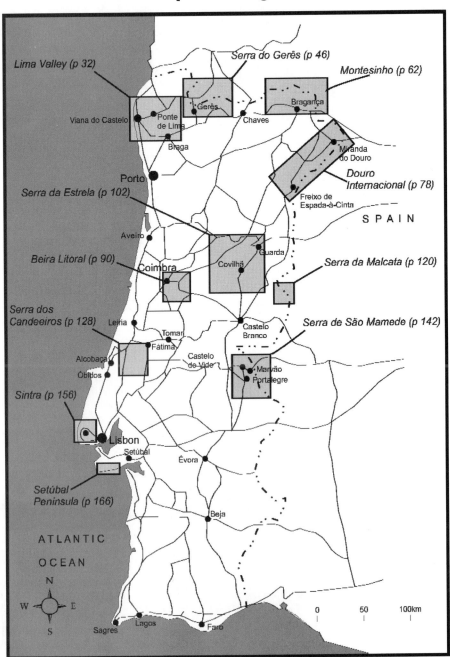

An Introduction to Portugal

Portugal lies in the southwestern-most corner of Europe, open to the Atlantic on two sides and hemmed in by Spain to the north and east along the longest land border in Europe. Constant battles with its larger Iberian neighbour and a spirit of adventure led Portugal to spend the last few centuries looking outwards to the Atlantic, voyaging to the Americas, Africa and Asia and spreading her language and culture across the globe. Emerging from four decades of insular dictatorship in the 1970s, the country's gaze turned inland towards Europe, and today Portugal is one of the strongest supporters of the European Union.

Walking in Portugal remains, for most visitors, a brief stroll along a beach in the Algarve before dinner, and more than 60% of overseas tourists head for the sea and sand of the country's over-developed southern coast. Outside this tourist mecca, Portugal is a country of contrasting landscapes. In the northwest, the striking green Minho region vibrates with the energy of local festivals and markets. Further east, the isolated Trás-os-Montes is dotted with ancient villages linked by well-trodden farm tracks. Travel south for about 150km and you'll reach Portugal's highest and most dramatic mountain range, the Serra da Estrela, which provides the country's most challenging hikes amidst bare plateaus that slide away into lush valleys. Elsewhere in Portugal, the scenery may be less grand, but the walking is always a pleasure, whether you're ambling around the Alentejo looking at megalithic ruins or wandering next to the Douro river along an abandoned railway line.

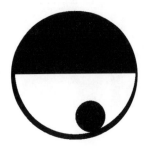

A Glimpse of Portugal

Walking

W alking for pleasure has never been a popular Portuguese pastime, and visiting hikers will be seen as a little soft in the head. Perhaps the Portuguese have been too engrossed in looking for overseas treasures to pay much attention to potential discoveries closer to home. By the time Cântaro Magro, a spire-like peak in the Serra da Estrela, was climbed in 1881, the Portuguese had been in India for almost four centuries.

This is not to say that the Portuguese don't walk. Despite the efforts of the national government and the European Union to modernize agriculture, there are still large pockets of land where subsistence farming is the norm and it's rare to see a tractor or combine harvester. To many farmers in rural Portugal, walking is the only means of transportation between villages and fields, and even a four-wheel drive won't help get your sheep to the high mountain pastures. This walking is generally a practical necessity rather than a principled choice, and if transportation is available, whether it's a daily bus or a lift in a neighbour's car, then locals see no sense in turning down the offer.

Think about it. Most Portuguese who walk do so to make a living, to buy food or to visit friends. You're travelling hundreds of miles just to walk around for a few hours and end up exactly where you started. Who's crazy here?

Aside from being treated as an eccentric foreigner, the lack of fellow walkers does present some practical problems. Walking boots, camping equipment and dried food are hard to come by, and there are very few specialist outdoor shops. Many maps are hopelessly out-of-date, and trail maintenance is practically non-existent. Turismos (tourist offices) and park offices have little or no printed information on local walks, and staff are unlikely to have any practical experience of walking.

However irritating some of these problems may prove, the benefits of Portuguese indifference to organized walking are tremendous. To anyone who has walked the Pennine Way in high season or trekked on a group tour in Nepal, the isolation of Portugal's mountain walking trails is a stunning, enlightening experience. Even in the most popular natural parks, you'll only need to walk a couple of kilometres to be entirely alone. The lack of noise makes birdwatching easier, and there's also a chance that you may glimpse one of the many shy mammals that live in Portugal.

Having said all this, Portugal is slowly getting used to the idea of walking as a leisure activity. More and more overseas operators are including Portugal in their brochures, and local tour companies are springing up across the country. Closer to the big cities, hiking is taking hold as an escape from urban drudgery, and areas like the Serra da Arrábida, just south of Lisbon, are attracting independent Portuguese walkers.

 Trails

Simply put, trail condition depends on the level of local use; if it's well-used, then it's well-worn. There's very little maintenance of natural park paths, although the Serra da Estrela does occasionally re-mark and clear its network of walking routes.

Agricultural modernization and economic development are having a major impact on the existence and quality of trails. In the 1980s and 1990s, both the national government and the European Union ploughed vast amounts of money into improving the country's infrastructure. Portugal is now well-set on an ambitious program of road building, and many tracks in and around rural villages are being paved and widened. Compounding this problem, rural people have been moving away from the countryside to big cities in Portugal, France and beyond. As villages and hamlets become depopulated, there's no one to walk the trails, and in a few short summers paths and tracks become overgrown and impassable.

Erosion is a problem on trails that pass through commercial forestry operations. As diverse deciduous forests are replaced by uniform blocks of pine and eucalyptus, there's no undergrowth to anchor the soil, and any rain just washes away another layer of countryside. It's a particular problem around the Serra da Arrábida in the south and Serra do Montesinho in the north, where tracks are severely rain-rutted.

Even in commercial plantations, there's very little restriction on where walkers can roam, and it's rare to see a path blocked by private property signs. Many of Portugal's farmers own only one field, and in some areas communitarian farming is still widespread, so the routes that link the fields and villages don't belong to a single farmer and are open to everyone.

Trail marking is becoming more uniform, with many parks and private tour operators using an equal sign (as in the symbol for this section) painted on posts, rocks or trees. Wrong turns are occasionally marked, usually by a painted X symbol. Yellow is the most popular colour on official trails, although tour companies and mountain bike race organizers use a rainbow of colours, which can get very confusing.

 Maps

There are two main topographic map producers in Portugal. The Instituto Geográfico do Exército (IGeoE), the army's geographic arm, publishes 1:25,000 and 1:50,000 maps, while the civilian Instituto Português de Cartográfia e Cadastro (IPCC) publishes 1:50,000 maps only. In this book we refer to IGeoE maps as military and IPCC maps as civilian.

Up until the 1990s, almost all the topographic maps available were so old as to be virtually useless. The IGeoE started systematically updating its 1:25,000 maps about a decade ago, although redoing the military 1:50,000 series seems to be less of a priority. The civilian 1:50,000 maps are even more outdated, and there are a few gems that have survived the 1950s.

Maps are generally accurate on tracks and trails, although roads have inevitably altered since the older maps were published, and you might suddenly be confronted with a reservoir or motorway where the map shows a pristine valley. Neither of the 1:50,000 series include paths much narrower than a car width, and while the 1:25,000 maps do include these in theory, in practice there are only one or two paths on each map.

In the last few years, IGeoE has started to get its act together, and the days when the complex bureaucracy involved in buying a single map could take hours off your day and years off your life are long gone. In its Lisbon headquarters, you can now walk in off the street (admittedly past armed security guards) and buy the map you want from a small, shop-like room. IGeoE headquarters are at Avenida Dr Alfredo Bensaúde in Lisbon (✆ 218 520063; www.igeoe.pt), open weekdays only. To get there, take the metro to Oriente, then jump on the #25 bus. Most of the military map series is also available in Livraria Porto Editora, a bookshop in Porto, at Praça Dona Filipa de Lencastre 42 (✆ 222 007681).

Bureaucracy is still rife in the civilian world. At IPCC headquarters, you must show ID, be issued with a security pass, and then request your map from a secretarial office. The IPCC is at 107 Rua da Artilharia Um, not far from Parque Eduardo VII (metro Parque;

✆ 213 819600; http://ipcc.pt) and is open weekdays only.

In Britain, Stanfords (12–14 Long Acre, London WC2E 9LP; ✆ (020) 7836 1321; e-mail sales@stanfords.co.uk) keeps some Portuguese topographical maps in stock, and can order both military and civilian versions with a month or two's notice. Information about maps needed for specific walks and places in this book is given in each chapter and at the start of each walk. For recommended maps of the whole country, see p 178, and for a translation of some common Portuguese map terms, see p 180.

Guided Walks

Rotas do Vento (Rua dos Lusíadas 5, Lisbon; ✆ 213 649852/9; fax 213 649843; e-mail rotas@rotasdovento.pt) offers reasonably-priced weekend hikes to destinations all over Portugal. Their excellent website (www.rotasdovento.pt) is bilingual and describes many of their walks in detail; you can also book online using their English language form.

Sistemas de Ar Livre or SAL (Avenida Manuel Maria Portela 40, Setúbal; ✆ 265 227685; e-mail sal@jgc.pt) organize remarkably cheap day walks, mainly in the Alentejo region. There's no need to book: just turn up at the right time and place and pay your money. You can find information on their website (www.sal.jgc.pt) or in leaflets in the turismo in Setúbal abut upcoming dates and destinations.

A few British companies offer tours of Portugal. Ramblers' Holidays (Box 43,

Welwyn Garden, Herts AL8 6PQ; ✆ (01707) 331133; fax (01707) 333276; e-mail info@ramblersholidays.co.uk) offers two-week holidays in the Douro valley, Alentejo and Minho. Explore Worldwide (1 Frederick Street, Aldershot, Hants GU11 1LQ; ✆ (01252) 760100; fax (01252) 760001; e-mail info@explore.co.uk) organizes a two-week walking tour of Portugal, taking in the Douro, Minho and Trás-os-Montes regions. HF Holidays (Imperial House, Edgware Road, London NW9 5AL; ✆ (020) 8905 9388; fax (020) 8905 0506; e-mail info@hfholidays.co.uk) combines sightseeing and walking in the Algarve and Sintra. Exodus' week-long holiday visits the Douro and Minho regions of the country (9 Weir Road, London SW12 0LT; ✆ (020) 8673 0859; fax (020) 8673 0779; e-mail sales@exodustravels.co.uk).

Naturetrek (The Cadcam Centre, Bighton, Nr Alresford, Hampshire SO24 9RE; ✆ (01962) 733051; fax (01962) 736426; e-mail sales@naturetrek.co.uk) focuses on the Algarve's flora and fauna in its week-long walking holiday guided by a naturalist. Winetrails (Greenways, Vann Lake, Ockley, Dorking RH5 5NT; ✆ (01306) 712111; e-mail sales@winetrails.co.uk) offers a five-night walking and wine-tasting itinerary in the Douro valley; the company's tours are self-guided.

 # Geography

Portugal is neatly divided in two by the Rio Tejo, which rises in Spain and washes into the sea at Lisbon, the country's national and cultural capital. South of this divide is the low-lying landscape of the Alentejo, Portugal's chief agricultural area, producing cork, olives and wheat.

The monotony of the southern plains is broken by beautiful mountain ranges such as the Serra de São Mamede in the east (p 142), and the Serra da Arrábida, just south of Lisbon on the Setúbal Peninsula (p 166). There's no danger of altitude sickness in these ranges: the highest point south of Lisbon, São Mamede, just sneaks over 1000m.

North of the Tejo, the land is higher and more varied, its mountain ranges the westernmost edge of a plateau that stretches from the French Pyrenees. Even so, Portugal is a low-lying country compared to its Spanish neighbour, and no mountain quite exceeds 2000m.

Torre, Portugal's highest mountain, lies in the Serra da Estrela, about half way between the Tejo and the Douro, Portugal's most important northern river. The Serra da Estrela is characterized by high plateaus of granite and schist, cut by deep, brilliant green valleys.

The Trás-os-Montes, in the northeast of the country, is made from similar stuff, but its isolated position within the country gives it more of a self-sufficient, frontier feel. Farming in both areas is small-scale and basic, and stone-walled smallholdings cling to the slopes of the stark landscape.

West of here, the more densely populated Minho region is Portugal's rainiest place. It's a more varied countryside, ranging from substantial vineyards surrounding elegant manor houses to tiny stone and tile villages.

Despite Portugal's inland delights, the country remains best known for its seaside, stretching for over 800km along its southern and western border. For more on regional geography, see the individual area chapters.

Environment

Portugal's environmental problems have gone largely unnoticed in the last few decades, both inside and outside the country. The few environmental groups that exist are very low key, and even national park staff have been slow to protest ecological damage.

As in much of Europe, Portugal's trees have been chopped down for centuries to make way for towns and clear fields for agriculture. In place of chestnuts and oaks, ugly tracts of pine were planted for quick and easy harvesting. Local consequences have been immense, reducing plant and animal diversity and contributing to soil erosion.

Dramatic as these changes are, they seem almost benign when compared to the devastating effect of widespread eucalyptus planting in the last couple of decades. Eucalyptus has been readily embraced by the forest industry, as it grows straight and fast and is ready for harvesting in about 10 years. The eucalyptus allows little to grow underneath its branches, and it guzzles scarce water at an alarming rate. The tree's insidious creep across the country is disturbing environmentalists and small-scale farmers alike. Portugal's enthusiastic adoption of European Union agricultural modernization has left the country's subsistence farmers with little recourse when their land is drained of water by huge, adjoining eucalyptus plantations. While the short-term economic benefits are hard to deny, the land is soon made sterile and unstable, unusable to future generations. It's an ugly sight: walk through a eucalyptus forest anywhere in Portugal and you'll see rivers of eroded soil and teetering trees whose exposed roots no longer provide an anchor for their slim trunks.

While soil runoff and fallen trees are clogging streams, rivers are being drained to irrigate the southern agricultural plains and to generate hydroelectric power. About half of Portugal's electricity comes from water power, and new reservoirs spring up annually. Portugal's mainly dry climate may be good for attracting tourists, but it can have drastic effects on its limited water supply. Most of the country's major rivers rise in Spain, an equally enthusiastic diverter of water. The Douro, Tejo and Guadiana rivers are being siphoned off to benefit Spanish agriculture, and conflict between the two countries over such a precious resource is coming to a head.

Water also bears the brunt of Portugal's ecological carelessness. Parts of the country's 800km long coastline and many of its major rivers have been ruined by industrial pollution, particularly around cities like Porto. Elsewhere along the coast, beaches and villages have been submerged under a tide of aggressive development. The Algarve is by far the most damaged area, but huge, ugly hotels and disgusting levels of litter mar the Tróia Peninsula near Setúbal and parts of the coast west of Sintra as well.

For more information on environmental issues in Portugal, contact Quercus, the National Association for the Conservation of Nature (℘ 217 788474; www.quercus.pt).

Parks & Reserves

There are more than 20 protected areas in Portugal, ranging from the vast Parque Natural da Serra da Estrela to the tiny Reserva Natural do Paúl de Arzila, a bird sanctuary not far from Coimbra. The Parque Nacional da Peneda-Gerês was the first area to be protected, created in the early 1970s in the dying days of the Salazar regime. Peneda-Gerês is also the most ecologically significant area. It's the only park deemed worthy of national status (the other parks are all called Parques Natural) by the World Conservation Union, largely due to its virgin deciduous forest north of Gerês, near the Spanish border.

All the protected areas come within the control of the Instituto da Conservação da Natureza (ICN). The parks are nominally controlled from ICN's head office in Lisbon, where there's little information available to the public (Rua da Lapa 73, Lisbon; ℘ 213 938900). The park's website (www.icn.pt) is an excellent source of information. It's in Portuguese and content varies from park to park, but you'll usually find information about regional flora and fauna, environmental concerns and local traditions.

In reality, each protected area is run as a fiefdom, independent of Lisbon and with dramatically different approaches to visitors and walkers. The Parque Nacional da Peneda-Gerês, for example, is reluctant to describe walking routes in case the region's fragile ecosystems are disturbed by lead-footed hikers, whereas parks such as the Serra da Estrela, Serra de São Mamede and Serras de Aire e Candeeiros map, mark and describe a varied network of trails.

Many areas have become protected too late, and cover stretches of land or coastline where pollution and industrial development have already taken hold. It's hard to believe that an area like the Sado Estuary, just south of Lisbon, is a natural reserve. Hotel complexes rise up from the Tróia Peninsula and industrial development scars the coast around Setúbal. Despite this, the reserve is a haven for storks and flamingos, and its coastal waters are home to a diminishing number of bottlenose dolphins.

Although organization can be haphazard, within Portugal's natural parks you'll find glorious, isolated scenery, unique natural and cultural attractions, and enough trails for months of walking.

When to Go

Portugal's weather is a complex blend of Mediterranean and Atlantic influences. The south of the country is hot in summer, mild in winter and dry year-round.

The Minho region in the country's northwest corner is famously rainy; the best time to visit is in the drier summer season, which also coincides with many of the region's lively festivals.

The Trás-os-Montes, further east, is divided into two distinct climactic zones. The northern part, called the terra fria (cold land), is always chilly in winter. Like the Minho, summers are generally warm, and may be the best time to visit. The terra quente (hot land), in the southern Trás-os-Montes, experiences wildly fluctuating weather; summers are long and blisteringly hot, winters very cold, so try to time a visit for spring or autumn.

There's little snow in Portugal, and the higher reaches of the Serra da Estrela are the only areas to get consistent snowfall. Summers are generally good in the Serra da Estrela, but come prepared for any weather, as fog and rain can creep up unexpectedly.

A climate chart for each area covered in this book, showing sun, rainfall and temperature, can be found on the first page of the area chapter.

People & Culture

History

Little is known of early Portuguese history, aside from some fabulous megalithic remains that show a thriving Neolithic culture, particularly around Gerês and in the Alentejo. Later settlers built hillforts or castros, most notably in the Trás-os-Montes, where strange-shaped mounds are the only evidence of the region's Iron Age peoples. Gradually, the hillforts grew more elaborate, until by around 700BC Celtic invaders refined the art into elaborate citânias like that in Briteiros, near Braga.

Even the Romans failed to leave much behind. Local guerrilla warfare held back the Roman push into Portugal, and the troops took a long time to quell dogged Lusitanian opposition. Some of the best remains are at the old Roman city of Conímbriga, near

Coimbra, and the stretch of Roman road from Campo do Gerês to the Spanish border, in the Minho.

Muslim invasion and influence in the last centuries of the first millennium were felt strongest in the Algarve and southern Portugal, where architecture and place names are distinctively Moorish. Christian reconquest began in earnest in the ninth century, when the land between the Douro and Minho became Portucale, independent from the Moors but inextricably linked with, and largely controlled by, Spain.

The fledgling country's identity continued to be in question until 1143, when Afonso Henriques was acknowledged as the first King of Portugal. Portugal's borders were expanded south to the Algarve in the thirteenth century, and its new frontier recognized by Spain in 1297. Despite this recognition, Portugal and Spain were in almost perpetual conflict until the beginning of the nineteenth century. Only when both Portugal and Spain started looking outwards towards the sea was the fighting put on hold.

The Age of Discovery, which began in Portugal in the fifteenth century, was the country's one moment in the world spotlight. Portuguese sailors travelled the world, inspired by Spanish tales of riches, a zeal to spread the Christian faith, and perhaps a national wanderlust bred from their proximity to the Atlantic ocean. Back home, Prince Henry the Navigator masterminded much of the exploration, raising funds and recruiting foreign experts in navigation.

The Portuguese were the first Europeans to sail the western Atlantic ocean, the first to cross the equator, round the Cape of Good Hope and see Australia. Even this may be an understatement, as Portugal sometimes failed to record her new conquests for fear that other countries would seize them. Portuguese explorers established colonies in South America, Africa, India and South East Asia, and brought back exotic spices, plants and animals. Although many of these treasures were paraded through the streets of Lisbon and Évora, the ordinary Portuguese saw little evidence of the country's wealth.

By the end of the fifteenth century, the orgy of discovery had calmed down, and in subsequent centuries Portugal looked to Europe once more, to intermittent conflict with Spain and increasing trade links with Britain.

When Napoleon came to power at the end of the eighteenth century, these links with Britain placed Portugal firmly on the anti-French side, and the country was invaded in 1801. The English and Portuguese, led by Wellington, spent a little over a decade driving the French and Spanish out of the land.

Although the English and Portuguese were victorious in the Peninsula War, Napoleon's republican ideals were taking hold in Portugal, and the rest of the nineteenth century was characterized by failed uprisings and constitutional reforms. A clutch of attempted revolutions in the first decade of the twentieth century culminated in the successful overthrow of the monarchy on October 5, 1910.

The first few years of republican Portugal were chaotic and unstable: between 1910 and 1926 there were 45 separate governments. The confusion ended in 1926 with the overthrow of the democratic government in a bloodless coup, leading eventually to the rise of power of António de Oliveira Salazar.

Salazar announced the creation of the New State in 1933, and his dictatorial, repressive regime lasted until the late 1960s.

The economy picked up a little in the 1950s and 1960s, but the Salazar period was a disastrous one for Portugal. The country became a one party state where opposition was stifled by a violent and pervasive police force. Censorship was rife, causing many authors and painters to flee the country, and education was seen as unimportant, with most Portuguese leaving school not long after their tenth birthday.

Salazar was effectively removed from power in 1968 when he suffered a stroke and was succeeded by Marcelo Caetano, though no one actually told Salazar this, and he died in 1970 still believing that he ran the country. The Salazar regime hobbled on without its figurehead for another few years until the growing colonial wars inspired segments of the army to stage a bloodless revolution on April 25, 1974.

Waking from Salazarist stagnation in the 1970s, Portugal had a lot of catching up to do. The first decade after the 1974 revolution was a turbulent time, not least because of the influx of more than a million refugees from Portugal's former colonies.

In January 1986, Portugal's luck changed when its membership of the European Community was accepted. With membership came investment in industry and infrastructure, attempts to modernize agriculture, and the continuing expansion of the country's growing tourist industry. Even so, Portugal was seen as far behind other European countries, and it was a surprise when its economy passed the stringent fiscal requirements for European Monetary Union in 1998.

Portugal today

The north-south divide along the Rio Tejo spills over into many aspects of Portuguese life. Most of industrial Portugal lies south of the river, largely concentrated in coastal areas around Lisbon, producing textiles and footwear, pulp and paper and metalwork. The south also gets the bulk of the country's 10 million tourists, most of whom head for the Algarve. Southern agriculture is made up of large estates (latifundias), a hangover from Roman times, and vast fields of olive or cork trees dominate the landscape. Even in the south, the population is largely rural, and only around 40% of Portuguese live in towns and cities.

Further north, farming is on a different scale, and often seems left over from a different era. Plots are small, often sliced from steep mountainsides, and provide enough food for the farmer's family, sometimes with a little spare to sell on market days. The harsh reality of northern agriculture and lack of other employment opportunities have ensured a consistent flood of migrants that peaked in the 1950s and 1960s. Workers largely head for construction sites in France and Germany, with the Minho, in particular, emptying citizens at a speedy rate.

The north of the country is also more traditional in outlook. Although Catholicism is practised throughout Portugal, religion is stronger here, and the people can be conservative and reluctant to change. But northerners are far from dour: religion and culture combine in riotous and colourful festivals, unchanged for centuries.

The Portuguese language is a unique and important part of national culture. Written down, it looks innocuous enough, and Spanish, Italian and French speakers will be able to grasp a good part of what's written in tourist brochures and newspapers. Spoken, Portuguese leaves most visitors stumped. It has hints of Hungarian, Finnish and Arabic, full of nasal, half-enunciated vowels and slurred consonants. See the language section on p 179 for pronunciation and vocabulary.

Football unites the north and south in national obsession. On match days, cafés and bars are brimful of supporters, and whether or not you're a fan, it's easy to get swept up in the excitement. The enthusiasm continues regardless of the form of the consistently underachieving national team and the big three clubs of Sporting Lisbon, Benfica and FC Porto, who all attract supporters from throughout the country. The Portuguese, as knowledgeable and generous connoisseurs of the game, are the ideal choice as hosts of Euro 2004; the party promises to be a spectacular one.

Arts

Portuguese literature is currently undergoing an international revival, fuelling and fuelled by José Saramago's 1998 Nobel Prize for Literature. Much of the credit for this has to go to publishers like Carcanet Press, who are publishing fresh translations of modern authors at a cracking rate.

Arguably the best, and certainly the most eccentric, of Portugal's poets is Fernando Pessoa, who lived and wrote, along with his four alter-egos, at the beginning of the twentieth century. Each of the five separate Pessoa personas wrote in their own individual style, and Pessoa went so far as to write conversations between his alter-egos. Between the five of them, their output was prolific: although little was published in Pessoa's lifetime, he left behind more than 25,000 articles, poems and stories. See p 178 for reading suggestions.

Portugal's chief musical contribution is fado, a melancholy, melodramatic marriage of voice and the twelve-stringed guitarra portuguesa. The lyrics and music combine in a melodious representation of saudade, a kind of national yearning or nostalgia.

The country's most famous fado singer, despite the genre's male-dominated history, was (and still is) Amália Rodrigues, who died in 1999. The public outpouring of grief at the news of her death was astounding: radio stations played wall-to-wall Amália, thousands lined the streets of Lisbon to see her funeral procession, and the government declared three days of official national mourning. There are fado concerts across the country, but it's music that's at its best when heard impromptu in a dingy bar in the early hours of the morning.

Folk music can be heard all over the country, particularly at festival time in the Minho and Trás-os-Montes. The sight of men dressed in traditional costume and marching from village to village playing sad romanceiro ballads accompanied by gaita de foles (bagpipes), bombo (bass drum) and the caixa (snare drum) is an echo from the time when many of these songs were sung while collecting the harvest and should not be missed.

Portugal's contribution to the visual arts has been unspectacular, with one notable exception. Throughout the country, on building façades, in churches and mansions, and on fountains, you'll see fine examples of painted tiles, called azulejos. Sometimes entirely in elegant blue and white, sometimes vividly coloured, these azulejos form a body of art work stretching back more than 400 years. Some of the best examples are in the art deco cafés of Lisbon and Porto, and in the quintas or manor houses of the Setúbal peninsula and the Lima valley.

For more about regional culture and people, see the individual area chapters.

 # Food

Portuguese food is solid, substantial and lacking in vegetables. It's also tasty and very cheap by Western European standards.

Traditionally, the Portuguese have followed the southern European pattern of a large main meal at lunchtime followed by a much-needed siesta, and although a heavy lunch is becoming less popular with city workers, it's still the norm in rural areas. Restaurants open from about 12pm until 3pm at lunch, and from 7pm onwards at night.

Soups are fabulous, often meals in themselves, and can cost as little as 150$. You shouldn't leave the country without trying caldo verde, a potato soup made with finely shredded couve gallego (a vivid green, thick cabbage), although vegetarians should note that it traditionally contains a few slices of chouriço sausage.

Most menus will include some kind of fried meat, usually pork and beef, often pounded into submission with generous amounts of garlic. Fried chicken is excellent and also available everywhere. Sausages and hams are popular throughout the country, especially in the north: try presunto, a smoked ham similar to Italian proscuitto, or chouriço, a spicy sausage.

And then there's offal. Ubiquitous in the north, and adding a hearty flavour to any stew, it can still be a stomach-churning experience to try and chew your way through a piece of tripe. If your idea of meat is a boneless chicken breast, avoid dishes such as cozido à portuguesa, which includes disturbingly recognisable ears, feet and innards, and tripas—just plain old tripe.

Despite this preponderance of meat, if Portugal has a national dish, it has to be bacalhau (salted cod). The tradition began in the sixteenth century, when the Portuguese began cod fishing off the coast of Newfoundland. Salt was added to the cod to preserve it on the long journey home, and the tradition has continued into the age of the fridge. Try bacalhau à Gomes de Sá, creamy, loaded with calories and garnished with olives and hard boiled eggs, or bacalhau à brás, made with scrambled eggs and fried potatoes. Bacalhau isn't the cheapest fish around: having eaten all the Canadian fish, Portugal now imports most of its cod from Norway.

Most restaurants will include a standby fried fish and chips, often very greasy. Lulas grelhadas (grilled squid) can be mouthwateringly tasty or bland and rubbery.

Vegetarians fare badly in cafés and restaurants, and will soon be sick of the sight of omelette and chips. There are some meatless alternatives in the cities, but elsewhere eating out is a disheartening experience best avoided.

In restaurants, you should leave about a 10% tip, and watch out for the little things: those tasty plates of olives and presunto will carry a hefty charge, and even bread and butter will be added to your bill.

After a few days of restaurant eating, when you might be hankering for something a little less rich, head for the local market. Most towns of any size boast a covered municipal market, bursting with noise and flavour, where you can buy fantastic olives, fruit and cheese for very little money. Stallholders will often sell just a few vegetables fresh from the family farm, yelling out prices and bargains to entice new customers. In the south, fruit stalls line the road, selling some of the cheapest, most delicious produce you'll find anywhere in the country.

Complete your picnic with some delicious Portuguese bread. Portuguese rolls are cheap and tasty, but to give your jaw a bit more of a workout try the delicious and amazingly heavy pão de milho (corn bread) or pão de trigo (made with wheat). Look for bread in a padaria (bakery) or pastelaria (pastry shop).

Pastries themselves are an integral part of Portuguese daily life. Start your morning by skipping the boring bread roll hotel breakfasts and heading for the nearest pastelaria. Choose from hearty chouriço-filled pasties, sticky buns and oozing custard tarts, and spend the day walking off the calories.

Regional specialities are found in the Food & Drink section of each area chapter.

Drink

Portuguese beer is light and refreshing, if a little insipid; the brands to try are Sagres and Super Bock.

Port, possibly the country's most famous export, begins life as Douro valley grapes, and is then fortified with brandy, before being left to mature in oak casks or in the bottle. Vintage ports, made only in selected years, are matured in the bottle and left for at least 10 years before drinking. For the very best vintages, look to 1994 (already disappearing fast), 1977 and 1963. For more general drinking, young ruby ports are cheapest, tawny ports lighter in colour and less syrupy, and dry white ports a refreshing, chilled alternative rarely available outside the country.

Although vintage port is held in high regard by the wine trade, Portuguese table wines are often compared unfavourably to those grown elsewhere in southern Europe. But comparison is difficult: more than 90% of Portuguese wine is made from grape varieties unique to the country.

Vines grow throughout the country, and most rural households will make their own wine each year. The house wine in a café or restaurant is solidly drinkable, although reds are generally better than whites. Moving up a notch, red wines from the Alentejo and Dão regions are gaining in reputation, and available throughout the country. In the northwest Minho region, the house speciality is invariably vinho verde, a young, semi-sparkling wine served in earthenware jugs, including a zingy and unusual red that's rare outside Portugal. Other wines worth sampling include the reds from Colares, near Sintra, and Moscatel, a sweet dessert wine made on the Setúbal peninsula.

The Portuguese take their coffee very seriously, and even the smallest café or bar will have an espresso-style machine to churn out the nation's favourite drink. Drink a bica standing at the counter; it's an intense, concentrated drink, bigger than an espresso but similar in taste. To be authentic, load the coffee with sugar and drink it in one gulp. If you have more time, go for the relaxed galão. Portugal's take on a latte, it's long, milky and perfect for an afternoon with friends.

Imported soft drinks are expensive, and local brands like Tri Naranjus are better. Bottled water is excellent and available everywhere, but it's still a poor second to drinking straight from the spring.

Flora

Portugal is one of Europe's richest botanical regions. The mix of Mediterranean and Atlantic climates and the varied underlying rock ensure a diverse collection of flowers, shrubs and trees. Geographically isolated from the rest of Europe by the Pyrenees, the Iberian peninsula's plant life developed at its own pace, helped along by windblown seeds from North Africa. The results are spectacular: of around 6000 species of flora in the Iberian Peninsula, about a quarter are indigenous to the region and occur nowhere else in the world.

Portugal was once covered by deciduous forests, dominated by Pyrenean oak in the north and by the evergreen cork oak in the south. Frequent forest fires and the introduction of faster-growing imported species such as pine and eucalyptus are rapidly destroying what little forest survived into the second half of the twentieth century. In the unforested areas that cover much of the country, the landscape is dominated by dense scrub as the land unsuccessfully tries to regenerate itself.

At higher altitudes gorse, broom and heather cover the ground. Hardy plants such as St Patrick's cabbage, mat grass and the insect-eating sphagnum mosses happily cope with strong winds, deep snow cover and extreme temperature change. In summer, especially in the Serra do Gerês, mountain pastures are transformed into sumptuous carpets of low-growing lilies and irises.

The vast, farmed landscapes south of the Tejo are dominated by three ubiquitous and useful species. Cork oak is widely grown and Portugal produces almost two-thirds of the world's supply. Vines are planted throughout the country, but are at their most concentrated and dramatic best in the steeply terraced vineyards alongside the Douro river. It's hard to picture the southern landscape without the outline of gnarled olive trees. Although not a native of the country, the olive was first imported more than 2000 years ago, and it's now firmly entwined with rural life.

In the flora section that follows, and in the fauna section on p 14, plant and animal names read, from left to right, English name, Latin name, Portuguese name.

Juniper   Juniperus communis   Zimbro

Leaves Needle-like, 1.2cm long, in groups of three; sharp, glossy, green white band on upper surface
Bark Red brown, peels in thin vertical strips
Fruit Berry-like, 6mm long cone; becomes black when ripe
Habitat Open spaces from coast to mountains
Height Up to 6m
Did you know? Juniper berries give gin its distinctive taste and are used as culinary flavouring

Cork Oak   Quercus suber   Sobreiro

Leaves 7cm long, 4cm wide, dark green on top grey underneath
Bark Gnarly, pale grey with thick ridges; vivid, smooth brownish-red when stripped
Fruit Acorn 3cm long
Habitat Rolling hills, mainly in the south of the country
Height Up to 20m
Did you know? Stripping the bark does not damage trees; bark harvested every decade or so

Pyrenean Oak   Quercus pyrenaica   Carvalho negral

Leaves 20cm long 10cm across, deep lobes, dark glossy green
Bark Pale grey and craggy
Fruit Acorn 4cm long, two years to mature
Habitat Mountains, particularly in the north
Height 20m
Did you know? Produces very strong lumber, used extensively in construction

Olive   Olea europaea   Oliveira

Leaves 2–8 cm long, narrow, grey-green above with delicate silver hairs underneath
Bark Pale grey
Fruit 1–4cm long
Habitat Farmland
Height Up to 15m
Did you know? Fruit is green the first year then turns black when ripe in second year.

Sweet chestnut   Castanea sativa   Castanheiro

Leaves 10–25cm long, oblong with pointed tip and sharp-toothed edges
Bark Grey ridges that seem to spiral around trunk
Fruit Edible chestnut
Habitat Farmland, plains and mixed woodlands
Height Up to 30m
Did you know? Chestnuts are a staple food in rural Portugal, used as a stuffing for meat or as a base for hearty soups

Beech   Fagus Sylvatica   Faia

Leaves 4–9cm long oval, with 7–8 parallel veins, silky hairs underneath
Bark Smooth grey
Fruit Triangular brown nuts
Habitat Farmland
Height Up to 40m
Did you know? Planted for timber because it grows tall and straight without knots

Fauna

Portugal is home to an assortment of rare animals. Nooks and crannies offer solitude to fire salamanders, Iberian lynx and a variety of wonderful creepy crawlies. Large tracts of remote wilderness, especially in the Trás-os-Montes, offer animals such as the wolf and golden eagle the space to roam unhindered. Agricultural underdevelopment has preserved unique ecosystems that are only now being studied for the first time.

Portugal is not just important for its resident population of animals; it's also a main refuelling stop on the north-south migration route for birds. For the keen birdwatcher these annual spring and autumn migrations are a fabulous time to visit. The Sado, Tejo and Minho estuaries, along with the lagoons near Aveiro and in the Algarve are the best places for viewing. Look out for sandwich terns, arctic terns, black terns, curlews, whimbrels, godwits and glossy ibises.

For the novice wildlife watcher, a few simple tips can greatly increase the chance of seeing animals. Try to time your viewing for dawn and dusk when most animals are active. There's also more chance of spotting animals if you're on the edge of two habitats, like on the fringes of a wood near a river or open farmland. As you walk along, stop every now and then to sit quietly and wait for a few minutes. Allow the animals time to get accustomed to your presence and resume their normal routines, and you'll gradually see undetected animals emerge before your eyes.

Wild cat   Felis silvestris   Gato bravo

Length 50cm **Tail** 30cm **Height** 35cm
Description Yellow-grey fur with black ringed tail
Habitat Woodland and scrubland
Voice Purrs and meows
Diet Mice, birds, fish and insects
Viewing tips Active in late afternoon, often seen sunning itself
Did you know? Persecution of cats in medieval times led to the spread of black death as rat and mice populations exploded

Genet   Genetta genetta   Geneta

Length 50cm **Tail** 40cm **Height** 20cm
Description Pale fur with well-defined dark spots, tail rings
Habitat Dark woods close to streams
Voice Purrs loudly
Diet Small birds, mammals, insects
Viewing tips Nocturnal, look for footprints near water
Did you know? Lives up to 21 years. Strong swimmer and climber; found up to an altitude of 2500m

Iberian lynx   Lynx pardinus   Lince Ibérico

Length 100cm **Tail** 25cm **Height** 70cm
Description Large and small black spots, black tip on tail, distinctive feathery tufts on head
Habitat Pyrenean and holm oak woods in rocky mountains
Voice Hisses and howls
Diet Rabbits, birds, young deer, fish, small mammals and reptiles
Viewing tips Very rare and difficult to spot; vast territory
Did you know? Most endangered carnivore in Europe

Wolf   Canis lupus   Lobo

Length 130cm **Tail** 40cm **Height** 80cm
Description Grey, bushy tail, alert ears
Habitat Woods and open country in mountains
Voice Silent when hunting; growls, yelps and drawn-out howls
Diet Large and small mammals
Viewing tips Footprint like a dog; best seen at dawn and dusk
Did you know? Wolves mate for life. Can travel up to 40km per day with a maximum speed of up to 50km per hour

Otter   Lutra lutra   Lontra

Length 80cm **Tail** 40cm **Height** 30cm
Description Brown fur; long, slender body with short legs
Habitat Rivers, lakes, marshes, estuaries and sea
Voice Clear whistle, sometimes growls
Diet Fish, birds, frogs and aquatic mammals
Viewing tips Look for remains of meals along riverbanks
Did you know? Good climber and jumper, can walk on land for long distances

Badger   Meles meles   Texugo

Length 60cm **Tail** 15cm **Height** 30cm
Description Silver-grey back; broad white stripes on face
Habitat Scrubland, farmland, woods
Voice Growls
Diet Small rodents, reptiles and plants
Viewing tips Nocturnal; listen for the sound of it digging
Did you know? Foxes and birds of prey often follow the burrowing badger to catch animals it disturbs while digging for food

Wild boar   Sus scrofa   Javali

Length 150cm **Tail** 15cm **Height** 90cm
Description Pale grey to black; tusks up to 30cm
Habitat Mixed, deciduous woodland; scrubland
Voice Snorts. Female barks and chatters teeth when angry
Diet Roots, vegetables, small mammals, insects
Viewing tips Mainly nocturnal but also active in mornings
Did you know? Litters of 4 to 12 piglets common, independent after 6 months and can live up to 25 years

Greater horseshoe bat   Rhinolophus ferrum-equinum   Morcego de ferradura grande

Length 6cm **Tail** 4cm   **Description** Red-grey back with pale underside
Habitat Woods and scrubland
Voice Loud shrill and squeaks
Diet Insects caught in flight or collected from leaves
Viewing tips Hunts throughout the night, flies close to ground
Did you know? Has one young at a time, which can fly after 4 weeks and matures in a year. Lives for 20 years

Large mouse -eared bat   Myotis myotis   Morcego rato grande

Length 7cm **Tail** 5cm   **Description** Grey-brown back with grey-white belly
Habitat Open woodland, parks
Voice Chirping and loud shrieks
Diet Insects caught in flight or collected from ground
Viewing tips Emerges to hunt after dark; flies straight and silent about 5m off the ground
Did you know? Migrates between summer and winter locations. Large nursing colonies consist of only young and adult females

European tree frog   Hyla arborea   Rela de moller

Length 4cm
Description Usually green but changes to grey or brown with temperature
Habitat Marshland, damp meadows, reed beds
Voice Croaks
Diet Insects and spiders
Viewing tips Easily spotted, active by day and twilight
Did you know? Female lays up to 1000 eggs; lives to be 15 years old

Natterjack — Bufo calamita — Sapo corredor

Length 8cm
Description Back covered with huge warts with brown and grey markings, belly white
Habitat Varied, especially dry sandy soil, up to 1200m
Voice Loud croak
Diet Insects, worms and spiders
Viewing tips Mainly nocturnal, occasionally active in day
Did you know? When the natterjack becomes alarmed, it inflates its body, lowers its head and sticks its bum in the air

Fire salamander — Salamandra salamandra — Salamandra de pintas

Length 20cm
Description Shiny black with yellow, orange or red markings
Habitat Damp woodlands, streams and meadows up to 1000m
Diet Insects and worms
Viewing tips Emerges at night or in bad weather, hides out of sight in sunshine
Did you know? Don't touch, as the oily slime that covers the body is poisonous. Can live for up to 42 years

Iberian wall lizard — Podaricus hispanica — Lagartixa-ibérica

Length 18cm
Description Flat head with long tail, upper parts grey to brown
Habitat Dry, stony places, especially walls and ruins
Diet Small insects and worms
Viewing tips Look and listen for them scuttling away as you approach!
Did you know? Lays eggs in hole in ground; can live up to 15 years

Green lizard — Lacerta viridis — Lagarto verde

Length 40cm
Description Males are a vivid green with tiny black dots, males have sky blue throat during mating. Females duller and brownish
Habitat Dry, sunny locations with shrubs, especially near walls and along roads
Diet Insects and fruit
Viewing tips Keep a look out for it running away as you approach!
Did you know? When threatened opens mouth and bites

Black stork   Ciconia nigra   Cegonha preta

Description 100cm, black with white belly, red bill and legs
Habitat Marshy land near forests
Voice Noisy, claps bill, random notes
Diet Fish, insects
Viewing tips Flies like white stork, only more gracefully as less reliant on thermals
Did you know? Nests high in the tops of trees. More solitary than white stork

White stork   Ciconia ciconia   Cegonha branca

Description 100cm, long bill and legs, white with black flight feathers, red bill and legs
Habitat Marshes, grassy plains
Voice Hisses and claps bill
Diet Fish, insects
Viewing tips Flies at high altitude with neck straight ahead
Did you know? Nests found on buildings all over northeast Portugal

Bee-eater   Merops apiaster   Abelharuco

Description 30cm, bright blue belly, yellow throat and shoulders, black eyeband
Habitat Open scrubland with some trees
Voice Prruep prruep prruep
Diet Insects
Viewing tips Sociable, likes to perch and watch the world go by. Good flier, with sudden accelaration and graceful glides
Did you know? Breeds in large groups in holes in the ground.

Chough   Pyrrhocorax pyrrhocorax   Gralha de bico vermelho

Description 40cm, red legs and long, thin, curved red bill
Habitat Rolling hills and mountains
Voice High-pitched cheeeaaah and chuff
Diet Mainly insects
Viewing tips Good flier, tumbles and twists during flight. Also frequently seen hopping on ground
Did you know? Nest in caves and on crags

Hoopoe   Upupa epops   Poupa

Description 30cm, crest on head, pinkish body, barred white and black body and wings, long bill
Habitat Farmland, open woodland
Voice Pooo pooo pooo
Diet Insects
Viewing tips Undulating flight as it open and closes wings
Did you know? One of our favourite birds. Nests in ruins and hollows of old trees

Goshawk   Accipter gentilis   Açor

Description 60cm, barred, grey belly, some white near tail and around eye
Habitat Woods on edge of open country
Voice Pee-lay or kik kik
Diet Wood pigeons and other forest-dwelling birds
Viewing tips Great flier, zooms 2–3m above the ground between and around trees
Did you know? Persistent; chases prey even if results in crashing

Short-toed eagle   Circaetus gallicus   Águia cobreira

Description 65cm, long wings and tail, white underneath except for brown chest
Habitat Mountain slopes, plains and coastal dunes
Voice Noisy; jee or peak-oh
Diet Snakes, lizards and frogs
Viewing tips Resembles osprey but without dark stripes
Did you know? Frequently hovers with legs dangling

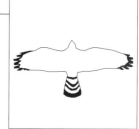

Booted eagle   Hieraaetus pennatus   Águia calçada

Description Two different varieties; can have either dark or white body with black wing edges
Habitat Forest clearings
Voice Keeee
Diet Small birds and reptiles
Viewing tips Always seen near trees; six obvious feathers at end of wings
Did you know? Smallest eagle in Europe

Golden eagle Aquila chrysaetos Águia real

Description 90cm, golden feathers on head, white patches on wings and tail
Habitat Mountains, forests, seacliffs
Voice Seldom-heard kya
Diet Rabbits, reptiles
Viewing tips Soars with wings in shallow V, solitary
Did you know? The largest eagle in the world and the emblem of ancient Rome

Bonelli's eagle Hieraaetus fasciatus Águia de Bonelli

Description 70cm, white body underneath, except dark tail band and wing
Habitat Rocky mountains, plains and wetlands
Voice Fast or slow kai kai kai
Diet Rabbits, birds up to heron size
Viewing tips Watch for spectacular, acrobatic courtship display in spring
Did you know? Pairs stay together even when not breeding

Imperial eagle Aquila heliaca Águia imperial

Description 80cm, similar to golden eagle but head appears white; white band on shoulders
Habitat Plains and marshes
Voice Rapid ark ark
Diet Scavenges carrion, also kills small mammals and birds
Viewing tips Hard to tell apart from other large eagles, look for white shoulder bars
Did you know? Huge nest, up to 3m across, in isolated trees

Buzzard Buteo buteo Águia de asa redonda

Description 50cm, dark with barred underside, broad wings and fat, round tail
Habitat Mountains, plains, farmland
Voice Peee-aah
Diet Birds, small mammals, insects
Viewing tips Common over most habitats
Did you know? Seen as the laziest raptor, it rarely chases prey and refuses to fly in the rain

Sparrowhawk   Accipiter nisus   Gavião

Description 35cm, long tail, barred underparts, grey above
Habitat Woodland and farmland
Voice Varies, makes lots of noise especially in breeding season
Diet Small mammals and birds
Viewing tips The sparrowhawk is a common sight hovering over fields looking for food
Did you know? Young birds and captive adults frequently resort to cannibalism

Kestrel   Falco tinnunculus   Peneireiro vulgar

Description 35cm, pointed wings, black band near base of tail
Habitat Coast, farmland, woodland, cities
Voice Kee kee kee in breeding season
Diet Mainly rodents, but also lizards and small birds
Viewing tips Often seen hovering patiently over fields checking the ground for prey
Did you know? Breeds in old nests of other birds, on cliffs or even buildings

Eagle owl   Bubo bubo   Bufo real

Description 65cm, rust colour with streaks and bars, big feathers look like ears
Habitat Rocky ledges on crags and mountains
Voice Ooo hoo
Diet Rabbits and other small mammals, birds up to game bird size
Viewing tips Active at dawn and dusk
Did you know? Easily mistaken for buzzard; uses other birds' abandoned nests

Peregrine falcon   Falco peregrinus   Falcão peregrino

Description 45cm, slate colour, thick black moustache, white belly with speckles. Female larger and darker than male
Habitat Open country, mountains, cliffs
Voice Hek hek hek or airk airk airk
Diet Small and medium-sized birds and mammals
Viewing tips Graceful flier, languid at rest but dramatic dive-bomb as attacks prey
Did you know? Attain speeds of up to 100km/hour when diving

Griffon vulture   Gyps fulvus   Grifo

Description 100cm, long broad wings, short stumpy tail, light lines under wings
Habitat All types of landscape but usually mountains
Voice Croaks and whistles
Diet Carrion
Viewing tips Flies gracefully by soaring, with only the occasional flap of wings
Did you know? Often breeds in caves

Egyptian vulture   Neophron percnopterus   Abutre do Egipto

Description 60cm, long wings with black edges, white body, wedge-shaped tail
Habitat Mountains and open country
Voice Largely silent
Diet Carrion
Viewing tips Easily confused with high altitude storks
Did you know? Most common vulture, often seen near rubbish dumps

Montagu's harrier   Circus pygargus   Tartaranhão caçador

Description 45cm, dark wing tips, male grey, female brown with black bars underneath
Habitat Marshes, farmland, plains
Voice Chattering kek kek kek
Diet Frogs, small mammals
Viewing tips Acrobatic flier as it patrols territory
Did you know? Winters in Africa and returns to same territory each year to breed

Quick Quiz
1. How many times did Prince Henry the Navigator sail round the Cape of Good Hope?

(answer on p 184)

Tourist Information

Getting to Portugal

For the best access to the walking areas in this book, fly to Lisbon or Porto. Algarve charter flights can still be a great bargain, but many low cost airlines now fly to Lisbon too.

Driving from Britain is a long haul of around a thousand miles once you've crossed the channel. Knock off around 600 miles of this trip by catching the ferry from Plymouth to Santander in northern Spain (a 24-hour sailing).

Eurolines runs bus services to a number of towns in Portugal, including Coimbra and Guarda, both convenient walking bases, but the journey takes around 40 hours and it can be just as costly as flying. Train fares are more expensive still, although the train is a good option if you want to see a bit of France or Spain on the way.

Red Tape

EU nationals can stay in Portugal indefinitely, and you won't need a visa if you're from Canada, the US or New Zealand and you stay for less than 90 days. As of 1999, Australians need to get a visa before entering the country.

EU nationals are covered by reciprocal health care arrangements; UK citizens should pick up an E111 form at a post office before they leave.

Travel insurance will give you extra health protection, and also cover your baggage, but be sure to read the fine print. Some policies specifically exclude walking accidents as a dangerous activity, particularly if you're walking on your own rather than in an organized group.

Money & Costs

Portugal is a member of the European Monetary Union, so its currency is in a state of transition. From 2000 until 2002, the currency remains the escudo, which is divided into 100 centavos.

The escudo-pound exchange rate generally hovers at around 300 escudos to the pound (200 escudos to the US dollar) and so the centavo's usefulness is limited.

Prices are normally written with a $ sign in between the escudo and the centavo, but some places are beginning to omit the centavos altogether. We follow this new convention, and so 250 escudos is written in this book as 250$.

The escudo-euro exchange rate is fixed at €1 = 200$48.

Many shops list both escudo and euro prices in tandem, and the euro is already in use electronically for credit and debit payments. Euro notes and coins enter circulation on 1 January 2002, then there's just a six-month overlap until the escudo is phased out on 1 July 2002.

The most convenient way to get Portuguese currency is to use your debit or credit card and take out money from cashpoints. Banks charge high commission fees and have limited opening times, and bureau de change rates are generally unfavourable. It's wise to bring a back up such as traveller's cheques, as Portuguese cashpoints are notoriously fickle. If your card is rejected, try using it again, or go to another machine. Make sure you get money out a few days before a public holiday, as cashpoints are frequently empty of cash at the end of a long weekend. We list bank and cashpoint locations in each area chapter.

Your costs can go down significantly if you're under 26, over 60 or a student. If you're a student, be sure to get an International Student Identity Card (ISIC) before leaving; these are recognized at some museums. More widely accepted is the Euro26 card, available from youth and student travel agencies throughout Europe. Over 60s also get discounts at museums and other sights.

There are generous discounts for children on railways and in hotels. In rural areas, young children may be allowed to stay for free in hotels or travel for free on buses: it's an incredibly child-friendly country.

How much will you spend?

Campsite, 2 people & tent	1000$ / €5
Cheap pensão, double room	4000$ / €20
Cheap lunch	1000$ / €5
3 course meal & wine for 2	5000$ / €25

 # Transport

Trains

Trains vary from international services that rush to and from Europe packed with InterRailers, to relaxed Regional trains that meander through the countryside stopping at every small town along the way. Train travel is fairly cheap, although the trains cover only limited routes: if you're in a hurry, take the bus. Most trains have both first and second class carriages, with old-fashioned, enclosed compartments seating from four to eight people and a corridor running down one side of the carriage.

Some of the lines are worth taking just for the ride: the Lisbon to Covilhã route hugs the Rio Tejo for much of its length, then turns north for great views of the Serra da Estrela.

There's not much food available on the trains themselves, but you'll normally be able to get a coffee and a sandwich at the station. Most stations are poorly signed, and platforms can change without notice. Keep your eyes open and ask as many people as possible if you're on the right platform.

Bus

Buses are a more flexible option than trains, as they run more frequently and go to more places. They can also a little more expensive, depending on the company. In small towns, bus schedules are haphazard and largely unwritten: ask at the tourist office and local cafés for the latest times.

Bus stations in large towns may look like a model of efficiency, but don't be fooled by appearances. Buying a ticket and finding your bus can be a frustrating experience. First, you have to find out which of the ten or so companies travel to your destination, then you need to work out when the bus leaves, and from which numbered bay. Even after you've done this, your bus may display a completely different destination, and leave from an entirely different bay. This all seems to make perfect sense to local people, so be sure to ask advice. There's generally no toilet or refreshments on board.

Hitching

Hitching long distances can be a long and frustrating experience, as foreign visitors are loathe to pick up hitchhikers and locals may only be travelling as far as the next village. For shorter distances, hitching may be a useful option, particularly on weekends when bus services are limited. Hitching does, of course, involve risk, so take care.

Car

Driving in Portugal may be the most stressful part of your trip, and after a few hours on the roads it's easy to see why the country's accident rate is the highest in Europe. Speeding and rash overtaking, especially on blind corners, are a badge of honour among some Portuguese drivers. Drinking and driving is commonplace, with bars attached to petrol stations and lorry drivers stopping every hour or so for a swift half. It's surprising to discover that the maximum blood-alcohol level is much lower than in Britain, and even that afternoon beer may push you over the limit. Narrow cobbled streets, unfathomable one-way systems and non-existent parking make city driving miserable; leave your car on the outskirts and walk or use the bus. EU and US nationals can drive using their home licences; nationals of other countries need an International Driving Permit.

Bicycle

Travelling by bicycle is a fabulous way to see the country. You'll stop for coffee at villages that car drivers whizz past, and see places undescribed in any guidebook (even this one). It can be tough-going in mountainous regions, particularly in the Serra da Estrela, Peneda-Gerês and Montesinho; make sure you load up on pastries before each big hill.

In remote areas, road condition is a big problem, and a mountain bike is a big advantage on potholed or gravel roads. You'll learn to hate city and town approaches, where smooth, easy-rolling tarmac suddenly gives way to frame-rattling cobblestones.

The notorious Portuguese drivers are in fact incredibly considerate of cyclists, quick to slow down and give lots of room.

Bringing a bike from overseas by aeroplane is surprisingly easy. It's generally free, and most airlines don't insist that you put the bike in a box, allowing you to simply take the pedals off, let most of the air out of the tyres, and turn the handlebars around.

There aren't many bike repair shops, especially in rural areas, so you should have some idea of how to fix the more common problems, and bring along spare inner tubes and cables. Hotels are extremely accommodating about bike storage.

It's expensive to put bikes on trains, sometimes three times the price of the ticket itself, and some stations won't allow it (Évora, for example). You'll have to fill in a couple of forms at the station office, so it's best to arrive about an hour before the train is scheduled to leave. Bikes are occasionally carried on buses, but this is always at the discretion of the driver.

Accommodation

Camping

Camping sites in Portugal range from basic, no-facilities summer campsites in some of the national parks to fully-equipped sites geared towards caravans. In between the two extremes, most sites will have hot showers and a small shop or café. Many Portuguese decamp to sites just outside the big cities on weekends, complete with ornamental plants, pets and artificial turf.

Often, sites are inaccessible by public transport; you'll need to walk, hitch or take a taxi. Wild camping is illegal in parts of the Serra da Estrela and Peneda-Gerês parks.

Hostels

There are about 20 youth hostels in Portugal; they're really busy in summer, so you'll need to book ahead. Apart from those in the Serra da Estrela and Campo do Gerês, none are that useful for areas in this book.

Dormidas

The cheapest option in any village or small town is privately-rented rooms, known as dormidas. Ask at the turismo or local cafés, or look for a dormidas sign in the window.

Pensões

The most popular budget choice is a pensão. Similar in style to a British B&B, these pensões often include a breakfast of rolls and coffee. They are officially graded from one to three stars, although the grading often measures superficial facilities like a TV rather than the cleanliness or atmosphere of a place.

Hotels

Hotels are generally larger, newer and better equipped than pensões, and more expensive. They can be a bit soulless, though, and Portugal is blessed with two far more characterful options, outlined below.

Turihab

One of Portugal's greatest inventions is the Turihab scheme, a network of mostly rural properties that rent a room, apartment or occasionally a whole building to visitors. Best of all is the accommodation within the Solares de Portugal group, concentrated in the Lima valley region, where you can stay in manor houses, rustic farmhouses or a converted windmill.

Rooms or properties are rented out by the owners, and you may find yourself sitting down to dinner with the family, or at least being offered a wealth of local advice on sights and walking routes.

Pousadas

Pousadas are top of the range, luxury establishments, often in converted historic properties located just outside town centres. The rooms are excellent, the gourmet food terrific and the wine lists superb. The prices match, and all the pousadas in this book fall within our $$$$ price rating.

Accommodation listings in this book

Within each area, we include accommodation suggestions for a range of budgets. We try to include hotels of character that are accessible by public transport and close to the walks in the text. In this book, accommodation is divided into price categories. The price given is for a double room in high season; prices may drop at other times.

$ up to 6000$ / €30

$$ 6000$ to 9000$ / €30-45

$$$ 9000$ to 15,000$ / €45-75

$$$$ more than 15,000$ / €75

Equipment & Supplies

For most of the walks in this book, good walking shoes are fine, though you may be glad of boots in soggy places like the Serra da Estrela's Torre plateau. As for clothes, see the When to Go section in each area chapter for details on weather, but note that evenings can be cool throughout the country. Don't rely on buying walking or camping equipment in Portugal, although basics like Camping Gaz canisters are readily available. You won't find any packages of dehydrated camping food, which is probably a good thing, and most village shops will stock packet soup and pasta mixes.

Health & Safety

Pharmacies are generally open from 9am to 6pm with a lunchtime siesta. There should be at least one pharmacy open outside these times, too; look at the duty rota notice posted outside each pharmacy. In an emergency, dial 112. Calls are answered in Portuguese, French and English. The local turismo can help find you an English-speaking doctor.

Walking hazards

Walking in Portugal presents few natural hazards, although for some of the walks in this book you'll need good backcountry navigation skills. Read the walk description and note the walk rating before you set out; for the more challenging walks in this book, make sure that you know how to use a map and compass.

Ask at your hotel or campsite about the weather forecast, and be prepared to delay or cancel the walk in case of fog or snow. If you're heading for the mountains, you'll need warm and waterproof clothes and a basic emergency kit with spare food, a torch and first aid equipment.

If you get lost, take the time to look around you for any obvious natural or man-made landmarks, and use these to pinpoint your whereabouts. If you're not sure where you are, if it's getting dark or if visibility is poor, stay put.

Specific health risks

The most common problems in Portugal are related to heat. Take good sunglasses and use plenty of suntan lotion with a high sun protection factor. Treat mild sunburn with cold water, ice or calamine lotion, and consult a doctor in more serious cases.

Wear loose-fitting, cotton clothes and bathe often to avoid prickly heat and fungal vaginal infections.

Drink lots of fluid and acclimatize gradually to hot conditions to stave off heat exhaustion. Rest often and leave more strenuous walks until your body is used to the heat. Symptoms of heat exhaustion include cold and clammy skin, nausea and dizziness. If feasible, get to a cool place, and be sure to sip plenty of water.

Heatstroke is a serious condition, prevented in the same way as heat exhaustion. There may be some early sensation of feeling unwell, but heatstroke usually occurs suddenly. Symptoms include lack of sweating, flushed skin, dizziness and restlessness. Try to move the sufferer to a cool place, cover them with a wet sheet, and fan constantly. Seek medical advice immediately, as the condition can be fatal.

Water from local springs is delicious; use your common sense about drinking water from streams and purify or boil it if there are villages or agricultural land nearby.

Most Portuguese snakes are harmless, but there are a couple of venomous, non-deadly vipers and adders. Wear long trousers tucked into your boots if you're walking through long grass, avoid poking around in holes, and make slow, deliberate movements if you spot a snake. If someone does get bitten, secure and support the affected limb. Seek medical help, armed with a description of the snake, if possible.

 Communication

Post Offices

Post offices are generally open weekdays from 9am to 6pm, with larger offices also open on Saturday mornings.

You can buy stamps at the post office, from the automatic machines outside, or at any shop displaying a red Correios–selos sign.

Phones

In 1999, Portugal introduced a new phone system. The initial zero in the old area codes has been replaced by a 2, and you have to dial this new version of the former area code for all calls, even local ones. For example, to call the Porto Editora bookshop, you need to dial 222 007681 whether or not you're in Porto. Cheap rate is evenings and weekends. Public telephones take money, credit cards or a phonecard, available at shops and telephone offices.

Many cell phones can now be used

throughout Europe, and they're a convenient, if irritating, means of keeping in touch. They're becoming incredibly popular in Portugal, and in campsite bathrooms the queue for the showers is generally shorter that the queue to charge up cellphones.

Internet

Internet cafés are springing up in towns across the country. They're frequently open late into the evening, and are a sociable place to hang out and check e-mail. Most charge extraordinarily low rates: ask at the turismo for an up-to-date list.

For information about Portugal on the Internet, click on to Pili Pala's website at www.pilipalapress.com.

Opening Hours

G et used to the siesta, and do your shopping before 12pm or after 3pm. Most shops and post offices will close for lunch; banks will generally stay open at siesta time but close for the day by 3pm. Museums and sights usually close on Mondays; they also usually shut down for the lunchtime snooze.

Public Holidays

Most shops and banks close on public holidays, and public transport is limited. If you're low on cash, take some out a few days before the holiday, as cashpoints can empty fast. For details of regional festivals, see Events & Festivals in each area chapter.

1 January	New Year's Day
Good Friday	March/April (varies)
25 April	1974 revolution
1 May	Labour Day
Corpus Christi	May/June (varies)
10 June	Camões Day
15 August	Feast of the Assumption
5 October	Republic Day (celebrating the end of the Monarchy in 1910)
1 November	All Saints' Day
1 December	Independence day (celebrating independence from Spain in 1640)
8 December	Feast of the Immaculate Conception
25 December	Christmas Day

Quick Quiz

2. How tall is the highest mountain in Portugal?

(answer on p 184)

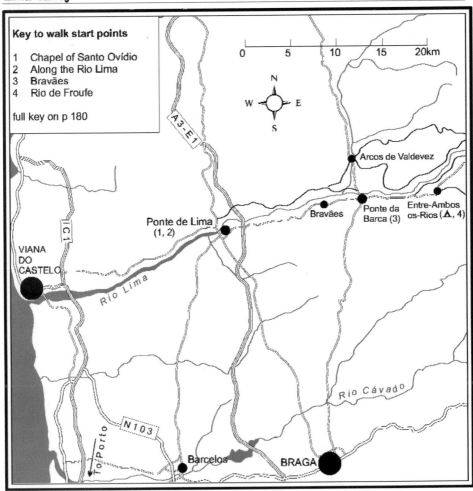

Key to walk start points

1   Chapel of Santo Ovídio
2   Along the Rio Lima
3   Bravães
4   Rio de Froufe

full key on p 180

What's the weather like?

	Jan	April	July	Oct
Sun	3 hrs	6 hrs	8.5 hrs	5 hrs
Rainfall	113mm	77mm	20mm	109mm
Maximum Temp	11°	18°	27°	20°
Minimum Temp	4°	8°	15°	10°

Average hours of sun, total average rainfall and average temperature in degrees celsius

Lima Valley

What's Inside

The Walks

Don't Miss . . .

Worship at the shrine to the patron saint of ears via the pilgrimage route to Santiago de Compostela (p 37)

Wander along the banks of the Rio Lima, passing charming manor houses and lush farmland (p 39)

Refresh yourself with a glass of sparkling vinho verde (p36)

Hospitable and colourful, the Minho region is a lively place to visit, especially in August and September when every tiny village organizes a festa. If you can find time for walking in amongst the celebrations you'll be strolling along gorgeous cobbled lanes that snake alongside broad rivers and centuries-old vineyards.

Walking

Geography

At the heart of the damp Minho region, the Rio Lima meanders through one of the loveliest valleys in Portugal. Around Ponte de Lima its broad banks are ideal for growing wine, and huge vineyards with their beautiful manor houses dominate the surrounding area.

Further east, the riverbanks rise and the scenery becomes more spectacular, until at Entre-Ambos-os-Rios small subsistence farmers must dig narrow terraces into the hillsides to make a living from the poor soil. The area around Entre-Ambos-os-Rios just sneaks into the boundary of the Parque Nacional Peneda-Gerês, described on p 48. The Lima valley's vivid green landscape owes much to the region's famous raininess: the Minho receives almost 2m of rain a year.

Trails

Trails range from tarmac roads to overgrown paths. The best wind along country lanes, passing under vines and alongside beautiful old quintas and espigueiros. The old farm trails are beginning to disappear as villagers move away, and there are noticeably fewer paths marked on the latest 1:25,000 maps.

Maps etc

The 1:25,000 maps (28, 29, 30) date from the 1990s, yet building and road work in both Ponte da Barca and Ponte de Lima has altered many trails. In Ponte de Lima, the construction of the motorway has dramatically affected access to the countryside, particularly east of town, and the 1:25,000 map doesn't show the new road. The turismo in Ponte de Lima prepared a series of walk descriptions a long time ago but is now reluctant to hand them out in the wake of inaccuracies caused by modern construction, especially of the motorway.

Guided walks

Gota Verde (℡ 253 616836) runs about six day-long walking tours a month to various points around the Rio Lima and into the Parque Nacional Peneda-Gerês. They're based in Braga, but the tourist office in Ponte de Lima has brochures, and there's no need to pre-book: just show up at the designated meeting place. The ADERE office in Ponte da Barca (℡ 258 452250) coordinates walks organized by various individual guides, mainly in the Parque Nacional Peneda-Gerês.

When to go

Whatever the season, come prepared for a downpour, as the Minho is Portugal's rainiest region. Summers are comparatively dry and hot, autumns are pleasant if you're lucky with the weather, and spring is dazzlingly green. The walks described in this section can even be done in winter, as they rarely stray above sea level or wander too far from civilization. Try to time your visit to catch some of the Minho's lively festivals (p 37);

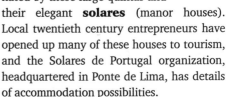

the best are in August and early September.

Flora & Fauna

There's excellent birdwatching all along the Rio Lima. Look out for the solitary **kingfisher** perched above the water or flying fast and dart-like just above it. In riverside rushes and marshy ground you may see the **fan-tailed warbler**, recognizable by its distinctive tzeep sound, always produced from the same point in its undulating flight.

Stocky, white-breasted **dippers** prefer faster-flowing waters, so look out for them along tributaries near Entre-Ambos-os-Rios. **Otters** are present in the Minho, although there's little chance of spotting them in developed areas. Over farmland, look out for **kestrels**, **Montagu's harriers** and **sparrowhawks**.

People & Culture

The distinctive architecture along the Rio Lima springs from the varying agricultural practices of the local people. In Entre-Ambos-os-Rios and the surrounding villages, crops are grown on steep terraces, and the subsistence farmers must make the food they harvest last all year. To protect corn and grain from rats, local people built stilted stone structures called **espigueiros**, and these curious containers can be seen throughout the region. The best collections are in the villages of Soajo and Lindoso, just east of Entre-Ambos-os-Rios.

The fertile soil and flat land around Ponte de Lima lends itself well to vine-growing,

and the town prospered as a result. The landscape is dominated by these large quintas and their elegant **solares** (manor houses). Local twentieth century entrepreneurs have opened up many of these houses to tourism, and the Solares de Portugal organization, headquartered in Ponte de Lima, has details of accommodation possibilities.

The Minho has always been the religious centre of Portugal, and while ornate churches and ecclesiastical politics are centred on Braga, the people around the Rio Lima celebrate religion in their own way. Much of the impetus for building the region's churches came from the large number of pilgrims heading north towards **Santiago do Compostela** in Spain. These pilgrim routes passed through the Minho to avoid the mountains to the east. Ponte da Barca was named for the boat that used to ferry Santiago pilgrims across the river, and the area is dotted with serene Romanesque churches, in particular the one at Bravães (p 42). Around Ponte de Lima, most villages boast a stone cross carved with conch shells, the symbol of the Caminho do Santiago.

The Minhotos aren't quiet and pious worshippers, however. The area is renowned for its religious **festivals**, and villagers pull out all the stops for their annual summer bash (p 37). The liveliness spills over into secular celebrations, too, and it's worth timing a visit to Ponte da Barca or Ponte de Lima to coincide with their fortnightly markets.

Food & Drink

Steel your stomach; this is **offal** country. Every menu in every restaurant offers delicacies such as tripe and rice cooked in blood, and even safe-sounding meat dishes contain disturbingly recognizable bits of animal. Unappealing though this may sound, many of the ingredients combine to make deliciously rich and satisfying dishes. Even so, after a few lunches and dinners even the most committed carnivore might be hankering after something different. Luckily for them (and more particularly for any hapless vegetarians who are still reading this), the region's markets and shops stock excellent bread, olives and fruit.

There's only one thing to drink in the Minho. The region's **vinho verde**, a young, semi-sparkling wine, is in light and delicate contrast to the heavy food. Almost every restaurant has its own blend, traditionally poured straight from the barrel into earthenware jugs or ceramic cups. White vinho verde has been successfully exported for years, but the wine is named for its youth rather than its colour, and the lesser-known red vinho verde is freely available throughout the Minho. It's worth getting over any reservations about drinking semi-sparkling red wine, as it's an oddly tart and delightfully refreshing drink.

Tourist Information

Tourist offices

Ponte de Lima turismo, Praça da República (☎ 258 942335), possibly the most helpful and patient in the country.

Ponte da Barca turismo, Largo da Misercórdia (☎ 258 452899), open sporadically in summer and closed in winter. Some information on the Parque Natural de Peneda-Gerês is available from the ADERE office (☎ 258 452250) on the first floor of the same building.

Transport

Public transport is pretty good to Ponte de Lima (frequent buses from Braga and Viana do Castelo), less frequent to Ponte da Barca and fairly sketchy once you move further east. There are generally a couple of buses a day to and from Entre-Ambos-os-Rios, but check times beforehand, especially on weekends and holidays.

Money

Cashpoints and banks in Ponte de Lima and Ponte da Barca.

Accommodation

Entre-Ambos-os-Rios campsite, signposted off the EN203 (☎ 258 588361). Well-equipped and beautifully situated on a bend in the river. Open May to September.

Unofficial camping along the Rio Lima just east of Ponte de Lima.

$ Pensão Gomes, Rua Conselheiro Rocha Peixoto 13, Ponte da Barca (☎ 258 452288).

$ Pensão São João, Largo de São João, Ponte de Lima (☎ 258 941288).

$$ Residencial os Poetas, Jardim os Poetas, Ponte da Barca (☎ 258 453578).

$$ Quinta da Prova, Ponte da Barca (☎ 258 453186), just across the bridge.

$$–$$$$ Solares de Portugal, Praça da República, Ponte de Lima (☎ 258 741672; www.turihab.pt). Central booking for rural properties all over Portugal, concentrated around the Ponte de Lima region; minimum two-night stay. See also Privetur, a similar organization on Largo das Pereiras in Ponte de Lima (✆ 258 741493). Best places include:

$$$ Casa do Arrabalde, Ponte de Lima (✆ 258 742829), just across the Roman bridge from the town centre.

$$$ Moinho de Estorãos, Estorãos, 12km from Ponte de Lima (✆ 258 742829). A renovated stone mill complete with water wheel, next to a Roman bridge; includes kitchen facilities. Open May to October.

Shopping

Ponte da Barca and Ponte de Lima have good grocery stores, and Ponte de Lima also has fabulous bakeries and pastelarias. There's a small shop in Entre-Ambos-os-Rios, but there's not much to buy there.

Ponte de Lima's Monday market, held fortnightly on the banks of the Rio Lima, is the oldest in Portugal, established in 1125.

Come early for the best in clothes, plastics and trinkets. Ponte da Barca's market is on alternate Wednesdays with nearby Arcos de Valvedez; it's a lively place to pick up anything from picnic supplies to cattle.

Events & Festivals

Vaca das Cordas (Ponte de Lima, early June), bull running festival; **Festa do Corpo de Deus** (Ponte de Lima, day after Vaca das Cordas), religious festival with flower paintings on the streets; **Nossa Senhora da Agonia** (Viana do Castelo, weekend closest to August 20), huge parades, firework displays and colourful costumes at one of Portugal's best festivals; **Festa de São Bartolomeu** (Ponte da Barca, week up to August 24), singing, dancing and fireworks at Ponte da Barca's annual bash; **Feiras Novas** (Ponte de Lima, mid-September), part market, part fair, one of the oldest and most popular festivals in Portugal.

1. Chapel of Santo Ovídio

Fast Facts

distance	10km	rating	easy to moderate
time	4 hours	map	28 (1:25,000)
	centre map page 2		

Ponte de Lima is encircled by cobbled streets and beautiful old mansions. This walk takes you high above the town to the strange church of Santo Ovídio, dedicated to the patron saint of ears.

Parts of this walk follow the Caminho de Santiago, the pilgrimage route to Santiago de Compostela in Spain, and there are frequent shrines and stone crosses incorporating the route's conch shell symbol. It's an easy walk, with just the one climb up to Santo Ovídio; bring a torch for a better look into the church.

Begin the walk by crossing over the Rio Lima via the elegant pedestrianized Roman bridge. Of the original bridge, five arches remain; the remainder date from fourteenth and fifteenth century renovations. Before the bridge existed, the river is said to have temporarily halted the inexorable march of the Romans across the Iberian Peninsula. Believing the Lima to be Lethe, the river of oblivion, the Roman troops refused to cross. Only after their commander, Decimus Junius Brutus, waded to the other side and shouted out their names to show that his memory was unaffected did the troops brave the water.

At the other side of the bridge turn right just before the Capela de Santo António. Ignore the cobbled road off to the left 200m later and instead turn left down a dirt track signposted Quinta do Arquinho. This inauspicious-looking track was once an important part of the network of Roman roads leading from the Minho to Astorga in Spain; since the early Middle Ages, it's been better known as a section of the Caminho de Santiago.

Pilgrimages to Santiago began in the tenth century to pay homage to the remains of Saint James, who had spent time preaching the gospel in Spain before being beheaded in Jerusalem. Pilgrims were attracted by the chance to test their faith against the danger and hardship of a route obstructed by wolves, bandits and Moors, and were encouraged by cathedral authorities who recognized the potential economic rewards early on.

The track narrows to a path after about 200m and you walk along the bottom of a field. Although the route here is overgrown, it's lined on either side by stone walls and fields so it's hard to lose your way. In any case, the overgrown section soon ends and you arrive at a junction with a broader track in a few hundred metres. Turn left here, and follow the track up to a tarmac road. Cross the road, following the sign to the Quinta do Sabadão, a beautiful mansion that you'll pass in 100m. Keep walking on the track, pass an abandoned building on your left, then take the grassy track off to the left 50m later.

In about 150m the track becomes cobbled and you arrive at a T-junction with a large stone wall. This wall encloses the Casa de Pomarchão, a handsome, eighteenth century Solares de Portugal property. To peer through the gates at the magnificent courtyard turn right; otherwise turn left to continue the walk.

In 200m, turn right on meeting a tarmac road, pass a café and restaurant then turn left up the road signposted Santo Ovídio 300m further on. It's a steep and twisting climb up with little shade but in just over a kilometre you'll reach the top. Below you the huge quintas nestle grandly in the Lima valley, their vast vineyards fanning out around them.

The chapel at the top of the hill is one of the oddest in Portugal. Dedicated to the patron saint of ears, it attracts the aurally afflicted in a steady trickle. Visitors walk a number of times around the tiny chapel, said by the turismo to be 500 years old, and finish the ritual by leaving behind a wax model of their ear. You can't get into the church and it's pretty dark inside, but once your eyes adjust to the gloom you can make out a revolting pile of wax ears just behind a grate. As a cure, it just might work, but you have to feel sorry for the person who cleans up the waxy gunk.

To return to Ponte de Lima, retrace your steps down the road for 500m, then turn left down a dirt track at the apex of a distinct right-hand hairpin bend. Veer left at a fork in the track 200m later, then turn left again at a T-junction with a cobbled road 200m further on. This is a lovely road, lined with small houses and quintas and shaded by trees and vines. The road curves around to the right then reaches a crossroads in 50m; turn left here to walk down a narrow tarmac road with high stone walls on either side.

In 500m you reach a T-junction at a large quinta, the Rego de Azal. It's a bit run down now, but its high walls and ornate doorway are still impressive. Turn left here, and in a few hundred metres you'll arrive at an elaborate stone cross in the middle of the road. The prominent conch shell indicates a connection with the Caminho de Santiago. Legend has it that when Saint James' body was brought back to Spain from Jerusalem by sea, his followers saw a man riding on horseback along the beach. The horse took fright and fled into the sea, but emerged a few minutes later with both horse and rider covered in shells.

Take the road straight ahead, just to the right of the church, passing a café on the left in 50m. Cross over the N201 and pass to the right of a shady village green, ideal for picnics. Head down the exceedingly narrow cobbled road, passing beneath overhanging balconies. The bottom of the street meets up with the old Roman bridge, but before heading back into Ponte de Lima spend some time wandering about this lively part of town.

2. Along the Rio Lima

Fast Facts

distance	13km	rating	easy
time	4 hours	maps	28 (1:25,000)
	centre map page 2		

West of Ponte de Lima, tiny hamlets and farmland line the banks of the river. The appeal of this easy stroll lies in the gentle, pastoral landscape and the friendliness of the farmers and villagers you meet rather than in any tourist sights of note.

The walk can be hot in summer, so take plenty of water. Start the walk at the café-filled Largo de Camões, one of Ponte de Lima's best spots for people-watching.

Facing the Roman bridge, turn left to walk along the waterfront boulevard, heading west out of town. This wide, elegant boulevard is shaded by trees and the kilometre walk to the Igreja de Nossa Senhora da Guia is popular with tourists and picnickers. Notice the conch shell above the church door, showing that you're walking along part of the pilgrim route to Santiago.

The trail continues to shadow the river and soon passes a weir with a fish ladder; keep straight ahead 40m later, ignoring the track off to the left. The trail becomes a cobbled road with stone walls either side, and overhead vines shelter the route from the sun. Pass the Quinta de Buraço on your right after about 500m, then keep on the road as the cobbles change to tarmac. Another 500m from the Quinta you pass the small chapel of Senhora das Neves; turn right immediately after the chapel to cross over the bridge. Keep straight ahead through the villages of Barros and Pedrosa, passing the church of São Francisco on your right. Among the cluster of old and new buildings that you pass is a stone cross that dates from 1636, another landmark on the road to Santiago.

In 50m the road forks; turn right here, then go straight across at a crossroads almost immediately afterwards. Keep straight ahead 100m further on as a road joins from the left. The houses start to thin out here as you approach farmland. Ignore the left-hand dirt track in 150m, and instead take the dirt track off to the left 100m further on, at a 45 degree angle to the road. There are olive trees and a low stone wall on your left-hand side. Follow this lane for 700m until you reach a T-junction with a cobbled road; turn right here and follow the road until you almost reach the Rio Lima.

Just before the river there's a track off to the left between a field and a small eucalyptus grove. Follow this track alongside the river, passing an electricity substation. There are lots of places to picnic around here, and a quick dip in the river is a welcome relief from the summer heat. Follow the riverside track for about a kilometre, until it curves sharply to the left and moves away from the river.

The fields around here are filled with corn in summer, and the hot, dusty tracks that thread through the tall plants are in sharp contrast to the cool, walled-in vineyards and olive groves that cover much of the rest of the land around Ponte de Lima. The tall corn is an excellent hiding place for small rodents, and this attracts birds of prey to the area; watch out for buzzards, sparrowhawks and kestrels.

Turn left at the T-junction in 100m, then take the track off to the right 500m later; this part of the walk can be muddy after rain. The trail curves around to the left in a few hundred metres. Ignore the first turning off to the right and keep to the lesser worn trail; instead take the right-hand track 500m further on, just before you pass under some powerlines. The trees that line this track are a welcome relief after the lack of shade in the cornfields. Stick to the main track as it winds through the trees, ignoring less obvious paths off to the right and left.

You'll eventually reach a fork in the trail marked with a large stone letter M; turn left here. Turn right at a T-junction in 300m, then left at the crossroads 100m further on. The large stone cross on your left here shows that you are back on the pilgrims' road to Santiago. In half a kilometre you'll pass a small shop where you can pick up a drink and a snack. Soon afterwards there's a shrine to Santo António; take the left-hand route here, down a cobbled road lined with stone walls and vineyards. In another 500m you'll find yourself back at the old stone cross; take the right-hand fork just afterwards, following the road across the bridge. Remember to turn left here past the small chapel of Senhora das Neves, then follow the road all the way back into Ponte de Lima.

3. Bravães

Fast Facts

distance 13km	rating easy
time 4 hours	maps 29 (1:25,000)
centre map page 3	

A delightful walk through farmland and over hills to the thirteenth century church of Bravães, decorated with some of the finest Romanesque carving in Portugal.

Leave Ponte da Barca by road, following the signs to Viana and Ponte de Lima, then at the small roundabout on the edge of town take the left-hand road that leads to Braga (note that this road isn't marked on the 1:25,000 map). Walk up this road for 150m, then turn right to go down a cobbled lane. Follow this lane over a beautiful stone bridge and up to a tarmac road that you'll reach in about 400m.

Turn left here and follow this road for almost a kilometre past a mixture of old and new houses, slowly climbing up above Ponte da Barca. Turn right at the junction, cross under some powerlines and turn right immediately afterwards up a dirt track.

Follow this track up to the small ridge, ignoring less obvious trails off to the right and left; once on top of the ridge the trail curves around to the left and flattens out.

About 300m after joining the track you'll come to a junction of five paths; take the second right trail that heads upwards just to the right of a small knoll. There are some huge boulders at the side of the trail rising above the scrub landscape, and excellent views of the surrounding farmland.

Half a kilometre further on, turn right on reaching a tarmac road, then keep right at a T-junction shortly afterwards. The road goes steeply downhill here and enters more cultivated farmland, and then in 600m reaches the village of Lobeira. Turn left to walk through the village, then turn right 300m later down a gravel road just as the village ends.

After 150m the road curves around to the right into the small hamlet of Airó. There are interesting old stone houses in Airó, some with split-level accommodation for animals and people, and all draped in vines or flowers.

At a right-hand bend in the road, turn left to walk down a small gravel track that quickly becomes a cobbled road. This is a shady part of the walk, passing through small vineyards and under overhanging trees. Stick to the main track as the cobbles end and the track traverses along a hill, before going steeply downhill to join a tarmac road. At the road, turn right and walk downhill into the village of Peneirada. Keep a look out for a small chapel on the right of the road after about 400m, and take the cobbled track off to the left about 50m after this.

Enjoy the pastoral scene that unfolds as you walk between villages along routes used for generations. After crossing a small stream, you'll come to the hamlet of Porta. Turn right at the group of three crosses next to a central washing area. These communal washing places are an interesting feature of Portuguese rural life.

Initially built to conserve water, many are maintained despite the presence of modern plumbing in most houses, perhaps as much for their social and communal value as for their convenience. Turn right at the tarmac road and follow it down to the main Ponte da Barca–Ponte de Lima road. Here, you'll find a small café-bar with a shop attached.

Turn left to walk down the road a short

way to the church at Bravães. Initially founded as a monastery in the twelfth century, it underwent a series of internal crises until by the fifteenth century it was practically uninhabited. In 1434, the archbishop of Braga revoked the monastic order, and the building became the church of São Salvador. The church is dominated by its intricate arch doorways carved with a glorious mix of local, exotic and mythical animals: you can see sheep, oxen and birds of prey amongst griffins and monkeys. There's more traditional Christian imagery here too, including Christ flanked by two angels above one of the doors. The whole place is in elegant and welcome contrast to the heavy gilt-dominated churches in much of the rest of Portugal.

The church may be locked: if so, ask for the key at the cottage behind. Inside, there are frescoes that date from the fifteenth and sixteenth centuries: St Sebastian on the left, and the Virgin and Child on the right. The church looks even smaller from the inside, with seating for just 30 people, and its walls are bare aside from simple wooden crosses. Back outside, you can see stone sarcophagi in the grounds to the east of the church.

To continue the walk, go back towards the café-bar, but take the gravel left-hand lane just before it. Walk past a stone gate on your right and a school on your left, and keep going as the gravel changes to tarmac. Follow the road as it curves around to the right, then turn left at a T-junction; 30m later, turn right down a dirt track. (Note that this road layout is different to that on the 1:25,000 map.) Stick to the main dirt track as it winds down towards the Rio Lima, ignoring side tracks off into the tiny fields that line the route.

As you approach the river, keep an eye out

for a stone structure that looks like a gate from the back, but is clearly a fountain when seen from the front. Walk around to the front of the fountain towards the dirt track you can see straight ahead, then turn right to follow the track for about a kilometre. There are lots of places to rest and swim along the river, although the best is near the fountain.

Ignore the first junction off to the right, but take the second one that winds past an ugly sewage works (separate from the river, which is lucky if you've just been for a swim) to join the Ponte de Lima road. You can turn left here to return to Ponte da Barca the quick way, but it's a narrow road with no pavement and can be busy in summer.

To detour around the main road, turn right, then turn left after 30m. Keep left at a junction 300m further on, and walk past houses and small-holdings up to a large electrical tower. Take the first left at the crossroads here, walk through the hamlets of Rua Nova and Barreiro, then turn right.

The road goes steeply downhill, crossing a small stream. Turn left 50m after the stream, keep left at another junction 200m later, then turn left again at the T-junction 50m further on. From here, you can look across the Rio Vade at Ponte da Barca's surprisingly impressive football stadium. You're now back on familiar territory; when the tarmac road ends, turn left down the cobbled lane to cross over the old bridge. Turn left at the main road and head back to Ponte da Barca.

4. Rio de Froufe

Fast Facts

distance	12km	rating	moderate
time	4 hours	maps	30 (1:25,000)
	centre map page 4		

A walk alongside the lovely Rio de Froufe, passing dilapidated farmhouses that are being reclaimed by the surrounding countryside, then through the gorgeous, timeless village of Lourido, before crossing barren hills and descending back into Entre-Ambos-os-Rios (also called São Miguel by locals).

The walk is overgrown in places, and there's a tricky section around the village of Froufe. Some of the walk has been marked with red and yellow paint by the Parque Nacional de Peneda-Gerês as a trilho interpretado (interpretive trail) and there is an accompanying booklet available at park offices.

From the campsite at Entre-Ambos-os-Rios, walk up to the main road and turn left. Cross over the bridge and turn right 500m later down a tarmac road that quickly becomes narrow and cobbled. The landscape around here is steep and craggy, and drought-resistant scrub plants dominate the hills. A little over a kilometre down this road, and just before a stone bridge crosses the Rio de Froufe into the village of the same name, turn left to go down some steps and join a path that follows a narrow levada (watercourse) high above the river. The path here can be tricky and narrow in places as it switches from one side of the concrete levada to the other, but the watercourse always shows the way.

After 500m, the watercourse and river meet next to a couple of dilapidated stone buildings. There's an old bridge below you, and this part of the river is a popular local bathing place. Turn left immediately after the houses to follow a distinct path uphill. The path initially passes between two stone walls and consists of large stone slabs, then curves around to the right and becomes a dirt track. In 300m, you'll reach a T-junction with a broader track; turn right here.

You're now walking on part of the trilho interpretado and the route for a while is marked with red and yellow equal signs (=). It's an ancient route between mountain villages and you can still see cartwheel grooves in the stone and the occasional incongruous streetlight. Ignore the track off to the right in 200m that doubles back towards the river.

Soon, the path moves back towards the river, sometimes a little too near it for comfort as there's an occasional sheer drop to the water below. This section of the walk is delightfully shaded, the deciduous trees unusual in this area's landscape of unremitting pine. You'll pass a number of abandoned fields next to the path, evidence of the Minho's population drain to urban Portugal and France.

The track begins to widen, then curves around to the right to cross over the river. The Rio de Froufe is broad and shallow here, and large, flat stepping stones have been placed across it. You'll need to cross two branches of the river to reach the track on the other side. It's a wonderful place for a paddle, although far too shallow for a swim.

Once safely across, walk uphill along a stone path flanked by high walls. At a T-junction with a broad track, turn right to keep going uphill, then turn right again at another junction 50m later. Keep heading in the same direction to pass under some overhanging vines and you'll reach a cobbled road soon afterwards. You're now in Lourida, an old stone hamlet perched on a hill; behind you, there are lovely views down into the Froufe valley.

As you climb up and away from Lourida, the cobbles change to tarmac, and there's a spectacular drop down to the Ribeiro de Carcerelho on your left. You can see for miles over the Serra Amarela into Spain but the landscape is depressingly barren and treeless. In 400m, turn right on to a track next to some electricity pylons. In 500m, the path loops around to the right back towards Lourida; turn left soon afterwards to cross over a tributary of the Rio de Froufe via an old bridge.

From here, Lourida's history is laid out beneath you. Old stone houses line the cobbled road through the village, and above them you can see a number of small stone constructions on stilts. These are espigueiros, built from the eighteenth century onwards to protect harvested corn or grain from rats, and still used today in places like Lourida. Often topped with a stone cross to add a little divine assistance to the anti-rodent struggle, their attractive design belies their rather mundane function.

Above the village are neatly terraced fields, the only way in which the villagers can grow crops on the steep slopes. Many of these are deserted, however, as people move away to try and earn their fortune in the cities. Some of the émigrés succeed in accumulating what is to the villagers that remain a fantastic amount of money, and return in retirement to build ugly, ostentatious reminders of their success.

Keep on the same path for a kilometre, until you come to a makeshift football pitch. Turn left here to go uphill, then keep straight ahead 200m later, ignoring the path off to the left. The landscape here is depressingly familiar; fire has destroyed the planted pine trees, leaving stumps and low scrub. Still, it's a popular enough place with the local livestock, and you'll see the odd herd of sheep or goats wandering about.

About 1km after the football pitch, there's a fork in the track as you approach a small river valley. Turn right here, going downhill, and in a few hundred metres you'll arrive at a tarmac road where you should turn right. Walk down the road for about 700m, then turn left down a cobbled road that leads into Entre-Ambos-os-Rios.

At a cross in the village, turn left to go down a tarmac road; there's a café-bar and bread shop on your left. Keep heading down this road, cross over the N203 and arrive back at the campsite.

Other walks

The turismo at Ponte de Lima gives out a leaflet describing a walk from Ponte de Lima to Valença on the Spanish border, part of the pilgrimage route to Santiago. Other walks around Ponte de Lima are possible, but the motorway just to the east of town cuts through many of the best walking areas, and there are very few ways around it. Further east, Soajo makes an excellent hiking base for walking in the Serra do Soajo and around the old villages of the region.

Rainy Day Options

If you have wheels, you're in luck. The local tourist region, aware of the area's propensity to rain, has mapped out themed itineraries such as a vinho verde route and a handicraft circuit; ask at the turismos in Ponte de Lima or Ponte da Barca, or at any of the large hotels for details.

There's not much to see in Ponte de Lima or Ponte da Barca if it's raining, although both are excellent places to stretch out a morning over a coffee and a pastry. If it's sights you're looking for, follow the Rio Lima to the sea and visit Viana do Castelo. Viana, as well as being an attractive town in its own right, boasts a couple of interesting churches, a good museu municipal and a castle. Above Viana, the Monte de Santa Luzia is worth the walk (or the funicular ride) to see the fascinating remains of a Celto-Iberian citânia, dating from around 500BC.

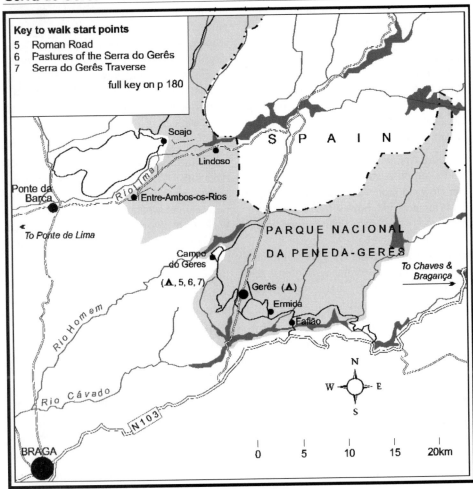

Key to walk start points

5 Roman Road
6 Pastures of the Serra do Gerês
7 Serra do Gerês Traverse

full key on p 180

What's the weather like?

	Jan	April	July	Oct
Sun	3 hrs	6 hrs	8.5 hrs	5 hrs
Rainfall	180mm	90mm	30mm	120mm
Maximum Temp	11°	17°	25°	20°
Minimum Temp	2°	6°	13°	8°

Average hours of sun, total average rainfall and average temperature in degrees celsius

Serra do Gerês

Don't Miss . . .

A classic, two-day alpine traverse across barren mountains and through deep, wooded valleys (p 57)

Avoid the crowds and spend a summer afternoon in a beautiful mountain pasture (p 54)

Follow in the steps of centurions along a Roman road complete with milestones that skirts around a cool, clear reservoir (p 52)

Serra do Gerês

The Serra do Gerês is a dramatic granite massif at the heart of the Parque Nacional da Peneda-Gerês in Portugal's far northern Minho region. Its fringes are popular with drivers and picnickers, but its desolate peaks rise amidst some of the most isolated wilderness in Portugal.

Walking

Geography

The serra consists of a series of huge granite mounds sliced through with breathtakingly steep wooded valleys. At the highest levels, a treeless plateau stretches into Spain. Lower down, there's a mix of almost vertical valleys and gentler slopes that contain some of the last virgin deciduous forest in Portugal. Most of the serra would be completely free of human occupation were it not for the road running north from the town of Gerês to the border with Spain and the Spanish Parque Natural Serra do Xures.

Parks & reserves

The Parque Nacional da Peneda-Gerês was created in 1971 as part of Portugal's contribution to the European Year for the Protection of Nature. Whereas the other Portuguese parks are classified as Parques Natural (natural parks) Peneda-Gerês is the only Parque Nacional in the country due to the presence here of important and undisturbed ecological areas. The park's main objectives are to preserve the natural environment, and in particular the most ecologi-

cally sensitive places away from the tourist centres nearest the border with Spain. It's a difficult battle in such a popular tourist area, and the inadequacy of the park's infrastructure is all too apparent in the busy summer months.

While visitors descend on the spa town of Gerês, most of the villages in the park are being deserted at an alarming rate. Farming here can be harsh and unprofitable, and most of the region's young people have moved to cities or emigrated to France to find work.

It's taken a while, but the park now seems to appreciate the interdependence between the traditions of rural village life and environmental protection. The Associação de Desenvolvimento das Regiões do Parque Nacional da Peneda-Gerês (ADERE) is a park-affiliated organization created to promote the region's rural traditions. From its office in Ponte da Barca (p 51), it co-ordinates accommodation from camping sites to the restored stone houses in the village of Soajo. ADERE also produces leaflets on the park's archaeological and architectural heritage, as well as on traditional products such as honey, wool and linen.

The park has sporadic printed information at its various offices, but offers little advice to walkers and discourages walking in the park in an effort to prevent environmental damage to sensitive areas.

Trails

The area around the Serra do Gerês was once criss-crossed by a network of shepherd paths and farm tracks. Since the movement to the cities earlier this century, however, the trails have become forgotten and overgrown

48

through lack of use.

In the early 1990s, the Parque Nacional put in place a coherent plan to map and clear trails in the park, centred on a long distance footpath called the Trilho Longo Curso. Stages of the route went from village to village, often to places off the usual tourist itineraries. The beginning of each stage was marked with a wooden map and the route was marked with yellow paint; the park office even provided a sketch map of the trilho. Unfortunately, this enlightened approach was scuppered by a government funded road-building program that paved over much of the route. By 1993 many of the tracks were either paved or so overgrown as to be impassable. Today the trilho seems to have been quietly abandoned: it's no longer mentioned in the park literature, and trails have been allowed to deteriorate.

Instead, the park is emphasizing shorter interpretive trails around villages on the fringe of the park, accompanied by attractive leaflets pointing out natural and cultural attractions en route. By 1999 there were just two marked and documented trails: one around Entre-Ambos-os-Rios in the west of the park, and the other around Pitões das Júnias in the east.

In the meantime, other organizations are starting to clear and mark paths in the region. Cerdeira campsite in Campo do Gerês (p 51) has marked a number of trails around the western flanks of the serra, while tour groups mark various routes in the eastern part of the park. Although these marked trails can be useful, the lack of a central coordinating agency means that there's no way of knowing where most of the routes lead, and there's also a danger that paths not designated by the park will pass through environ-mentally sensitive areas. The upshot of all this is that it's never wise to rely on trail markers alone: always take a map and a compass with you and know how to use them.

Maps, etc

The 1:25,000 maps of the park (30, 31, 43, 44) all date from the 1990s; the main tracks and roads are present, although there's little logic to which paths are marked and which are not. The 1:50,000 maps (military 5I, 6IV, civilian 5B, 6A) are insufficiently detailed for walking in a mountain area like the Serra do Gerês, where you may have to navigate using key landmarks.

The park publishes an overview map marked with villages and points of interest, which includes brief information on the park's ecology and culture. It's available at park offices, as is the Portuguese language *Flores do Parque Nacional*. The colour photographs of the region's flora in this book are useful even for non-Portuguese speakers.

Guided walks

There are a number of local places offering guided walks within the park. The ADERE office in Ponte da Barca (℘ 258 452250) coordinates walks organized by various individual guides, while other walking trips can be booked at both the campsite (℘ 253 351005) and the youth hostel (℘ 253 351339) in Campo do Gerês.

Many walking tours to Portugal include at least a couple of days near Gerês; see p 4 for contact information.

When to go

Summer sees the best weather on high

ground, with the least chance of rain. Unfortunately, everyone else knows this, and although the walks will be deserted, the campsites and pensions will be cramped. On the other hand, pensions and the campsite in Gerês shut down outside peak season. Early autumn and late spring may be a good compromise between fairly predictable weather and availability of accommodation.

Flora & Fauna

One of the most ecologically important areas in the Serra do Gerês is the **Mata de Albergaria**, an old growth deciduous wood next to the Vilarinho das Furnas reservoir and bordered on two sides by road. The ancient **oaks** and **chestnuts** here are important in their own right, but they also provide vital shelter for animals such as the **Leisler's bat**, rarely found this far south.

Higher up, the barren mountains are brightened by a succession of wildflowers. In spring, the hillsides are carpeted with vibrant **heather** and **gorse**. Later in the year head to the mountain pastures to see the **quita-merendas lily** (*merendera pyrenaica*), a single purple or pink flower growing close to the ground. If you're lucky, you might also see the **Gerês iris**, unique to the serra. It's a delicate, bluer version of the common iris, with smaller flowers and long, narrow leaves, and generally grows singly up through the scrub.

The fauna in the Serra do Gerês is among the richest in Portugal, and although the last of the brown bears disappeared at the end of the nineteenth century, there are still **wolves**, **wild boar**, **roe deer** (the park's symbol) and **otters** in the park. Most of these shy creatures live in the inaccessible areas of the park near the Spanish border. The park is also one of the best places in Portugal to see birds of prey. When you're high up in the mountains look for **golden** and **short-toed eagles** and **peregrine falcons**. Lower down, you might see the tiny **scops owl**, which generally lives near human habitation; its soft, repeating call is distinct among owls and sounds remarkably similar to that of the **midwife toad**, also found in the park.

People & Culture

The park's initial focus on the natural side of things led to some friction with local farmers and shepherds. Park officials were seen as unsympathetic to farmers' needs, especially when there were delays in compensation for attacks on livestock by wolves and other animals.

Today, there's not much left of traditional life in the Serra do Gerês. Waves of **migration** have emptied the villages of most people under 65, and those that remain are increasingly employed in tourism rather than agriculture. The belated attempt by the park to define and promote traditional culture may stop a few people moving away, but the seasonal nature of tourist employment can't compare with the lure of steady city work.

Away from the tourist centres, life goes on for the villagers that remain in much the same way as it always has. Tending a small plot of land or a flock of goats occupies daylight hours, then it's home to make wine or cheese, or to spin wool into yarn by the fire. Water is collected from a communal village fountain and clothes are washed by hand. There are cars, but these compete for cobbled road space with ox-drawn carts. In summer, many shepherds migrate along with their flocks to the high mountain pastures, remaining there for weeks or months on end.

Food & Drink

Traditionally, the food around the Serra do Gerês mirrored that of the Lima Valley (p 35). Tourist tastes are taming the local fondness for offal, however, and restaurants in Gerês tend to offer identikit menus of fried fish or meat served with chips.

If you're looking for authentic Gerês produce, try the local **honey**. As elsewhere in Portugal, the locals claim that their bees and flowers conspire to create the finest honey in the land. Here, it's just possible they may be right.

The serra's steep slopes and rainy climate preclude most vine growing, so the local **vinho verde** generally comes from further west. What's bad for the wine is ideal for producing clear mineral water, however, and the brand named after the mountain range is particularly good.

Tourist Information

Park Offices

Park headquarters, Avenida António Macedo, Braga (✆ 253 6003480).

Information office, Avenida Manuel Francisco da Costa, Gerês, just north of the town centre (✆ 253 391181).

Tourist Office

Gerês turismo, Avenida Manuel Francisco da Costa, in the colonnade at the north end of town (✆ 253 391133).

Transport

Public transport into the park is sporadic: a few buses a day run from Braga to Campo do Gerês, more to Gerês. Within the park, transport is hopeless—it's impossible to go either east or west from Gerês, and there's no way of reaching Soajo, Lindoso or Entre-Ambos-os-Rios without returning to Braga.

Money

There's one bank and two sporadically-working cashpoints in Gerês.

Accommodation

Parque Campismo Vidoeiro, 1km north of Gerês (✆ 253 391289). Steep site, small pitches, river swimming, noisy and crowded in summer, open year round.

Parque de Cerdeira Campsite, Campo do Gerês (✆ 253 351005). Sells and distributes walking information, some 1:25,000 maps; bar, shop, excellent restaurant.

$ Vilarinho das Furnas Youth Hostel, Campo do Gerês (✆ 253 351339).

$ Casas Abrigo, Gerês. 2 mountain huts, each with 4 bedrooms and minimal facilities can be rented for two days minimum. Contact ADERE in Ponte da Barca (✆ 258 452250, e-mail aderepg@mail.telepac.pt).

$–$$ Rooms. Rooms are available for rent in many of the serra villages. In Gerês they're often the cheapest choice, and in villages such as Ermida and Fafião they provide a fascinating insight into rural life.

$$ Residencial Stop, Campo do Gerês (℘ 253 351291).

$$ Pensão da Ponte, Rua da Boa Vista, Gerês (℘ 253 391121).

$$ Pensão Adelaide, Rua da Boa Vista, Gerês (℘ 253 3900020).

$$$ Hotel Universal e Termas, Avendia Manuel Ferreira da Costa, Gerês (℘ 253 391170).

Shopping

Amidst the tacky souvenir stands in Gerês, there's an indoor market with a couple of good fruit and vegetable shops and bakeries. Head down to the two minimarkets at the bottom of town for the best selection of tins and packets. Shopping in Campo do Gerês is difficult: there are a couple of shops in the village and one in the campsite, but neither of them sells much of anything. The closest place to buy petrol is in Rio Caldo, 10km south of Gerês.

5. Roman Road

Fast Facts

distance	12km	rating	easy
time	4 hours	map	30 (1:25,000)
	centre map page 4		

The Romans have little to show for the 600 years they spent in Portugal, but this stretch of Roman road, the best-preserved part of the 215 mile route from Bracara Augusta (Braga) to Asturica Augusta (Astorga), is one of their more impressive legacies.

The road runs alongside the lovely Vilarinho das Furnas reservoir, providing glimpses of the submerged village of the same name; bring binoculars for a closer look. This walk largely follows the route described in the leaflet produced by Cerdeira campsite.

Turn right out of Cerdeira campsite to walk along the tarmac road. In 400m you'll come to a T-junction; ignore the left-hand road to Vilarinho das Furnas and the right-hand road to Portela do Homem and instead take the track straight ahead of you, that's signposted Geira Romana.

You soon have great views of the Vilarinho das Furnas reservoir, a beautifully-situated body of water created when the village of the same name was flooded in 1972. In summer when the water level falls, you can make out the remains of the village on the far side of the reservoir. Vast stretches of farmland were also submerged, and countless stone walls edge down the hillsides before disappearing into the water.

The sunken village was once a model of communitarian living, a true democracy where property was owned in common and decisions were reached by a consensus of the people. There's an excellent museu etnográfico in Campo do Gerês containing artefacts donated by the villagers (p 61). The villagers also played a large part in preserving the road; well-built and sturdy, they saw no reason to build a new track or cover the stone slabs.

It's almost immediately apparent that you're walking along an old Roman road: large blocks of stone pave the way, and centuries of cartwheels have etched definite grooves into the stone. The Romans first came to the Iberian Peninsula in 218BC, but it took them more than 200 years to subdue the significant resistance from the local people. Once settled in they quickly began organizing trade, establishing metal mines and fish salting works, and creating a sophisticated network of river and road routes. Roman road Number XVIII, called Geira, linked Bracara Augusta (Braga) to Asturica Augusta (Astorga in Spain) over the Serra do Gerês.

In about 300m you reach the cluster of milestones at mile XXIX. The Romans marked every mile of their roads with stone columns inscribed with the distance to certain cities and the name of the emperor who decreed the construction of the road; some also bear the name of the governor of the region.

A total of 86 milestones have been found between here and the Spanish border at Portela do Homem, dating from the 1st to the 4th centuries AD; many of them were restored in 1992. This first group consists of 13 stones in total, some fragmented and most on their sides; two of the milestones are in particularly good condition with clear inscriptions.

The stretch following this first group of milestones is the best-preserved part of the route and you can clearly see cartwheel grooves in the stone. Although Roman roads were famously built to the width of a chariot, it's likely that these marks were made by more modern vehicles. The road here is beautifully shaded by trees and bordered on either side by stone walls.

After about 700m the road emerges from the shade and veers towards the edge of the reservoir; in winter, parts of the path become submerged by the water but it's easy to detour via the broad, flat rocks. You soon cross over a stream on stepping stones, then arrive in 100m at mile XXX, where there's just a single milestone. Closer to the water you can see more substantial remains that have yet to be fully excavated: it's thought that this may have been a station for resting and changing horses.

In 300m the path becomes grassy and a little overgrown, although there are a number of yellow paint stripes here to show you the way. Soon, you'll arrive at a dirt road, which despite being subject to traffic restrictions can be dusty with cars in summer. Walk up this road until you reach a group of milestones at mile XXXI.

In spite of the road, this is a lovely setting, with a bridge over the Ribeiro do Pedredo and a couple of shady spots for a picnic. There are 21 stones here of which around 10 have legible inscriptions. It's unusual to see such a large number of stones in one place, and it's been suggested that the stones were grouped together recently, possibly when the forestry road was built in the 1940s. Mile XXXI is the turnaround point of the walk; try to time the walk back to the campsite so that you catch the sun setting over the eerie remains of Vilarinho das Furnas.

6. Pastures of the Serra do Gerês

Fast Facts

distance 6km	rating difficult
time 5 hours	map 30 (1:25,000)
centre map page 5	

High above Campo do Gerês, the western edges of the Serra do Gerês are a spectacular combination of strange granite shapes and steep-sided valleys.

While the paths are fairly easy to follow, the walk is rated difficult because of the steep climbs and the isolation. It's hard to find your way to the next shepherd stone in bad weather, so always be aware of a change in the weather. A map is essential, as are good navigation skills. This route is based on a walk mapped by the people at the Cerdeira campsite (p 51); it's marked with red paint, yellow paint and shepherd stones.

Turn left out of Cerdeira campsite to walk along the road, then turn left at the T-junc-tion in 400m following the sign for Braga; if you're not staying at the campsite begin here, at the village bus stop. Just after crossing a concrete bridge 200m later, turn left on to a dirt track.

This track has stone walls and fields on either side and is shaded by oak and pine trees. Many of these fields are no longer used and ruined buildings line the route; it's clear that Campo, as the locals call the village, is increasingly a tourist-driven rather than a farm-based economy.

The trail narrows to a single track after about 150m, shortly after passing under an old vine trellised across the path. You'll pass a rock on your left painted with a red and yellow equal sign (=); 100m later keep left at a junction. The trees start thinning out here as the path begins to climb and you'll begin to see piles of shepherd stones that mark the route from now on.

Ignore the path to the right marked with a yellow dash in 50m; instead, take the path off to the right 50m further along, this time marked with a red painted dash. To your left, a path leads to a popular spot with the local beekeepers for keeping hives. Honey is still widely produced in the Serra do Gerês; you'll find the end products in stalls that line the main street of Gerês itself.

Continuing the walk, cross over the stream bed of the Ribeiro da Roda 75m later and follow alongside it up the valley; there's another stream immediately to your right and soon these streams split the mountain into two distinct valleys: be sure to keep to the left-hand valley, passing a dry stone wall and gate on your right. All the while, your route is marked with red paint dashes, although these can be far apart and occasionally difficult to spot. Note too that this trail is not marked on the 1:25,000 map.

The path is occasionally overgrown but, on the whole, it's a well-worn route still used as an approach to the high pastures by local shepherds.

Soon after the valley splits, cross the streambed once more; this is only about 150m after you first crossed the stream. The valley narrows into a bottleneck at a large boulder, then opens out again as you pass a dry stone wall on your left. In another 50m,

you get the first distinct view of your path up the mountain, which heads up the barren U-shaped valley to your left towards the large boulders clearly visible at the head of the valley.

The path begins as a broad stone track and zigzags up the slope following the red markers. About two-thirds of the way up, the path gets much steeper and the trail veers off to the left, before swinging back to the right to pass underneath the boulders you saw from the valley floor.

The trail finally emerges at the saddle marked Fraga do Suadouro on the 1:25,000 map. You're standing amongst low scrub in barren, rocky country, high above Campo do Gerês, but there's still a good bit of climbing left. There's a large rock marked with a red equal sign here, showing where you should start your climb up the mountain, heading east.

The trails zigzags upwards, still following shepherd stones, initially on the right-hand side of the valley, then it crosses the face of the mountain heading for the granite spires above you. Soon you'll see the long line of a stone wall straight ahead, looking distinctly out of place in an otherwise barren and empty setting. Head up towards the middle of the wall, then turn around and stop.

The views from this part of the walk are glorious: down to the Vilarinho das Furnas reservoir and beyond it to the radio masts on the peak of Louriça mountain. In summer, with binoculars, you can see the ruined buildings of the village of Vilarinho das Furnas (p 9) sticking out of the water.

Cross over the wall, then head straight up and over the ridge and you'll soon arrive at a mountain pasture. This is a beautiful spot, dotted with oak trees and, in late summer and autumn, the delicate pink lily the Portuguese call quitamerendas. All that's visible at this time of year is a single flower growing close to the ground; the leaves don't appear until the spring, after the flower has disappeared.

Looking across the valley ahead, a single granite spire dominates the landscape, and at the base of the spire you can see the clear line of the trail you will eventually join. The shepherd stones continue out of the bottom of the gently-sloping pasture then the path veers to the left-hand side of the small valley, climbing slightly.

The trail maintains its height and curves around to the left, then flattens out and passes a huge boulder with a very pronounced overhang that looks disturbingly like Barney the purple dinosaur. Soon you come to a narrow rock pass, and 30m further on there is a junction in the trail; in total, you've walked about 1.5km since leaving the saddle at Fraga do Suadouro.

You've now finally linked up with the trail that's marked on the 1:25,000 map. The route straight on heads to Pé de Cabril and Portela de Leonte (see the Serra do Gerês Traverse on the next page); you should turn right, heading towards the granite spire you saw from the pasture. The path here is well-worn but only intermittently marked with stones.

The trail curves around the base of the granite spire then heads uphill to another saddle, around 700m on from the junction. You're walking on fairly level ground through low scrub and there are magnificent views across the Gerês valley to Borrageiro moun-

tain. To orient yourself on this part of the route, notice the dirt road that is further along the ridge, and keep to the path that runs in a line a little to the right of this road. About 400m after the saddle you cross a stone wall. The trail soon joins up with another stone wall and follows alongside it until you reach a couple of houses at Junceda.

About 50m further along from these houses, there's a yellow dash painted on the wall. Here, you should turn right and head across a meadow just to the right of a large lump of granite, following the yellow dashes that will lead you all the way back to Campo do Gerês.

This path isn't marked on the 1:25,000 map, and although it was once an easy trail and formed part of the park's Trilho Longo Curso, it's been a bit neglected in recent years and is getting overgrown in places. You should see yellow dashes at frequent intervals: if you haven't seen one for a while, try retracing your steps to the last one.

The path goes downhill and can be a bit slippery in wet weather, so take care. Soon, Campo do Gerês comes into view and you zigzag down to a rocky meadow. There's a fascinating shepherd's hut at the end of this meadow, carefully built into the surrounding flat rocks, maximizing heat and minimizing construction time. For some reason, there's a large yellow Number 90 painted on one wall.

On leaving the hut, the path curves right in about 50m and heads more steeply downhill, giving views of the U-shaped valley that you climbed earlier in the day. Always keep a sharp lookout for yellow markers, particularly in one spot where the route you're following veers off the main track: there's a large yellow arrow marking the distinct right-hand turn. By now, you're approaching the treeline once more. It's a bit of a scramble to cross over the Ribeira da Roda a little further on, but in 30m you'll link up with the trail that

began this walk. Turn left here and follow the path back to the tarmac road, then retrace your steps to the campsite.

7. Serra do Gerês Traverse

Fast Facts

distance	31km	rating	difficult
time	2 days	maps	30, 31, 43, 44 (1:25,000)
	centre map pages 5, 6, 7		

The wildest and most isolated scenery in Portugal lies within easy reach of two of the main tourist centres of the Serra do Gerês. This walk links Campo do Gerês to Gerês via a long and tortuous route over craggy mountaintops and across isolated high pastures.

The surroundings are breathtakingly majestic, the walking exhilarating and exhausting. Most of all, you need good map reading skills. As you need to navigate using distant landmarks, it's best not to attempt this walk in bad weather or poor visibility. Note that it's also possible to walk from Gerês to Campo do Gerês via an easier route; see p 61 for details.

Day 1

Follow the Pastures of the Serra do Gerês walk up until the Pé de Cabril junction (p 56). Continue straight ahead instead of turning right towards Junceda, following the trail marked on the map. It's sometimes diffi-

cult to find the path so keep a close eye out for the shepherd stones.

In 100m you climb over a pass into a meadow, which can be waterlogged in spring. Above you, the Pé de Cabril dominates the landscape, a huge jutting granite mountain, unnamed on the 1:25,000 map, although its spot height (1235m) is marked. Head across the meadow towards a stone shepherd hut, aiming just to the right of the shoulder of Pé de Cabril.

The views from the meadow are stunning, and fairly close is the looming Borrageiro mountain, where you'll head later in this walk. On a clear day you can see across to the Serra da Estrela 140km away, and north

57

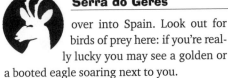
over into Spain. Look out for birds of prey here: if you're really lucky you may see a golden or a booted eagle soaring next to you.

The path out of the meadow curves to the right to skirt around the mountain, then heads through a rocky pass into another meadow. Head straight up through the meadow and keep going through the rocky boulder field above it; there are worn stone steps here to help you find your way. On reaching a third meadow, veer right and scramble across some rocks.

You're now immediately below the main granite rock face of the Pé de Cabril, with fabulous views down into the Gerês valley, dense with trees. The route starts to descend across broad flat rocks; up ahead you can see a dirt track that you'll link up with soon. The path gets steeper and more distinct as you go down and soon you'll find yourself below the treeline.

Eventually the path ends at a T-junction with a broad dirt track; turn right here and you'll arrive at the road in 400m. Despite stopping restrictions, this road is choked with cars in summer as tourists head for the viewpoint at the border with Spain. The road cuts through one of the most ecologically sensitive areas in the park and the damage being done to the fragile environment is causing park officials to rethink their vehicle access policy.

Cross the road and join the stone path on the other side near a No Fishing sign. The path climbs steadily and is in excellent condition, intricately constructed from large stone slabs; it's quite shady too, a welcome relief in summer. As you get higher, you're treated to yet more fantastic views of the Gerês valley, and the distinctive Pé de Cabril looks particularly impressive from here.

On passing through a gap in a stone wall the shepherd stones, which have been absent since the road, begin to reappear. After about 1.5km the trail arrives at a mountain pasture. This is a fantastic place for a picnic, complete with stone table and chairs under an old oak tree. The gently sloping meadow is filled with quitamerendas lilies that form a sumptuous blanket of pink in late summer. From the meadow, you can see the radio masts at the top of Borrageiro; the trail climbs up the series of small river valleys that lead down from the top of the mountain.

On leaving the meadow, cross a small stream. Turn right 100m later to follow another stream for 200m up to a saddle where there's a pyramid-shaped stone and more great views. The trail traverses left for about 400m and skips over yet another small stream, then turns right and follows a fourth stream (where there's usually water) for about 600m up to a ridge. At the top of the ridge, the trail splits in two. The right-hand trail leads down into the Rio do Camalhão valley; you should take the left-hand trail that keeps heading uphill for the last real climb of the day.

In 300m you'll arrive at an arid plateau strewn with boulders; the view stretched out before you is a vast progression of craggy peaks. Cross over a stream and enter a meadow. At this point, the walk leaves the trail marked on the 1:25,000 map; your eventual destination is the broad-bottomed valley to the east of the outcrop marked Roca Negra (N23°1', W73°8') on the map.

As you cross the meadow, look for the

small ridge topped by two cairns about 45 degrees to your right; leave the meadow and climb up to the ridge. Just behind the ridge there's a small stream; turn right and follow this stream for about 300m until you're in a bowl at the head of the small valley.

Notice the series of three small peaks on your left, marked on the 1:25,000 map as spot heights 1401m (N24°, W73°5'), 1404m (N23°8', W73°7') and 1413m (N23°7', W73°7'). Climb up between the second and third peaks, then once at the ridge veer right to walk across a saddle.

Straight ahead of you are two distinct twin summits of Roca Negra (1381m and 1386m); walk towards these for about 100m, then turn left to walk towards another large rocky summit (1353m, N23°3', W74°6'). After about 150m the valley you're heading for is clearly visible below.

Pick your descent into it carefully, then once you're at the valley bottom, turn right and head towards a group of oak trees in the pasture. You're now back on a good trail and the tricky navigating is at an end. The meadow is an oasis of green, although the more distant views are still dominated by the now familiar craggy landscape.

Walk through the pasture, passing shepherd huts on your left. In summer you'll see the odd herd of beautiful reddish-brown cows up here; their huge curving horns may look ominous but the animals tend to be too engrossed in chewing to pay much attention to hikers.

Shepherds come up to the Serra do Gerês' mountain pastures for long stretches of time in the summer, but it's a dying occupation. The villages' young people increasingly reject the isolation of the hills in favour of more lucrative work; three quarters of Parque Nacional inhabitants are over 65 and the population is, quite literally, dying off.

Traverse through a series of valleys, following the frequent shepherd stones. About a kilometre on from the first valley, you reach an exceedingly narrow saddle where the ground plunges giddily down to thickly wooded valleys.

Cross the saddle, then walk through the rock pass straight ahead, ignoring the shepherd stones that lead across the bare rock on your left. About 100m after the pass, the trail heads up to the rocky ridge on your right.

Views open up ahead of you south towards the Rio Cávado in welcome stretches of green. Cross a small meadow, passing a conical shepherd hut and you'll arrive at the top of a rocky spur. Follow the trail down this spur, looking out for the shepherd stones that mark your route.

At the end of the spur, the trail emerges at a large, wide meadow; walk across it heading for the coniferous trees at the far end. The trail is now wider and dusty; it zigzags steeply down the mountain through patches of coniferous forest. At the beginning there are ugly gaps where forest fires have devastated the landscape, but as the path becomes less steep you enter established forest with more diverse trees.

You're coming to the end of today's walk now, some 4km after crossing the narrow saddle. The path appears to end at a small rocky spur, but if you look carefully you'll see stone steps leading downwards; follow these until you join up with a wide path that leads down to the Rio de Fafião.

The river is an idyllic spot for swimming, with cool waters, chest-high pools and large, flat rocks on which to dry off. The area tends to get a bit crowded on summer evenings but you're sure to find a quiet place if you move further upstream. Camping is tolerated here, although it's officially prohibited by park regulations. Alternatively, it's only another 1.5km to the hamlet of Fafião where there are rooms to rent; to get there, walk up to the dirt road, then turn left to cross over the bridge.

Day 2

To return to Gerês, walk up to the dirt road a little way on from the river pools, and turn right. It's a quiet road as the rickety bridge you reach in 2km discourages traffic. After crossing the bridge, you start to climb steeply; turn right at a junction 100m later, following the signposts to Gerês. In another 1.5km, turn right again, this time following the signs to Ermida, and in 500m you'll reach the village itself.

Ermida's a lovely place, seemingly frozen in time. Its steep cobbled streets overhang with vines, and there are fabulous views down to the Rio Cávado. At the end of the village, there's a café-bar and a small shop; turn right at the T-junction just beyond the shop.

You're now back on a dusty road, still climbing through forest. In a couple of kilometres, you'll reach a junction; turn right to detour to the impressive Arado waterfalls, about a kilometre away, or left to continue the walk. There's still a bit of climbing left, although it's less steep than before.

In another few kilometres you reach a junction near the viewpoint at Pedra Bela; turn left here for stunning views down into the Gerês valley and over to the Caniçada reservoir; otherwise go straight ahead. You're now finally heading downhill for the first time today. This stretch of road can be busy in summer as the Pedra Bela viewpoint is popular with tourists, and there's a chance you could hitch a ride down if it's late enough in the day.

The road emerges at a picnic site just above the town of Gerês. Turn left here to reach Vidoeiro campsite in a few hundred metres, and the town of Gerês in another kilometre.

Quick Quiz
3. In which year was Lisbon largely destroyed in an earthquake?

(answer on p 184)

Other walks

There's a quicker and easier way to get from Gerês to Campo do Gerês than by following the walk on p 57. From Gerês, follow the Rua da Boa Vista uphill, then turn right to walk along the road. Turn left at the next junction, and follow the road for a couple of kilometres until you reach the Fonte da Quinta da Buraca. About 200m further on, there's a steep dirt track off to your right; follow this for just over a kilometre until you rejoin the road. Turn right, and follow the road into Campo do Gerês. Alternatively, you can turn off the track about 100m after passing the houses at Lamas and follow this path to the houses at Junceda. From Junceda, you can take the route described in the Pastures of the Serra do Gerês walk on p 56.

Another popular walk is to the fabulous viewpoint of Pedra Bela high above Gerês. You can approach the viewpoint following the road that leads up from the picnic area above the town, or take the more attractive but steeper path that leads up from various points on the main street. Try to time the walk for early in the day, when there are fewer cars and tourists.

East of Gerês there are a multitude of farm tracks around the attractive villages of Cabril and Fafião, looping down towards the Rio Cávado or ambling through forest. You'll need your own transport to get here, and you can stay in one of the many dormidas in the villages.

Rainy Day options

The spa in Gerês is the ideal place to soak away your hiking hangover. There are some baths in the colonnade near the tourist office and others further down the road near the Hotel Universal e Termas; they're open daily except Sunday.

If you're in Campo when the rains come, visit the Museu Etnográfia de Vilarinho das Furnas, a fascinating look at the village life that ended in 1972 when the reservoir was built. The museum includes photographs and artefacts donated by the villagers, and is a poignant memorial to their communitarian society. It's open daily except Mondays.

Once you've exhausted the options around Gerês, take the bus to Braga for an overdose of churches—the self-proclaimed religious capital of Portugal boasts dozens of religious buildings. Easily the best is Bom Jesus, a short way outside town, approached by a massive granite stairway decorated with symbolic gargoyles and fountains.

Further afield, and sadly inaccessible by public transport, is the Citânia de Briteiros is an atmospheric Celtic settlement, occupied from about 300BC and the site of determined resistance against Roman attacks. It's fascinating to wander around the remains of the site; houses, streets and water systems are all clearly discernible, and two of the stone huts have been reconstructed.

Quick Quiz

4. In which year was the Carnation Revolution?

(answer on p 184)

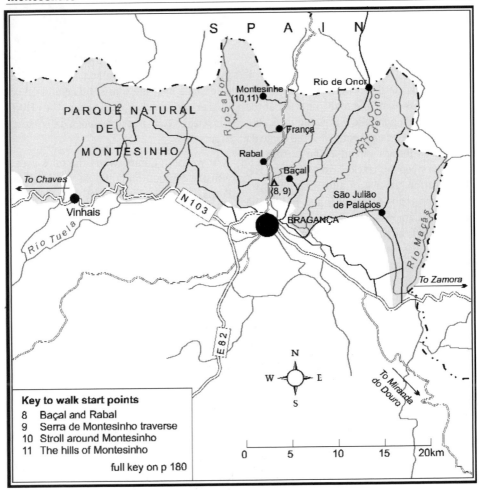

Key to walk start points
8   Baçal and Rabal
9   Serra de Montesinho traverse
10 Stroll around Montesinho
11 The hills of Montesinho

full key on p 180

What's the weather like?

	Jan	April	July	Oct
Sun	4 hrs	8 hrs	9.5 hrs	6.5 hrs
Rainfall	150mm	73mm	21mm	79mm
Maximum Temp	13°	19°	25°	21°
Minimum Temp	4°	9°	15°	11°

Average hours of sun, total average rainfall and average temperature in degrees celsius

Montesinho

What's Inside

The Walks

Don't Miss . . .

Sample the region's famous sausages and smoked meats. The best include **salpição** and **presunto** (p 66)

Spend three days walking up and down the **rolling hills** of the Serra de Montesinho (p 71)

Wander lazily through mountain hamlets

The Parque Natural de Montesinho lies in the Terra Fria of the Trás-os-Montes. It's aptly named on both counts: Trás-os-Montes means beyond the mountains, and Montesinho is squeezed into the northeastern-most corner of the country, bordered on three sides by Spain, while Terra Fria (cold earth) alludes to plummeting winter temperatures and the biting, chilly winds that sweep across the mountains.

Don't be put off; Montesinho is a beautiful, isolated pocket of Portugal, warm in summer and a great place to see wolves and birds of prey. Scattered amongst the wilderness are around 100 tiny villages, and exploring their individual quirks and characteristics can occupy the walker for weeks.

Walking

Geography

The land of schist and granite falls from its heights of more than 1000m at the Spanish border to the lower, more populated areas around the towns of Bragança and Vinhais. The park is crossed by a huge number of rivers running north to south, and the scenery is an alternating mix of high, barren mountains and lush valleys.

Environmentally, the major problem in the region is forestry. Ever since the Middle Ages, indigenous deciduous forests have been destroyed to make way for profitable, fast-growing pine. This dramatic destruction accelerated in the first half of the twentieth century, when Salazar's Campanha do Trigo (wheat campaign) dictated that forests should be chopped down and replaced with wheat and other cereal crops. The climate and landscape of the Trás-os-Montes was completely unsuited to growing wheat and as local farmers abandoned the now-sterile land, the old cereal fields were replaced with yet more pine plantations.

Parks & reserves

Montesinho park staff were quick to recognize the inextricable link between the health of the natural environment and the traditional life of the park's human residents.

Efforts to encourage tourism focus on locally-driven projects such as accommodation in park villages and initiatives like the centro hípico in França, where visitors can rent horses or mountain bikes. The park promotes local handicrafts, and organizes agricultural competitions to maintain the high farming standards associated with traditional methods.

The main conservation effort is geared towards rejuvenating deciduous forests of oak and chestnut. The park funds the study, development and application of techniques to reintroduce indigenous species, offering subsidies for farmers who plant deciduous trees and help with thinning and clearing. The park also promotes small-scale, high quality wood production rather than fast-growing commercial forestry.

The staff at the park office in Bragança are helpful and knowledgeable, although they have little information on walking.

Trails

Trails throughout the park are generally still in use by villagers and farmers, so their condition is excellent. Most are wide enough for a cart or tractor, and are ideal for mountain biking. There's some trail deterioration and redirection around the large forestry projects, although this is generally short-term and avoidable. There are no trail markings or signs in the park.

Maps etc

The 1:25,000 maps of the park (10, 11, 12, 23, 24, 25) are all up-to-date. The civilian 1:50,000 maps (3C, 3D) are fairly useful, but the military equivalents (3II, 3III) date from the early 1970s.

The free, English-language *Montesinho Natural Park* sketch map includes brief information on the park's wildlife and culture and is an useful overview if you're driving or mountain biking. Roads marked as unpaved on the map can be in very bad condition, especially after rain, and are best attempted in a four-wheel drive or on a mountain bike.

More comprehensive information can be found in the Portuguese language Parque Natural de Montesinho book, available from the park office and filled with details of environment, people and culture. The book includes three walks, three mountain bike routes and three car tours, all with maps clear enough to be useful to non-Portuguese speakers.

Guided walks

Not many tour groups venture into the natural park, although Rotas do Vento (p 4) organizes infrequent weekend hikes in the area.

When to go

The Terra Fria lives up to its name in winter, with snow and thick fog on the highest eleva-

tions from December to March. Summers are generally sunny and warm, but be prepared for the occasional storm if you're hiking.

Flora & Fauna

Despite the widespread planting of pine, some deciduous natural forest remains. The most important area is a tract of relatively undisturbed **Pyrenean oak** between the Sabor and Tuela rivers, one of the largest forests of its kind in Europe. The oak forests harbour plenty of plant life; look on the ground for flowers such as the **hairy violet**, **Martagan lily** and **cranesbill**. Present too, but more difficult to spot are the mammals: the forest is home to **genets**, **pine martens**, **wild cats**, **badgers** and **wild boar**.

The other major undisturbed habitat is the high altitude region closest to the Spanish border. The **wolf** is firmly established at the apex of the food chain here, its territory stretching from the eastern border of the park through the Parque Natural Peneda-Gerês and almost to the Atlantic. The 200 or so wolves that live in this part of Portugal need the space: they can move 20–40km in a single day, smell prey or a potential mate 2km away and hear things that are up to 10km distant.

In isolated areas of the park, the wolf feeds on wild boar, roe deer and red deer, although some packs have adapted to human presence, and members of one pack that lives close to Bragança supplement their traditional diet with domestic animals such as sheep and goats.

Along with these adapted wolves, more populated areas in the park are home to **white storks**, **redstarts** and **house martins** and in winter, are sometimes visited by bramblings and citril finches. Above the fields, look out for **Montagu's** and **hen harriers** and the **northern wheatear**.

People & Culture

The first inhabitants of the Parque Natural to make an impression were the Zoelas people, who built at least 30 **hill-forts** in the area during the Iron Age. Up close, these forts look like any of the other rolling hills in the park, but from a distance the defensive rings around them become distinct and impressive.

These Iron Age peoples were among the first to farm the area, and agriculture is still the dominant industry in the Parque Natural. Little seems to have changed in the last couple of millennia, and most of the inhabitants of the region's hundred or so tiny villages continue to survive through small-scale, subsistence farming.

Within the villages, **traditional architecture** is being encouraged, and much government-funded restoration is going on. Spruced-up Montesinho is attractive in a picture postcard kind of way, but it's often lesser-known villages like Baçal, an earthy mixture of old and new, that are more interesting to explore.

As elsewhere in isolated rural Portugal, **migration** to the cities is depleting the population. In the last decade or so, the park's efforts in encouraging traditional farming methods, handicrafts and tourism have started to pay off, and while the village populations are noticeably dominated by the elderly, there are far fewer abandoned villages in Montesinho than in other remote regions of the country.

Food & Drink

Montesinho's gastronomic highlight is its various smoked meats. **Presunto**, a smoked ham similar to Italian prosciutto, is dry-cured in a mixture of red wine, spices and salt, then smoked for about a week; the best is said to come from Chaves, just east of the Trás-os-Montes. **Salpição** is similarly-treated smoked pork tenderloin, great for barbecues. Try the local sausages, too: there's an excellent butcher shop in the market in Bragança filled with meats of all description, hanging next to reminders of the owner's glory days as a local football star.

The **chestnut** groves that dot the region contribute tastily to some regional specialities, including chestnut and potato soup and pork stuffed with chestnuts.

Be careful what you order after an afternoon walk, as you may end up eating that cute animal you passed in the woods earlier: **rabbit** and **wild boar** are popular. Trout is abundant in local rivers and popular in restaurants; try the stunningly-good **truta à moda de Bragança**, in which the fish is wrapped in presunto and baked.

Eating out may be tortuous for vegetarians, but the food at Bragança's daily market more than makes up for the hardship.

Tourist Information

Park office

Park office, Bairro Salvador Nunes Teixeira 5, Bragança (℘ 273 381234; website www.icn.pt/parques/pnm/pnm.html), down a left-hand road 200m past the turismo.

Tourist office

Bragança Turismo, Avenida Cidade de Zamora (℘ 273 381273).

Transport

Bragança is easy to get to by public transport from Lisbon, Porto, Braga and Vila Real. Once in the park, your options are more limited. Infrequent STUB buses run to and from the villages north of Bragança, but many of these services disappear outside the school term. Ask at the turismo, park office or campsite for up-to-date schedules.

Money

Banks and cashpoints in Bragança.

Accommodation

Campismo Sobre Águas, Bragança (℘ 273 331535), 6km north of Bragança on the França road. Bar, restaurant, small shop, lake; infrequent buses. Open May to October.

$ Residencial Poças, Rua Combatentes 200, Bragança (℘ 273 331428).

$ Pensão Rucha, Rua Almirante Reis 48, Bragança (℘ 273 331672).

$-$$ Casas de Abrigo. The park office can book you into a number of casas de abrigo (mountain huts); call well in advance.

$-$$ Rooms. Many villages have rooms for rent. Ask at the park office before setting out, or in village cafés and shops once you arrive.

$$ Residencial São Roque, Rua Miguel Torga, Bragança (℘ 273 381481).

$$ Residencial Santa Isabel, Rua da República, Bragança (℘ 273 331427).

$$$ Classis, Avenida João da Cruz 102, Bragança (℘ 273 331631).

$$$$ Pousada de São Bartolomeu, Estrada de Turismo, Bragança (℘ 273 331493), 1km out of town.

Shopping

Bragança's market is one of the best in the country, packed full of fruit, vegetables and Tupperware. The town also has a couple of hypermarkets, including one just outside town at the turning to the campsite.

Events & Festivals

There are lots of fairs in the park villages in summer, when there's generally traditional music (including bagpipes) and dancing. The biggest festivals include **Feira do Fumeiro** (Vinhais, February); **Feira Franca da Moimenta** (Moimenta, weekend closest to 25 April); **Feira das Cantarinhas** (Bragança, early May), traditional handicrafts; **Feira da Lombada** (São Julião, 2 August); **Nossa Senhora do Carmo** (Moimenta, 19–20 August); **Festa dos Rapezes** (whole region, Christmas or Twelfth Night), single young men dress like psychotic morris dancers in rags, bells and masks and skip around the village performing initiation ceremonies said to go back to Roman times.

8. Baçal & Rabal

Fast Facts

distance 17km	rating easy
time 5 hours	map 25 (1:25,000)
centre map page 8	

An easy walk on good farm tracks through three small and seldom-visited villages. As you walk among the gentle, rolling landscape, you'll pass an Iron Age hillfort and a hilltop shrine.

Despite these lofty constructions, the highlight of the walk is in and around the villages themselves, where precarious balconies mix with beautiful communal buildings and pombals, the Trás-os-Montes' trademark horseshoe-shaped dovecotes. Sundays are hunting days, so save the walk for another time if you're after a bit of peace and quiet. The walk begins and ends at the Sobre Águas campsite, 6km north of Bragança, where there's free parking and a bar-restaurant.

Turn left out of the campsite to walk along the tarmac road. After 200m take the road on the right that soon loops around to go back under the tarmac road; follow the track as it curves first left, then right to cross a bridge. Look out for kingfishers on the river here, easily recognizable by their squat body shape, bright blue and green colouring and dagger-like bill. If you don't see one helpfully perched on a branch for easy spotting, watch for a brilliant flash of colour out of the corner of your eye as the kingfisher speeds low over the water.

The dirt track follows a wire fence for a

while, then continues straight on 200m after the bridge as the fence curves around to the left. Ignore the right-hand track 50m later that leads to a house. Climb uphill, and you'll soon be rewarded with views of layers of undulating hills; to the south you can see Bragança, its imposing old centre just distinguishable amongst the modern suburban sprawl. In a further 300m keep straight ahead, following the line of pylons. There are views over to the Alta Lombada in the west of the park, a more mountainous and forested region than the agricultural hills you're walking over now.

As the track goes downhill slightly, you enter pockets of deciduous wood, and overhanging trees and bushes provide some shade. This in an excellent place for seeing and hearing songbirds, particularly in the early morning. The more open agricultural land is home to a number of birds of prey, including the hen harrier, Montagu's harrier and buzzard. Soon, the village of Baçal comes into view as the track begins to climb once more. Look out for frogs in the small ponds that line the trail here; even in summer, when the water has almost dried up, there's a good chance of seeing a European tree frog.

The first houses in Baçal are modern, simple and surrounded by the rusting hulks of farm vehicles. Soon after you pass the houses, turn left next to a fountain at a T-junction with a broad dirt road. The road becomes cobbled and in a couple of hundred metres you're in the centre of Baçal.

Unlike prettified villages such as Montesinho, Baçal is still very much a farming community. Tourist-led gentrification has yet to reach the village, and architecturally, it's a rag tag mix of old and new buildings, cobbled together and half-finished. Despite, or maybe because of this lack of renovation, Baçal is an interesting village to wander around.

They don't see many visitors here, so be prepared for a barrage of questions and a convoy of villagers curiously following you around.

Go left at the stone cross in the village, pass a church and you'll soon reach the end of the houses. Go straight ahead along a dirt track as the cobbled road you're on curves around to the right next to a shrine. Look out for a horseshoe-shaped small building on your left, one of a huge number of pombals (dovecotes) scattered about the Trás-os-Montes.

The buildings look much too good for pigeons, whitewashed on the outside with sloping roofs. The roofs are made of overlapping slates and are constructed in three different levels with gaps in between so that the birds can fly inside and nest in holes in the walls; small, whitewashed stones are sometimes fixed along these gaps to act as a pigeon-like lure.

The birds are fed by way of a small door at the front of the pombal. Most of the pombals are no longer used, but those that remain provide local farmers with valuable pigeon-dropping fertilizer as well as a year-round food supply.

Keep on the main track for half a kilometre and you'll reach a chestnut grove, ideal habitat for tawny owls and rock sparrows. Chestnuts are a winter staple in the Trás-os-Montes, stuffed into meat or cooked with root vegetables into hearty stews. In the grove, keep straight ahead, ignoring a track off to the left and also one to the right 30m later. Walk downhill, ignoring another right-hand track in 100m, and heading for the Ribeira de Baçal. There's lots of tree-planting going on here, part of the park's efforts to regenerate indigenous deciduous forest.

Just before you reach the river, the track dog-legs to the left. Cross a stone and concrete bridge, then in 75m take the left-hand rocky track going steeply uphill. At the top of the rise, ignore the track to the right as you see the church of Santa Ana on the hill ahead of you.

Keep straight ahead 50m later, ignoring a track to the left, then take the left-hand track at a fork in the trail 200m further on. The track follows the river and there's a well-preserved pombal on your right. In a few hundred metres, cross a stone bridge over the Rio Sabor, then turn left on joining a tarmac road.

In 100m you'll arrive at the village of Rabal, one of the most attractive settlements in the park with the added bonus of a couple of cafés. Turn right at the cafés along the lower of two cobbled roads. On your right is the Casa do Povo, the communal town hall common to most villages in the Trás-os-Montes. Historically, the casas were used to store villagers' possessions and were dedicated to a saint: as a religious building containing communal property, the possessions then remained tax-free.

Turn left just after the Casa de Povo, then keep on the main cobbled street and cross over a concrete bridge. There are fabulous buildings in this part of Rabal; balconies jut out into the street, often resting on improbably large stone monoliths, and doors are marked with carved red crosses to ward off evil spirits.

At a drinking fountain, turn left to go uphill, follow the road as it curves around to the right, then take the track off to the left 30m later. This dirt track climbs steeply, giving an unusual perspective of the village's varied roofs; as you climb, keep to the main track, ignoring the multitude of smaller paths off to the left.

Once you've climbed for a while, turn around and look at the hill behind Rabal. On the hill, called the Alto do Castro, you can clearly see the remains of the concentric earthwork circles of an Iron Age hillfort. The defensive systems of this hillfort, one of around 30 in the park, consisted of stone walls alternating with steep trenches and parapets. The inhabitants farmed the surrounding countryside and retreated to the hillfort for protection from frequent attacks.

About a kilometre after leaving Rabal you'll reach the sanctuary of Santa Ana, packed with the picnicking faithful during religious holidays. The church itself is fairly modern and uninteresting, but there are great views of the endless rolling hills from the top and lots of shady stone benches where you can eat and rest.

From the large cross just below the church, follow the dirt and gravel track downhill. The track winds down the south-facing slope, one of the few places in the Parque Natural that's sheltered enough to grow olives and grapes, although neither look particularly healthy. In 700m a track joins from the left, then the trail becomes cobbled and you enter the village of Meixedo. Turn left when you reach the main cobbled road to detour to the village café; turn right to continue the walk.

Meixedo is another appealing village with fine examples of traditional architecture. Turn left at the tiny village chapel, then take the left-hand fork 50m later, passing an old barn. At a junction 300m further on, turn left to go downhill. Ignore the track that joins from the left 250m later, then turn left in another 50m to follow a small stream. There's some welcome shade here, and a remote chance of seeing a shy otter or water vole.

In another half a kilometre, ignore the track to the right heading uphill. Soon afterwards, you begin to leave the stream; keep to the main track from now onwards, ignoring tracks off to the left that lead back towards the water. The track heads steeply uphill to open ground then flattens out before going downhill past a couple of houses and joining the Bragança–Rabal road. Turn left here, and in 600m you'll arrive back at the campsite.

9. Serra de Montesinho Traverse

Fast Facts

distance	65km	rating	moderate
time	3 to 4 days	maps	11, 12, 24, 25 (1:25,000)
		centre map page 9, 10, 11	

The Parque Natural de Montesinho is an attractive mix of traditional villages, beautiful river valleys and unpopulated, windswept mountain plateaus. This walk swings from farm track to riverside trail to high, boulder-strewn route and back again, taking in some of the loveliest scenery in the park.

The timing of the walk varies, depending on where you want to stay and how far you want to walk each day. There's accommodation available in Rabal, França, Montesinho, and casas de abrigo (mountain huts) at Lama Grande and on the Rio Sabor; book in advance at the park office in Bragança (p 67). While liquid refreshment is available at every small village along the way, there's not much in the way of more substantial sustenance: take enough food for the whole trip. There are many variations on this walk; see the end of the walk for some alternatives.

Follow the Baçal and Rabal walk to the village of Rabal (p 68). Once in Rabal, turn right to go steeply uphill along the cobbled road just before the Casa de Povo. Take the right-hand fork in 100m; the cobbles soon end and you're walking on a dirt track. Keep on this main track, ignoring a series of smaller tracks (off to the left in 100m, right 200m further on, and left in another 300m).

About a kilometre after leaving Rabal, the track goes steeply uphill, becomes more stony and curves sharply to the right at a gate. Turn off the main trail to continue straight on at this bend along a less distinct track. Turn left at a junction in 500m, then take the middle of three paths 100m later. In another 250m you'll reach a water tank and a concrete building just below a rocky outcrop. Follow the main track here as it curves first to the right, then back around to the left; ignore the left-hand track that leads off from the right-hand bend.

The trail follows the line of a hill to cross first one, then another river valley; both can be muddy even in summer. The track rises to meet a gravel road; turn right here, where there are clear views of the dramatic hydroelectric power station on top of the hill to your left. Follow the gravel road as it changes to tarmac and then arrives at the village of França. Turn right at the village, pass a mini-mercado on the right, and you'll reach the main Bragança–Portelo road in 100m.

França's a small, laid-back village with a couple of places to rent rooms and some old, odd-looking buildings. There's also a park-run centro hípico where you can rent horses and mountain bikes.

Turn left at the main road, pass an unnamed café-bar, cross a concrete bridge over the Rio Sabor, then turn left to walk down the road that follows the river. The road soon changes to a dirt track, climbs steeply at first, then levels out to a more gradual climb. The difference between this lush, deep river valley and the barren hills that surround it is immense.

The river is a great place to see wildlife and if you're lucky, you may catch a glimpse of a wild boar or a black stork. About 3km after leaving França, pass a trout farm on the left, then walk under a huge water pipe that's part of the extensive hydroelectric network in this area.

In another 2km there's a signpost pointing left to Soutelo. Note that this will be your return route, but carry straight on here, leaving the river behind. The track begins to climb uphill, winding through horribly uniform pine plantations and scarred, harvested patches of land towards the top of Montesinho mountain. About 3km further on as the track flattens out, turn left at a crossroads on to a broad dirt road; there are fewer tracks here than are marked on the 1:25,000 map.

In 2km you'll arrive at another crossroads where you have two options. If you're staying at Montesinho, turn left here to go to the village. Otherwise, go straight ahead.

Continue along the dirt road, which climbs slowly in a few kilometres to the Barragem da Serra Serrada, a huge reservoir surrounded by rocky open country. It's one of the best places in the park to see wolves, and local shepherds are wary of leaving their sheep alone here.

Walk over the dam via a concrete bridge, keeping to the main track. The terrain in this part of the walk is in green and vivid contrast to the barren hills immediately surrounding Montesinho. It's an otherworldly place, where bizarre boulders rise up from carpets of heather.

Birds of prey seem to like it here, too. Look out for the rare golden eagle, a massive 90cm from bill to tail. Smaller and more common raptors include the hen harrier and Montagu's harrier, both white and pale grey in colour, and with stable populations in the park.

Around 3km after the reservoir, there's a junction to the right that leads to the casa abrigo at Lama Grande; turn here, next to a bizarrely-located shrine, only if you're staying at the mountain hut. Keep straight ahead to continue the walk.

Soon after the Lama Grande turning you'll pass the inauspicious beginning of the Rio Sabor, one of the most important rivers in Portugal, which eventually links up with the Douro near the Côa Valley rock engravings (p 89). After walking across the plateau for a while, you'll see more cultivated land up ahead as the trail starts to go downhill. Descend for about 3km until you reach a left-hand junction signposted França and Montesinho.

Turn left here, following the dirt road for 2km downhill to the Rio Sabor, now much fuller and more impressive than at its source. Cross over the bridge, and turn right to keep following the dirt road alongside the river; the Rio Sabor casa abrigo is off to the left. Follow the road for about 3km and you'll reach the signposted junction that you passed on your way out of França. Keep straight ahead, and you'll arrive back at the village in about 5km.

To return to the campsite, follow the beginning of the walk in reverse (12km), or follow the main Bragança–Portelo road back instead (7km).

Alternative 1

Start the walk in França (without your own transport, hitching is fairly easy, or there are occasional buses from Bragança) to make a shorter 38–40km circuit.

Alternative 2

To avoid walking over the same ground you can follow a shorter circuit (56–58km) via the villages of Soutelo, Carragosa and Meixedo. Unfortunately, much of this route is now on tarmac road. Instead of turning left at the signpost to França and Montesinho, keep straight on, heading towards Soutelo.

On reaching Soutelo, turn left to go through the village, passing a café on the way. The cobbled road through the village soon becomes paved; follow this for just over a kilometre, then turn left at a T-junction with another tarmac road. In about a kilometre you'll arrive at Carragosa. There's a café here, next to a fountain on a side road off to the right, and a church with an interesting external stone staircase leading up to the belltower.

Keep to the tarmac road for about 2km, then take the left-hand dirt track shortly after crossing a small bridge. This good track passes through large fields cultivated using modern machinery, entirely different from the surrounding small-scale farms. In 500m you'll arrive at the village of Meixedo. From here, follow the last part of the Baçal–Rabal walk (p 70) back to the campsite.

Quick Quiz

4. In which year did Fernando Pessoa die?

(answer on p 184)

---

10. Stroll around Montesinho

Fast Facts

distance	2.5km	rating	easy
time	1 hour	map	12 (1:25,000)
	centre map page 11		

A short stroll around the lovingly-restored village of Montesinho, with splendid views of the surrounding hills. It's an easy walk on good track and a great way to build up an appetite before dinner.

Getting to and from Montesinho is a struggle without your own wheels, and a steep haul if you're cycling. If you're reliant on public transport, you'll need to catch a Bragança–Portelo bus, then walk the extra 5km to the village. If you're staying at the campsite, ask a neighbour for a lift, as Montesinho is a popular destination.

Montesinho is wholeheartedly embracing the park's concept of tourism. Most of the houses in the villages have been renovated in traditional style, although many of the residents now seem to be burnt-out office workers or professors rather than local farmers. The buildings themselves are lovely, and the restored café is an excellent place to while away a couple of hours, but there's a certain sanitized air to the place that was absent a decade ago.

Begin the walk at the stone cross and fountain in Montesinho. Straight ahead of you is the Casa de Povo de Montesinho (town hall), built using traditional methods in the 1990s. Next door is the old village blacksmith that dates from the 1800s. You can peer inside and look at the centuries-old equipment that was used right up until the blacksmith closed in the early 1990s.

Take the cobbled lane that goes to the right of the Casa de Povo and follow it as it climbs out of the village. The scenery here is barren, dominated by rocky, unproductive soil and, in season, brilliant swaths of heather. Here and there, you'll find the occasional determined patch of farmland, but on the whole the countryside is left to its own devices.

In about a kilometre you'll come to a broad, flat area. There's a fork in the trail here, although it's difficult to spot at first. Ignore the right-hand trail that leads towards a pump house, and take the left-hand trail heading downhill instead.

In 200m you'll reach an aqueduct; cross over the concrete bridge here, then turn immediately left to follow the line of the aqueduct. Keep walking until the aqueduct crosses over a stream via a bridge. Just before this you'll see a short, steel ladder that will take you over the aqueduct.

About 30m after crossing the aqueduct, keep to your right and a well-worn rocky track will take you between two fields and over a stone bridge. Walk uphill for a short while then turn left at a T-junction. In about 200m you arrive back in Montesinho, pass-

ing a church on your right. A little further along is the Café Montezinho, a cosy café-bar with unusual, hand-made wood furniture, and just around the corner is the fountain where the walk began.

11. The Hills of Montesinho

Fast Facts

distance 8km	rating moderate
time 3 hours	maps 11, 12 (1:25,000)
centre map page 11	

The hills behind the village of Montesinho are barren and deserted, and within a few kilometres of the welcoming Café Montezinho, you're in isolated territory ideal for seeing birds of prey. From here, there are fabulous views down into the village and across the whole Trás-os-Montes region.

Begin the walk at the stone cross and fountain in Montesinho, following the cobbled road to the right of the Casa de Povo (town hall).

The road soon becomes a track and curves around to the left. Ignore the trail that leads off to the right at this left-hand bend and take the next right-hand track about 30m later. The trail winds its way up and over rocky scrubland, becoming faint in places; stick to the most well-worn path. There are occasional fields on either side of the trail, fenced in using huge slabs of

the abundant local stone rather than the dry stone walls seen elsewhere in Portugal. The fences look more like majestic, megalithic monuments than a practical means of keeping animals penned in.

The trail continues up and over the left-hand shoulder of the Alto do Falgueirão before meeting up with a stream a little over a kilometre after leaving Montesinho. Silver birch trees line the narrow stream in this lovely spot; the path, which sticks to the right-hand side of the stream, is overgrown in places.

Montesinho

In a couple of hundred metres follow the path as it crosses over the stream. The trail almost doubles back on itself for about 40m before curving around to the right and heading diagonally uphill. The stream that's next to this section of the trail on the 1:25,000 map is dry in summer.

In about 150m you'll find yourself at the saddle of the mountain. The trail veers right here, heading up the mountain just to the right of the stone peaks on your left-hand side. Although the trail is sometimes indistinct, it's still fairly easy to follow.

Follow the trail for about 600m across a flat area strewn with boulders. Abruptly, just as the trail seems to head straight for a large rock you'll find yourself at a well-maintained stone track. Turn left here to head for the Açude das Gralhas, the lower and smaller of the two reservoirs above Montesinho.

The reservoir is a good place for a picnic, sheltered from the high winds that frequently tear across the Serra de Montesinho. While you're picnicking, keep a look out for birds of prey.

To continue the walk, cross the concrete bridge over the reservoir and veer left, then keep left at a T-junction 20m further along. The trail curves around and passes underneath the aqueduct that transports the reservoir water past Montesinho and on to the hydroelectric station, feeding Bragança with electricity.

The walking is easy as the broad track skirts around the mountain, gradually revealing fabulous views of the barren hills and densely wooded valleys that characterize the Serra de Montesinho.

About 3km along from the reservoir you reach a junction, where you should take the lower left-hand track. This steep, stony trail zigzags down the mountainside, keeping to the left of a large water pipe.

Near the bottom of the hill you'll pass a rickety old bridge, and 30m later a new concrete bridge takes you over the Ribeira das Andorinhas. Pass a pump house on your right, then follow a track uphill to a broad, flat area.

From here, you have two options. Either turn left to follow the dirt track back into Montesinho, or turn right and follow the instructions in the Montesinho stroll on p 74.

Quick Quiz

5. In which year were women given the vote in Portugal?

(answer on p 184)

Other walks

The Parque Natural is riddled with farm tracks that connect the region's tiny villages to each other and the surrounding fields. You're never too far from civilization, and it's easy enough to spend a whole day wandering between café-bars.

An excellent starting place for just such an aimless walk is Rio de Onor, a gorgeous village straddling the border between Spain and Portugal. Some locals still speak Rionorês, a unique dialect that borrows from the languages of both countries, and the village's communitarian systems of justice and agriculture remain independent of either state.

The Lombada region on the eastern edge of the park is one of the best places to see wolves, and the *Parque Natural de Montesinho* book (p 65) details a walk that begins in Quintanilha and hugs the Spanish border along the Rio Maçãs. Further west, there's good walking near the Rio Tuela around the villages of Moimenta and Mofreita.

Rainy day options

Bragança, the only town of any size near the Parque Natural, is well-placed to entertain soggy walkers for a couple of days. It's no longer a dull backwater, and fashionable clothes shops and expanding suburbs are testament to the city's new-found wealth. Despite this, the centre retains a distinctly uncity-like feel, helped by the impractically narrow streets and popular local market.

Start your explorations at the cidadela (citadel), where medieval walls enclose tiny houses and cobbled streets. A walk along the top of the wall is a great way to get a feel for the miniature town inside, and provides fantastic views of the Parque Natural and the surrounding countryside as well.

Dominating the cidadela, however, is the castle, built in the late twelfth century and expanded when the Duchy of Bragança, soon to provide Portugal with a string of kings and queens, was created in 1442. The castle contains a rather dull military museum, and is subject to constantly changing opening days: ask at the turismo for the latest information.

Just outside the castle, look out for the bizarre sight of a medieval pillory rising up from the back of an ancient stone pig (porca). These porcas (minus the piercing pillory) are found throughout the Trás-os-Montes; their purpose remains a mystery, although archaeologists' suggestions include land boundary markers, fertility symbols or statues of Iron Age gods.

Also within the walls of the cidadela is the Domus Municipalis (town council chamber), a simple, pentagonal building and one of the few surviving examples of civil Romanesque architecture in Portugal.

Back in downtown Bragança, the Museu do Abade de Baçal is well worth a visit; there's a cluster of porcas in the gardens, and inside there are interesting displays of regional archaeology and ethnology.

Douro Internacional

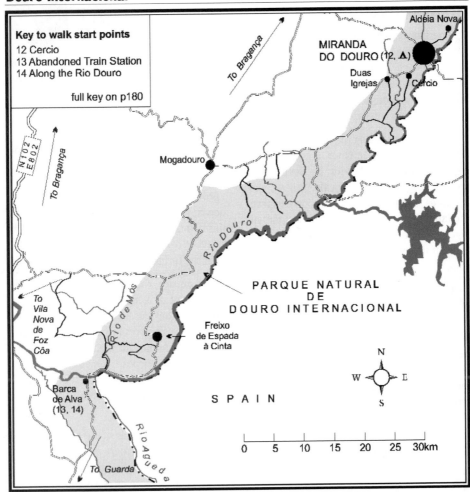

Key to walk start points
12 Cercio
13 Abandoned Train Station
14 Along the Rio Douro

full key on p180

What's the weather like?

	Jan	April	July	Oct
Sun	5 hrs	8 hrs	11 hrs	7 hrs
Rainfall	100mm	76mm	13mm	87mm
Maximum Temp	14°	21°	29°	23°
Minimum Temp	5°	10°	15°	12°

Average hours of sun, total average rainfall and average temperature in degrees celsius

Douro Internacional

What's Inside

The Walks

Don't Miss . . .

Walk along the rim of Portugal's own **'grand canyon'** (p 84)

Follow an old **railway track** to the eerie, abandoned station at Barca d'Alva (p 88)

Look up! You're in one of the best places in Portugal to see **birds of prey** such as Egyptian vultures and peregrine falcons (p 81)

Leave the tourist trail behind to follow the string of isolated fortress towns that lie forgotten amidst the endless expanse of the high plateau of the Trás-os-Montes. The Douro river's canyon cuts a deep, 122km-long groove that contrasts with the surrounding barren plains. The steep walls provide ideal habitat for nesting birds of prey and the Douro valley is considered one of the best sites in Europe to see large raptors.

Walking

Geography

The Douro river snakes through Iberia for just under 1000 kilometres, and drains an area of 58,200km², making it the largest river basin in Iberia. Over the millennia the force of water has cut a deep gorge in the natural barrier of the Trás-os-Montes, in some places as much as 400m below the level of the plateau.

The greatest threat to the gorge's unique ecosystem is the ongoing effort to build more dams on the river that's already the largest provider of hydroelectric power in Portugal.

Parks & reserves

The Parque Natural do Douro Internacional was created in 1997 to preserve the biodiversity and safeguard the architectural heritage of this region. Straddling the border, it's inextricably linked with the Spanish Parque Natural de Arribes del Duero, inaugurated as a natural park in 1998.

As yet, there's not much of an infrastructure in place, and information for visitors and walkers is thinly spread over a wide area with little coordination between facilities. There are plans for the park to follow the example of other recently-created parks and develop an interpretation centre with marked trails but details aren't yet available.

Trails

In 1999, when this book was researched, there were no official marked trails in the park, so the walks in this chapter follow dirt country lanes or abandoned train tracks. The sheer walls of the Douro gorge prevent easy access to the river for much of its length north of Barca d'Alva. There are some old paths marked on the 1:25,000 maps that descend steeply down to the river but you'll have to retrace your steps back uphill; for the most part it's easier and safer to stick to the paths on the edge of the gorge.

Maps etc

The 1:25,000 maps needed for the walks in this section (142, 81) date from the mid-1990s and are great for navigation. Sadly, the same can't be said for the 1960s vintage 1:50,000 civilian maps (8C, 15B). The military 1:50,000 maps (8III, 15I) are a little better, dating from the 1980s.

The wonderful *Entre Duas Margens: Douro International* is a fantastic guide to all aspects of life in the park. It's a hefty coffee table book, beautifully illustrated with photos and hand drawn maps, and a great souvenir even if you can't understand the Portuguese text.

There's also some good information in the

bilingual, well-designed *Guia da Região do Vale do Côa*, available at turismos.

Guided walks

Rotas do Vento (p 4) organize walks in the southern section of the park along the railway lines near Barca d'Alva. Sabor, Douro e Aventura (Rua Abade Tavares, Torre de Moncorvo, ✆ 279 258270) run theme tours which highlight various aspects of life in and around the park, and also visit the Archaeological Park near Vila Nova de Foz Côa (p 89); you may have to gather a group of enough people together yourself.

When to go

Come in early spring to see thousands of almond trees in blossom. From mid-March the bird migration begins with the arrival of white storks from Africa and the return of many birds of prey to breed. By summer the heat can be too much to bear: this part of the Trás-os-Montes lives up to its name of Terra Quente (hot earth), so stick to early morning or late afternoon when it's cooler for walking, and avoid the midday heat with a well-earned siesta.

Autumn is mild and pleasant. Try to time your visit from mid-September to late October when the harvest is gathered; the spectacle of lorries loaded with olives and grapes will make your jaw drop.

Flora & Fauna

The park is currently under consideration as a candidate for protection by the International Council for Bird Protection, and by the European Union's Important Bird Area program. The canyon walls provide safe breeding for **Egyptian** and **griffin vultures**, **golden eagles**, **Bonelli's eagles**, **black storks** and **peregrine falcons**. In total, close to 200 different species of birds are found here. The thermal updrafts created by the canyon help carry these feathered hunters high over the surrounding land in their quest for food.

Birds are not the only animals that find protection here: **wolves**, **wild cats** and **otters** also roam the canyon, though you'll be lucky to spot one of these shy creatures.

The region's flora looks distinctly out of place, as the Mediterranean climate suits species that would otherwise not venture this far north, most obviously in the cultivated **olive** and **almond** trees. Rare species of **snapdragon**, **lily**, **figwort**, **jonquil** and **love-in-a-mist** exist only in this part of the Iberian peninsula. At present the park is trying to catalogue the many different species of animals and plants that are found in the park, which will hopefully result in this unique area receiving special protection.

People & Culture

The people of this region are a hardy lot, having been cut off from the rest of Portugal for centuries. In the Middle Ages, **convicts** could be spared imprisonment if they agreed to internal banishment to populate and protect this forgotten frontier. **Jews** fleeing persecution from the Inquisition settled in this remote region, practising their religion in secret. Not long after the collapse of the Salazar regime in the 1970s, anthropologists identified groups of people whose beliefs and customs were closely connected with Judaism. Although the meaning behind some of the rituals had been lost during the years of isolation and secrecy, the practices were clearly recognizable as Jewish.

Isolation has helped preserve many traditions long forgotten in the rest of the country. The bellow of **bagpipes**, accompanied by colourful **pauliteiros** (stick dancers) can be heard at fiesta time, and an old language called **Mirandês** is still spoken. There's some beautiful local architecture here, too. As you walk through the countryside, horseshoe-shaped **pombals** (pigeon houses) are a common sight. The pigeons are not only a source of food, but their droppings also provide much needed fertilizer.

Romantic as this might be to the visitor, life can be harsh for the local people. The hot, arid summers and cold winters make farming difficult and unpredictable, and there are few job opportunities for young people. As in much of rural Portugal, the population is both shrinking and ageing, and while tourism may help in a small way, it's seasonal and unpredictable work and the waves of migration seem likely to continue.

Food & Drink

Local wine is a rare treat, rarely available outside the region. Many of the table wines have a distinctive taste that's recognizably from the same grape as port, though without the sweetness. **Port** is, however, what the region is famous for. From Barca d'Alva west, the land on either side of the Douro is crossed by regimented lines of grapes, ready to be sweetened and matured in the port lodges downriver in Porto.

While the region may produce the finest ports in the world, it's hard to find the quality vintages here unless you take an organized tour, and the selection in cafés and restaurants is disappointingly ordinary. You're better off buying from shops or lodges in Porto.

Alheira sausages are a tasty history lesson. Made with an intoxicating mix of garlic, hot peppers, chicken and partridge, the sausages were cooked by Jewish settlers to disguise the fact that they continued to abstain from eating pork during and after the Inquisition. The king of sausages around here is the **azedo sausage**, a delicious combination of beef, pork, hot peppers and paprika. **Amêndoas cobertas** (sugared almonds) are a local treat at Easter.

Tourist Information

Park office

Head Office, Figueira de Castelo Rodrigo, Largo Mateus de Castro, just off main square (www.icn.pt/parques/pndi/pndi.html).

Tourist offices

Miranda do Douro turismo, Largo do Menino Jesus da Cartolinha, on main square (✆ 273 431132).

Freixo de Espada à Cinta turismo, Avenida do Emigrante (✆ 279 653480).

Transport

Public transport within the park is limited to a couple of buses a day that travel between Miranda do Douro and Freixo de Espada à Cinta. The best way to approach the park is via Bragança to the north. It's difficult to get from Barca d'Alva to Freixo de Espada à Cinta and vice versa as the buses rarely run anymore: hitching may be your only option. Ask at the turismos before setting out for the latest bus times.

Money

Cashpoints and banks are available in Miranda do Douro, Mogadouro, and Freixo de Espada à Cinta.

Accommodation

Santa Luzia Campsite, Rua do Parque de Campismo, Miranda do Douro (℘ 273 431273); 1km south-west of town, see Cércio walk on p 84 for directions.

$ Residencial Flôr do Douro, Rua do Mercado Municipal 7, Miranda do Douro (℘ 273 431186).

$ Pensão Santa Cruz, Rua Abade de Baçal 61, Miranda do Douro (℘ 273 431374).

$ Pensão Paris, Largo do Outeiro, Freixo de Espada à Cinta (℘ 279 652785).

$$ Hotel Turismo, Rua 1 de Maio 5, Miranda do Douro (℘ 273 438030).

$$ Baga d'Ouro, Barca d'Alva (℘ 279 35126).

$$$$ Pousada de Santa Catarina, Miranda do Douro (tel 273 431005).

Shopping

Miranda do Douro's new and old town shops are well-equipped with supplies and trinkets, and on the first weekday of the month the town holds a large fair. There's a colourful market once a week in Freixo de Espada à Cinta at the new municipal market building. If you miss the market, there are plenty of small grocery shops scattered all over the town.

On a more unusual note, this is a great area to buy the curious Portuguese hoe that you see used by farmers throughout the country. A cross between a shovel and a pick, it would make a fitting reminder of this remote region.

Events & Festivals

Festa de Santa Bárbara (region-wide, third Sunday in August), pauliteiros (stick dancers), drums and bagpipes, most famously in the village of Duas Igrejas, near Miranda do Douro; **Romaria Nossa Senhora do Nazo** (Miranda do Douro, 7–8 September); **Festa das Morcelas** or **Festa da Mocidade** (region-wide, week between Christmas and New Year), a strange mix of pagan and Christian traditions, with stick dancers, of course.

12. Cércio

Fast Facts

distance	9km	rating	easy
time	3 hours	map	81 (1:25,000)
	centre map page 12		

This walk visits the tiny village of Cércio, typical of the region with its multitude of sixteenth century Gothic and Manueline houses. On the way, visit the small aqueduct that once supplied Miranda do Douro with water.

Pack lunch with you for the return leg where a detour leads to the lip of the Douro canyon. Find a pleasant spot for a picnic and watch for raptors riding the thermals.

From Praça Dom João III in the heart of Miranda do Douro's old town, walk down Rua da Costanilha, and leave the old town through the stone gatehouse. Once outside the city walls, turn left to walk along the tarmac road, then turn right in 100m to double back on yourself heading downhill. The lane leads down to the river with small terraces and allotments on either side. Cross the Fonte dos Canos, the medieval bridge that takes its name from the eighteenth century fountain you'll pass on your right, once you reach the far bank.

Take the first left after 100m at an out of place, postmodern, white house on the opposite side of the road. Follow this road, passing the campsite on your right as the road changes to a dirt track. Walk 50m further to a crossroads and look off to your right, where a medieval aqueduct is worth a brief detour.

Carry straight on at the crossroads, then soon after on the left-hand side pass the old gates of the Quinta do Vilarinho. Follow the wide dirt track for 2km as it passes fields and orchards, ignoring the many tracks that branch off right and left. Look behind for dramatic views of Miranda do Douro sitting beside the steep gorge.

The Sé is clearly visible, as is the castle's keep—the only structure that remained after the castle's ammunitions store caught fire in 1762, killing 400 people. The Duke of Wellington had a close-up view of the gorge in 1813 as he was hoisted across the river in a makeshift hammock. Any humiliation proved worthwhile as the forces he met on the other side helped swing the war decisively in his favour a few months later.

Pass a cross on the right-hand side that is known as Cruz de Miranda and once marked the medieval city boundary. In another 100m, note the track off to the left that will be your route on the return leg.

Continue on to the village of Cércio,

which you'll reach in 300m. This is a village to savour slowly. Locals are justly proud of their fine houses, and even though the village streets are largely made of dirt or gravel, many of the buildings show subtle touches of finesse. Modern buildings are made in the same style, and dilapidated buildings are being renovated instead of being torn down.

The vegetable patches next to the houses are a gardener's delight, and self-sufficiency has been elevated to an art form, producing a vast array of vegetables. Meanwhile, cows are herded into the centre of the mammoth village square to drink at the stone cattle trough in its centre. Find the café just off the square and watch the ebb and flow of daily life.

Retrace your steps towards the edge of the village and turn right down the track you noted on your way out, just after the last house. Follow this along, ignoring a track to the left just under the power lines.

S top to check out the tall, old-fashioned well on right-hand side of the track. Of a design found throughout the Trás-os-Montes, it's simply and ingeniously constructed from a large pivoting pole that rises diagonally from the ground, with a rope hanging from its tip to which the bucket is attached.

Hoopoes, subalpine warblers and spectacled warblers can be seen along this section of the walk, fluttering along the field edges.

Follow the track for another 500m and turn left at a well-worn track. If you wish to have a closer look at the Douro gorge continue straight on, take the left hand fork 100m later, then return by doubling back to this point. The gorge is regarded as the best place in Portugal for viewing raptors, and during the spring breeding season, booted and short-toed eagles migrate here looking for love. The rare golden eagle, the largest of European eagles, may also be glimpsed. Although similar in shape to a buzzard, it's easily distinguished by its great size and the distinctive shallow V its wings make as it soars above the canyon.

Follow the main track, shaded by trees at first; it's a little overgrown in places but still passable. In 750m rejoin the track you set out on, turn right and head back to Miranda do Douro. If you're returning at dusk watch out for the huge, fast-flying eagle owl. Measuring 70cm in height with distinct "ear" feathers, this giant of an owl roosts in holes or old nests of birds of prey.

Quick Quiz

6. What do the years 1994, 1983, and 1970 have in common?

(answer on p 184)

---

13. Along the Rio Douro

Fast Facts

distance 11km	rating	easy
time 4 hours	map	142 (1:25,000)
	centre map page 13	

Walk along a disused railway line on the south bank of the Douro river. Abandoned farmhouses sit among olive trees and vines, as the path winds its way back through parched farmland to the forgotten last stop of the now defunct Douro line at Barca d'Alva.

Leave sleepy Barca d'Alva heading west along the cobbled road at the bottom of the village. On the way out pass the few small cafés that are jammed in between terrace houses and follow the Douro downstream. At the edge of the village the cobbled road changes to a dirt track. At this point, hop up the small path alongside the last building to walk along the railway track.

There's no path as such, and you're mainly stepping from sleeper to sleeper along the railway line. The gravel used to build the track has so far prevented it from becoming too overgrown since the line was decommissioned in the 1980s.

Early morning or late afternoon, when the sun catches the shimmering Douro, is a delightful time for this section. Herons inhabit the riverbanks and stand like sentries, patiently waiting for fish to swim within range. Look up for griffon vultures that breed on the escarpments: common in this region, the vultures are often seen riding the thermals in groups as they search for food. The Egyptian vulture, smallest of the European vultures, migrates here in spring to breed, when it can easily be confused with the high-flying storks that also breed here.

Follow the track for 4km to a collection of abandoned buildings marked Quinta de São Cibrão on the 1:25,000 map. Just past the derelict farm buildings an old metal bridge crosses a small tributary of the Douro. If you're brave enough to cross the rusty bridge, it's possible to continue along the railway as far as Pocinho, where trains from Porto along the Douro now end. This would be an interesting way to get to Vila Nova de Foz Côa and the fascinating archaeological park there (p 89).

To continue the walk, leave the railway track just before the bridge and head up the path towards the abandoned houses. Once there, follow the track towards another abandoned building that's set back from the rest, then take the right-hand fork in 50m, along a well-worn dirt track. The farmed landscape is full of olive and almond trees with little land untouched or left fallow. In early spring hordes of Spanish tourists flock to this section of the Douro and up to Freixo de Espada à Cinta to see the almond trees in bloom. In a further 700m carry straight on and ignore a track that heads off to the left between two hills.

Autumn brings the countryside to life with the grape and olive harvest. The fields are dotted with small groups of farmers who cover the ground beneath the olive tree with a large sheet. One person then steps forward with a large stick to whack the trunk and branches until the olives have fallen on the sheet below. The olive pickers wear huge straw hats to keep the sun off, which from a distance make them look like animated mushrooms. Don't be tempted to try an olive straight from the tree: they're bitter and hard, and have to be soaked in oil, vinegar or brine before they become edible.

Turn left at a T-junction after 2km of walking along the track. Look out for frogs in the shallow streams on the right after this junction. Keep on the track as it curves around to the left, ignoring the right-hand turning which heads straight on.

Follow the track up to the brow of the hill where the Douro becomes visible for the first time since leaving the bridge back at Quinta de São Cibrão. Take time to soak in the fantastic view of the Douro valley. Notice the white marks high on the cliffs opposite, the telltale signs of griffon vultures that build their nests and nurture their young perched out of predators' reach.

At the next fork in the path, turn right. The walk soon enters the first vineyards of the walk so far, then traverses around a hill, revealing the main road and a group of modern houses. As you approach the road the dirt track becomes cobbled.

Turn left at the main tarmac road and pass the old olive factory on the left, which for some reason has hundreds of citrus trees in front. Follow the main road back to Barca d'Alva, passing underneath the old railway bridge and heading back towards the Douro.

Quick Quiz

7. How many strings does a guitarra portuguesa have?

(answer on p 184)

14. Abandoned Train Station

Fast Facts

distance	2km	rating	easy
time	1 hour	map	142 (1:25,000)

centre map page 13

A very short walk exploring the old railway station and the banks of the Douro River around Barca D'Alva. This is a great way to build up an appetite before settling down to dinner at the village's single restaurant. You need a good head for heights to cross the two short bridges along the way.

Leave Barca d'Alva as in the Along the Rio Douro walk on p 86. On reaching the railway track, turn left to double back on yourself, following the tracks back through the village. Barca d'Alva lies in a slight depression. To keep the railway track level, large earthworks were built along the length of the village, so that the track is now at the height of the surrounding rooftops.

It's an unusual and fascinating perspective: look out across the roofs at the enormous nests built by the white storks that migrate to this region to breed in mid-March. These nests are thought by local people to bring good luck and are left undisturbed. In places along the track, chicken coops and small gardens are beginning to encroach on to the former railway property, but a clear path through the poultry remains.

The height of the old railway means that you cross over the village streets by way of a couple of bridges. Crossing these bridges is an act of faith: they are no longer being maintained, and the street below looks an awfully long way down. Be careful, and keep your eyes straight ahead!

In a few hundred metres you reach the old train station, once the last stop before the train crossed over into Spain. The buildings have been left just as they were when the line was decommissioned, and the strange feeling lingers that the last conductor has only just left.

Further past the station the old turntable is still clearly visible in front of the engine sheds. This mammoth, cast iron circle once guided the engines into the sheds and turned them around for the return trip to Porto. Further down the line the train bridge to Spain still stands; it's worth seeing up close, but ask local advice on its safety before crossing.

After looking at the bridge return to the engine sheds and take the track just to the riverside of the turntable, leading down to

The Centre Map Pages   1

The maps in these centre pages correspond to walk descriptions in the rest of the book.

At the top of each map, there's a key to the walks with the page number in the book where the walk description can be found

	lake / sea
	river
	main road
	minor road
	unpaved or single track road
	track
	path
	unclear or overgrown path
	railway
	route of first walk
	route of second walk
	route of third walk
	start point of first walk
	start point of second walk
	start point of third walk
	church
	town
	village
	hamlet
	campsite
	mountain name
	point of interest

1900–2000
1800–1900
1700–1800
1600–1700
1500–1600
1400–1500
1300–1400
1200–1300
1100–1200
1000–1100
900–1000
800–900
700–800
600–700
500–600
400–500
300–400
200–300
100–200
0–100

2

N 202

Rio Lima

N 203

Anta

Pedrosa

N 201

Santo
Ovídio

Salgueirinho

Quin
Pom

N 201

PONTE
DE LIMA

0 1 2 3 4km

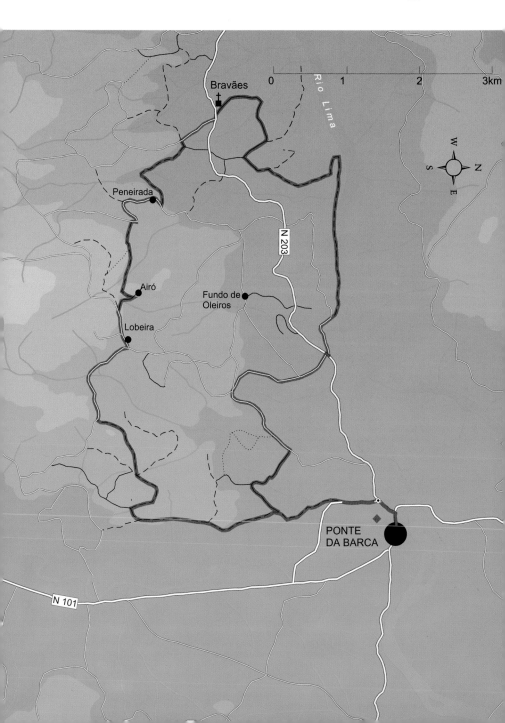

Lourido

Froufe

Entre Ambos-os-Rios

Rio Lima

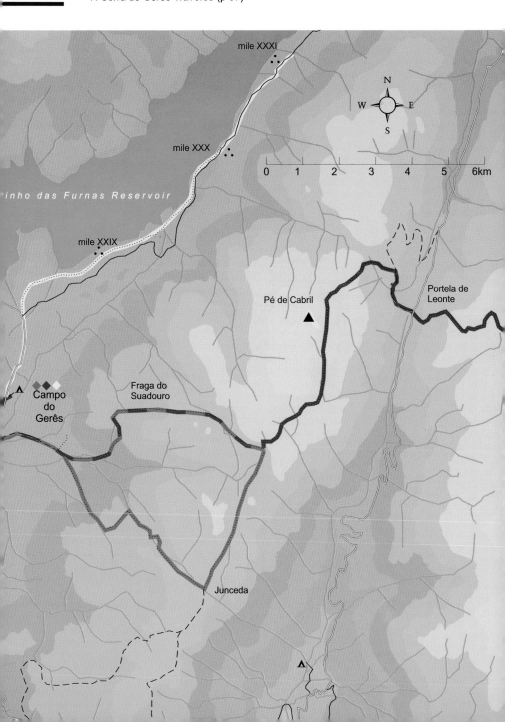

5

mile XXXI

mile XXX

N
W E
S

0 1 2 3 4 5 6km

inho das Furnas Reservoir

mile XXIX

Pé de Cabril

Portela de Leonte

Campo do Gerês

Fraga do Suadouro

Junceda

Fafião

Rio de Fafião

Ermida

Gerês

11

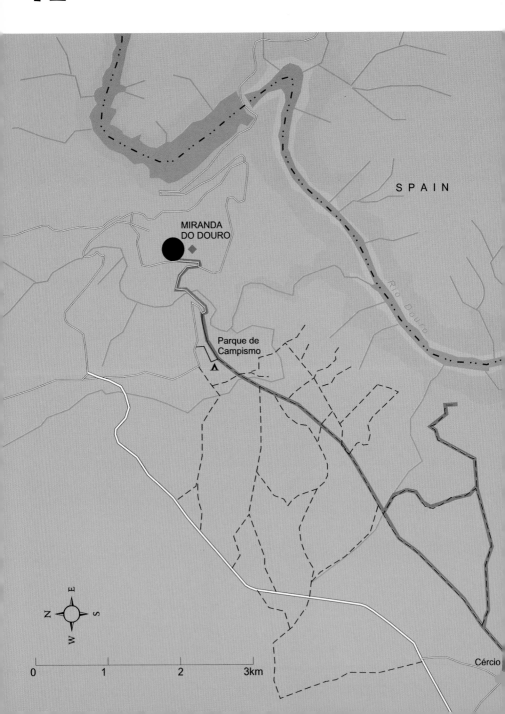

13

Quinta de
São Cibrão

0   1   2   3km

W
N
S
E

Rio Douro

Barca
d'Alva

Barca d'Alva
Train Station

14

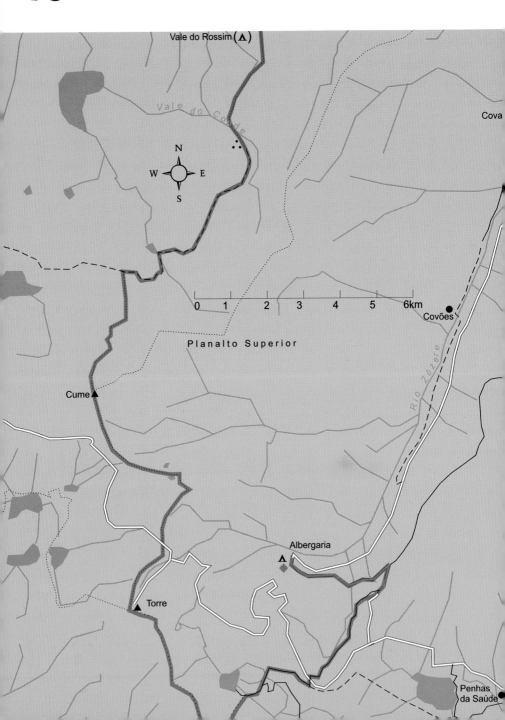

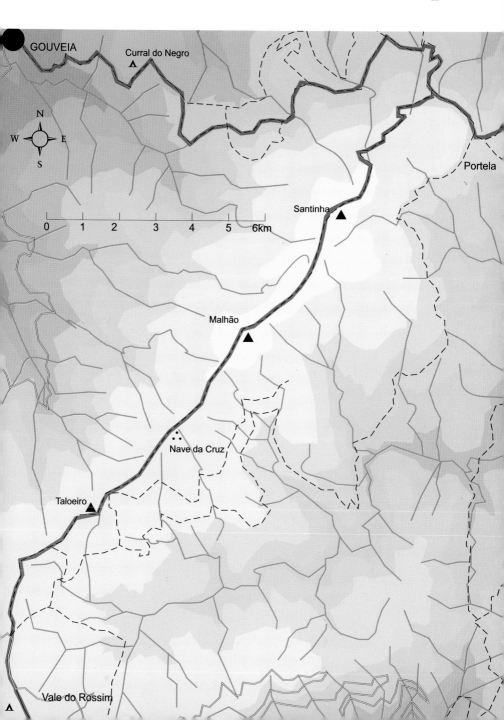

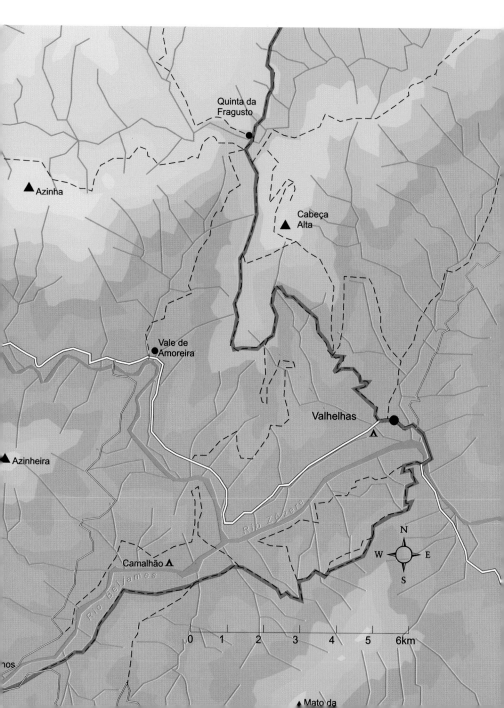

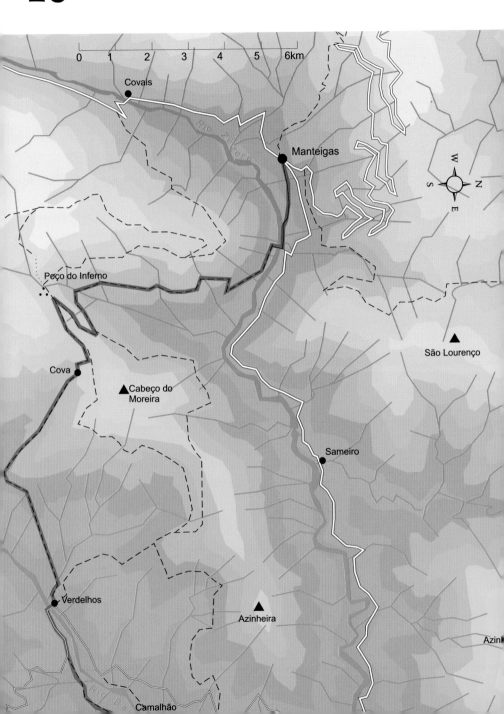

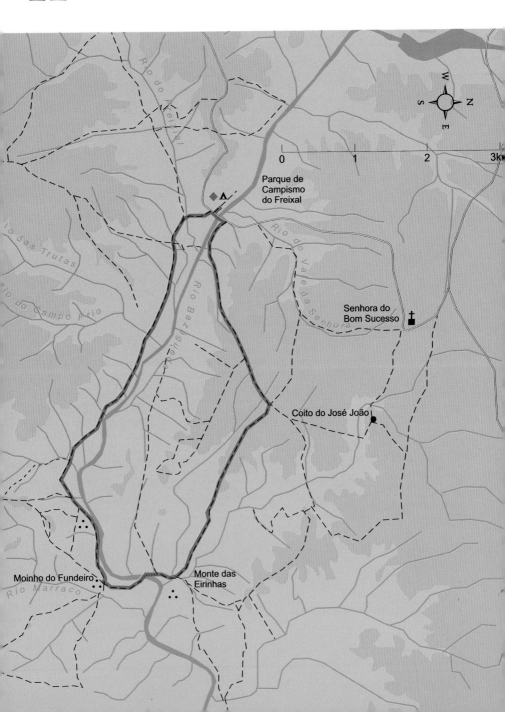

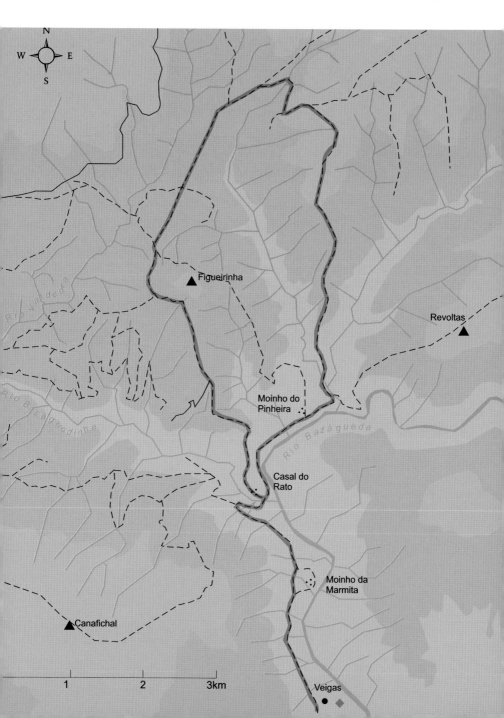

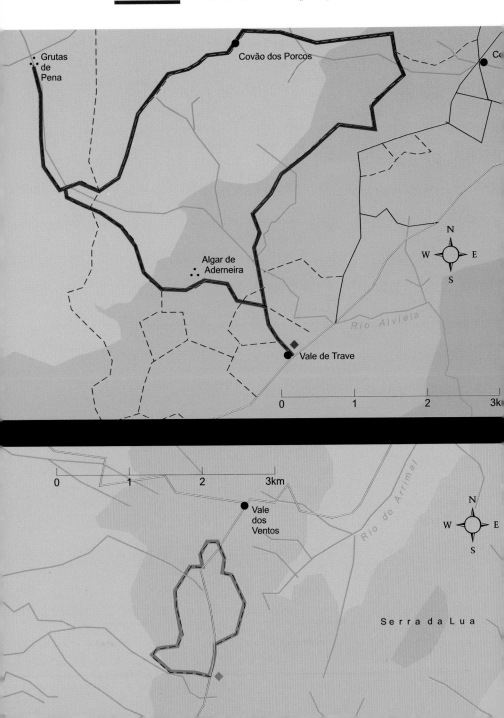

Grutas
de
Pena

Covão dos Porcos

C

Algar de
Aderneira

Rio Alviela

Vale de Trave

N
W E
S

0   1   2   3k

0   1   2   3km

Vale
dos
Ventos

Rio do Arrimal

N
W E
S

Serra da Lua

25

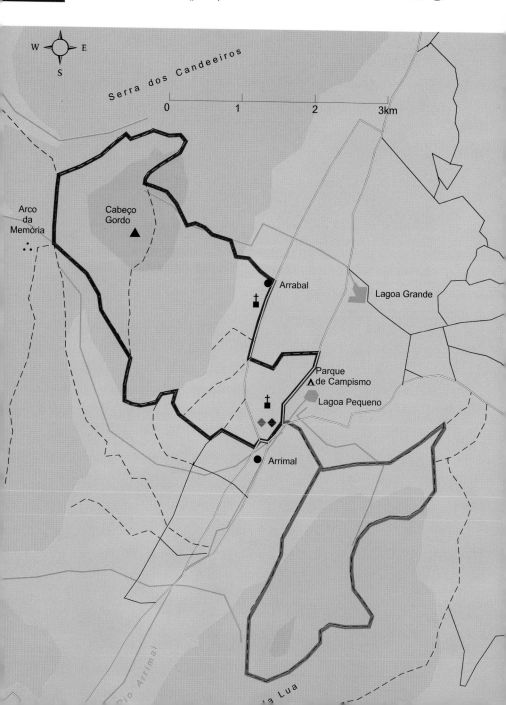

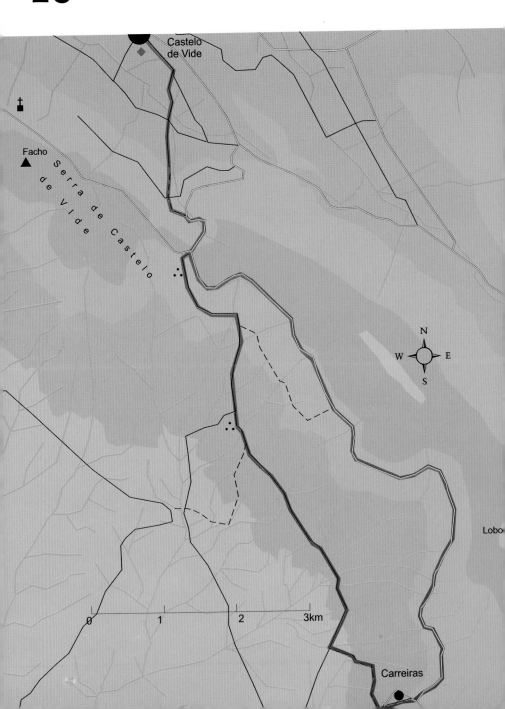

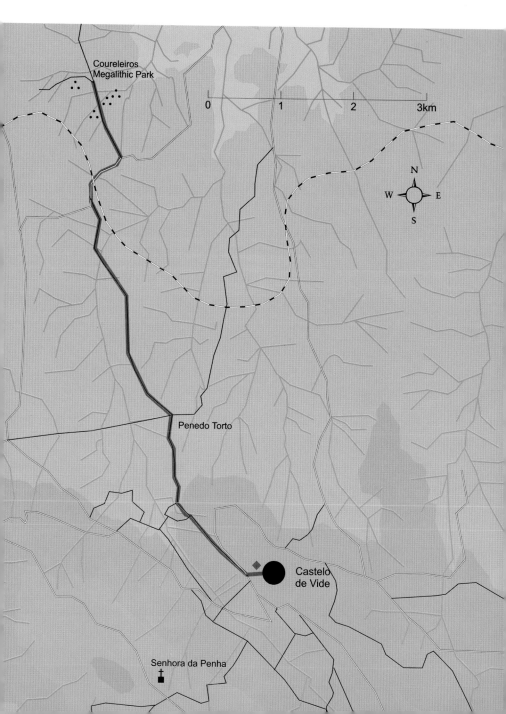

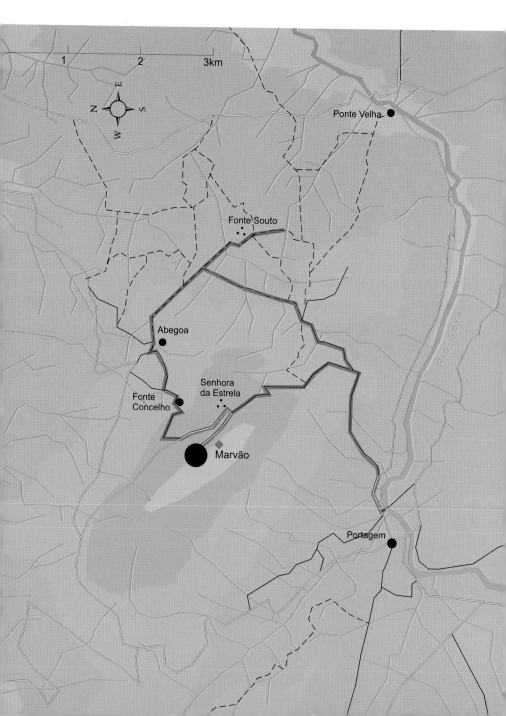

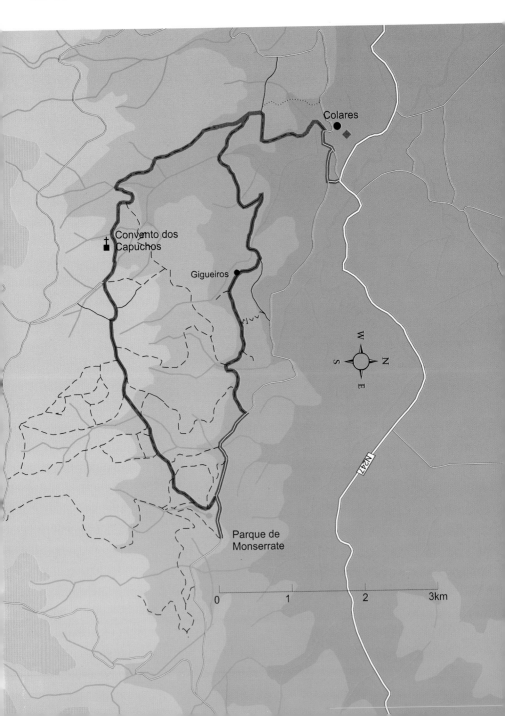

Colares

Convento dos
Capuchos

Gigueiros

Parque de
Monserrate

N247

0   1   2   3km

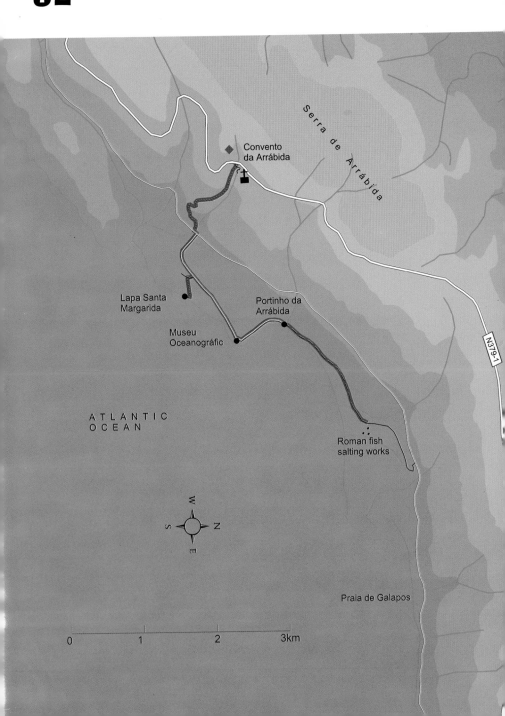

the Douro. Once at the river turn left to head back slowly to the village, passing small allotments and watching out for herons and fish among the reeds of the riverbank.

Other walks

The parque natural is largely uncharted walking territory. Although the steep canyon walls limit access to the river for much of its length there are a number of walking possibilities along the park's fringes.

From Miranda do Douro strike out north-east following the edge of the canyon towards the small town of Vale de Águia. A few more kilometres will bring you to the village of Aldeia Nova, from where you can walk to the tiny chapel of São João, perched on the rim of the canyon and offering dramatic views down into the gorge.

In the middle of the park, set off south-west from Freixo de Espada à Cinta, heading up the Serra de Poiares towards the town of Poiares. Once at the top of the serra, head a few more kilometres south for bird's eye views down over the Canada de Nasce Água to the fields of vines that produce some of the world's finest port.

In the south of the park, it's still possible to walk along the abandoned railway line between Barca d'Alva and Pocinho, an attractive and roundabout route to the Parque Arqueológico do Vale de Côa. It's at least a two-day trip with nowhere to buy supplies along the route, so make sure that you're prepared.

Rainy day options

Book ahead to see the largest collection of rock carvings in Europe at the Parque Arqueológico do Vale de Côa. The site wasn't discovered until 1992, and was narrowly saved by a national petition from being flooded to make way for a hydroelectric dam in 1995. The site contains petroglyphs that span the history of the human occupation of Portugal from prehistoric to medieval times. For more information about tours, contact the archaeological park headquarters (Avenida Gago Coutinho 19, Vila Nova de Foz Côa; ℘ 279 764317).

Miranda do Douro has enough attractions to keep the wet walker happy for a day or two. Check out the Sé, home to the Menino Jesus de Cartolinha, a statue with an endlessly revolving wardrobe, but not an awful lot else. The wonderful Museu da Terra de Miranda in the old part of town contains curious artefacts about the local culture, including Hebrew inscriptions dating back more than 500 years.

Some port lodges in the area are open for tours but many are geared towards pre-booked groups: check with the turismo to find out which ones are open during your visit.

Beira Litoral

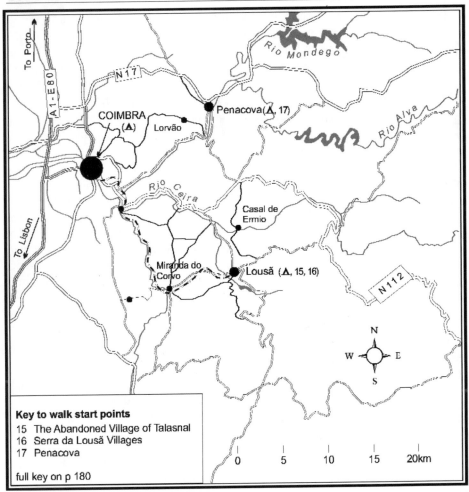

Key to walk start points

15 The Abandoned Village of Talasnal
16 Serra da Lousă Villages
17 Penacova

full key on p 180

What's the weather like?

	Jan	April	July	Oct
Sun	4.5 hrs	8 hrs	11 hrs	7 hrs
Rainfall	130mm	76mm	13mm	87mm
Maximum Temp	14°	21°	29°	23°
Minimum Temp	6°	10°	15°	12°

Average hours of sun, total average rainfall and average temperature in degrees celsius

Beira Litoral

What's Inside

The Walks

Don't Miss . . .

Explore mysterious, abandoned villages in the lovely setting of the Serra da Lousã (p 97)

Stroll around the rolling hills of Penacova (p 99)

Start your day off right in Lousã at one of the best pastelarias (pastry shops) in Portugal (p 94)

Half way up Portugal, not far from the coast and centred on the historical university town of Coimbra, the Beira Litoral is perfect wandering country. You won't find any natural parks or protected areas here, but the countryside contains some of the most fascinating, beautifully-situated villages in all of Portugal. In the Serra da Lousã, enjoy the eerie sensation of exploring mountain hamlets abandoned for decades, then head north for a visit to the still-inhabited, narrow cobbled streets of the villages around Penacova.

Walking

Geography

The Serra da Lousã are an extension of the better known Serra da Estrela range further to the east. Moist Atlantic air is caught by the high peaks, feeding the many rivers that carve steep valleys throughout the serra. Roads wind painstakingly through the range, villages stick precariously to abrupt slopes, and farmers must slice terraces into the hillsides to give their crops a chance to grow.

The serra is startlingly green at its lower levels closest to the town of Lousã; higher up, it's made barren by forestry and blackened by frequent forest fires.

Penacova sits dramatically high above the meandering Mondego river; across the water villages have sprung up on the gentler eastern banks. As at Lousã, farming and forestry dominate, and the landscape is alternately lush and dust-dry.

Trails

Trails in this part of Portugal follow routes that have linked villages and farms for centuries. In many places the old paths have been paved as the internal combustion engine became more popular than the beast of burden.

In the Serra da Lousã, the lower abandoned villages are connected by good stone trails occasionally damaged by over-zealous local forestry, while higher up the walking is mostly on wider, drivable tracks that can be hot and dusty in summer. Blue and yellow paint stripes mark the trails; these correspond loosely to the sketch map given out at the turismo in town.

Many of the old trails around Penacova have largely disappeared, replaced by tarmac roads or forestry tracks, but the route between Sanguinho and Carvoeira (see the walk on p 99) remains a peaceful, wooded exception.

Maps etc

The 1:25,000 map of Penacova (231) is only a few years old, but even so new trails and road upgrades have made much of the map inaccurate; neither 1:50,000 map is of much use as both the 19B civilian and 19I military date from the early 1970s.

The useful Lousã 1:25,000 map (252) was published in 1999, while the military (19I) and the civilian (19D) 1:50,000 maps also date from the 1970s.

The turismo in Lousã (p 94) produces a free sketch map of the serra: it's not particularly detailed, but it gives a general idea of where the trails are when used in conjunction with the 1:25,000 map.

When to go

Summers can be hot in Lousã and you'll feel the sun on the steep climbs around the abandoned villages. The campsite at Lousã is quiet even in summer.

At Penacova, the campsites are busy with families in the school holidays; if you don't mind crowds and queues for the showers, it's not too hot here and there's great river swimming right at the campsite.

Avoid coming in the winter, as most accommodation closes down and ankle-deep mud makes the mountain trails precarious.

Flora & Fauna

It's a fairytale heard all over Portugal: once upon a time the hillsides around Lousã and Penacova were covered with ancient forests of oak and chestnut.

Now, however, it's monotonous swaths of **pine**, **eucalyptus** and **acacia** as far as the eye can see, and the effect of the forestry industry is dramatic even for Portugal. Around Lousã it's rare to see a summer sky unblemished by smoke from forest fires, and throughout the region widespread erosion and frequent landslides scar the otherwise beautiful landscape.

The pine forests aren't totally devoid of life; among the more common crows and jays you may see an **azure-winged magpie** with its distinctive black cap, blue wings, long tail and pinkish-brown underside.

In the farmland around Penacova, watch out for hovering birds of prey, especially **sparrowhawks**.

People & Culture

Lousã would probably be just another small mountain village were it not for the **paper factory** built in the early eighteenth century. The factory owed its early success to the Marquês de Pombal, the supreme organizer best-known for rebuilding Lisbon after the 1755 earthquake, who brought in paper-making experts from across Europe to teach their craft to the local people. Paper prosperity inspired local people to build beautifully understated mansions, and the long façades of these **casas brasonadas** can be seen throughout the town.

Higher up the mountain, life was grim. For centuries, farmers struggled to make a living from the steep, infertile land and built beautiful villages nestled in the rocky slopes, but by the 1950s, most of these **mountain villages** had been abandoned, their inhabitants looking for an easier life in the valleys or overseas. Although locally-driven tourism is now repackaging the simple stone houses as alternative holiday accommodation, the villages are still dominated by ghostly ruined buildings.

The people around Penacova were also mainly **farmers** until the latter part of the twentieth century, when the thin, acidic soil was given over to **forestry** instead, and what little farming remains is confined to the fertile strip of land alongside the Rio Mondego. Aside from food, the best-known

local products are the rather eccentric, intricate **willow toothpicks**; they're unique to the town, and sold almost everywhere.

 Food & Drink

Penacovan cuisine is dominated by the products of the Rio Mondego, from the eel-like **lampreys** in winter to **truta grelhada** (grilled trout) in the spring.

It's almost worth skipping a couple of meals, though, to fill up on the region's **pastries**. In Penacova, the **almond tarts** from the nearby Lorvão monastery are delicious, while in Lousã, no morning would be complete without a visit to one of the three branches of Pastelaria São Silvestre, which rival even the pastry shops of Lisbon for variety and mouthwatering sweetness. Perhaps it's all down to the delicious local **honey**, which is celebrated along with **chestnuts** in an annual November fair.

Northeast of Penacova and Lousã is **Dão wine** country, producing the most consistently drinkable red in the country; Dão wine is available throughout Portugal, but locals say it tastes different here. Alternatively, splash out on a visit the Buçaco Palace Hotel (p 101) and sample the superb house wines, exclusively available inside the hotel's gourmet restaurant.

Those after something a little stronger should be well-pleased with Lousã's ubiquitous **Licor Beirão**, a herb-based concoction with a dynamite kick.

 Tourist Information

Tourist offices

Lousã Turismo, Town Hall, Rua João de Cáceres (☏ 239 993502).

Penacova Turismo, Town Hall, main square (☏ 239 477114).

Transport

Trains run from Coimbra to Lousã A at least once an hour. There are about five buses daily from Coimbra to Penacova; if you're heading for the campsite, ask for Ponte Penacova, below the town.

Money

There are banks and cashpoints in Penacova and Lousã.

Accommodation

Lousã campsite, Rua Professor António Batista de Almeida, Lousã (☏ 239 991052). Small quiet site, open March to October.

Penacova campsite, across the river from Penacova (☏ 239 477464). Shop, café, river beach; crowded in summer.

$ Pensão Bem Estar, Avenida Coelho da Gama 11, Lousã (☏ 239 991445).

$ Residencial Martinho, Rua Forças Armadas, Lousã (☏ 239 991052).

$-$$$ Serra da Lousã houses. Price and availability varies. Contact the turismo in Lousã for an up-to-date list.

$$ Casa da Eira, Casal de Ermio, 4km north of Lousã (☏ 239 991712).

$$ Pensão Avenida, Avenida Abel Rodrigues da Costa, Penacova (℘ 239 477142).

$$$$ Quinta das Lágrimas, Rua António Augusta Gonçalves, Santa Clara, Coimbra (℘ 239 441615).

Shopping

Penacova's big market takes place on the second Thursday of the month; at other times there's a tiny but excellent municipal market just off the main square. Lousã's municipal market is packed with stalls and many of the small producers offer just one or two food items; honey and nuts are particularly good

here, as are the sales tactics of the savvy stallholders.

Events & Festivals

Queima das Fitas (Coimbra, May), Coimbra's energetic end-of-academic year celebrations with the traditional burning of academic ribbons and wall-to-wall fado; **Festa de São João** (Lousã, June 24); **Festa de Rainha Santa** (Coimbra, beginning of July every even-numbered year), major religious festival in honour of Queen Isabel.

15. The Abandoned Village of Talasnal

Fast Facts

distance 9km	rating easy to moderate
time 3 hours	map 252 (1:25,000)
centre map page 14	

High above Lousã, the village of Talasnal was abandoned to encroaching weeds after the last of its resident farmers left in the 1950s. After decades of solitude, however, Talasnal is experiencing something of a revival as a rural holiday destination and the village is now an attractive juxtaposition of ruined buildings, overhanging vines and lovingly restored stone and wood homes.

The route begins and ends in Lousã, passing the Castelo de Arouce and following paths cut into steep valley slopes hundreds of years ago. It's an easy walk on good paths, although there are a couple of steep uphills

just beyond the castle and around Talasnal itself. Bring a swimsuit for a dip in the river pools below the castle.

From the town hall in Lousã, go up Avenida Coelho da Gama past the

Residencial Bem Estar. Turn left to follow the Castelo sign, walk past the Residencial Martinho, then turn right in 100m up Rua Professor Correi de Seixta. Notice the azulejo (tile) sign for this road, which includes a drawing of the long-lived professor—born in 1859, he finally died in 1963. This road is lined with the houses of Lousã's wealthier residents; the town has been fairly prosperous ever since the paper factory opened in the eighteenth century and these newer houses are presumably the modern day equivalent of the infinitely more attractive paper-funded mansions in the centre of town.

Many of the houses here are fronted by bright green lawns, a rare and arresting sight in a country where most gardens are dominated by fruit trees and vines, and where dry summers make hard work of maintaining such manicured squares of grass. The road bends to the right, and in a few hundred metres you'll pass the most bizarre front garden of the lot, adorned with an assortment of military hardware. After another few hundred metres take the road off to your right signposted Castelo. As the road climbs the mountains start to close in and you follow the line of the steep, wooded Arouce valley, passing a water fountain popular with locals.

In 2km you arrive at the Castelo de Arouce, said to date from the twelfth century. Close up, it's an unimpressive collection of semi-restored buildings, although further on in the walk there are lovely views that emphasize its defensive location on top of a small spur deep within the Arouce valley.

Follow the narrow road from the castle as it goes steeply downhill and ends in about

100m at a group of river pools. Cross over the stone bridge and walk up the wide stone path past the Azenha restaurant (closed Sunday evening and all day Monday) and a small chapel. At the functional picnic area in 100m, take the path off to the left marked Casal Novo, Talasnal, Vaqueirinho and Catarredor. Climb sharply uphill on this narrow, stony path past a large white cross until you reach a junction in about 200m; take the left-hand path, following the blue paint stripes and signpost to Talasnal.

The landscape here is badly charred by some of the thousands of forest fires that occur annually in Portugal. The numbers of fires throughout the country are on the increase due to arson and carelessness. The inaccessible slopes around here make fire-fighting particularly difficult. From this part of the walk you can see the summit of Lousã mountain marked with radio masts, and below you in the valley Arouce castle exudes photogenic charm. The stiff climb soon gives way to a flatter path that's easier to walk on, although the sheer drop on your left may cause you to tread carefully.

About a kilometre after the Talasnal junction, the village itself comes into view. Perched on a steep slope, it blends effortlessly into its surroundings and manages to look both natural and improbable at the same time. The effort required to build streets and houses here and to hack out the narrow terraced fields that fan out from the village must have been immense: the results are a stunning testament to the craftsmanship and industry of the local people.

Soon after your first sighting of Talasnal, the path curves around to cross the Ribeira da Vergada via a gorgeous stone bridge. The trail is now cobbled and lined with stone walls; looking back you can see your route snaking around the mountains. In 100m you arrive at the outskirts of Talasnal; bear right just before a burnt out building, then turn right to climb up to the village (the route straight ahead, marked with yellow paint, will be the way back to the castle).

Talasnal, despite being partly renovated, retains an unearthly charm. The main stone path curves up the hill past ruined and restored houses and ducks under vines and bougainvillea, with branches heading off in all directions. As you wander around look for the many splendid viewpoints and try to find the old communal bread oven, off to the right of the main street. Although some of the restored houses in Talasnal are reserved for groups, others can be rented privately: the turismo in Lousã has a list of properties.

When you've finished poking around, retrace your steps back to the junction at the foot of the village; turn right here, then right again 30m later. The path is narrow and eroded in sections; keep an eye out for yellow or blue paint stripes that show the way down. You'll reach a junction at a white electrical building in 400m; turn left to keep following the blue and yellow paint stripes (the right-hand route is marked in red). A metal bridge takes you across the Ribeira de São João, then you pass through the verandah of an electrical power station and emerge at a gravel road, which arrives back to the castle in just over a kilometre.

Before returning to Lousã by way of the outward route, overheated hikers can refresh themselves in the fabulous river pools below the castle. It's a beautiful setting with a shady picnic area, snack bar and restaurant, and the line up to the tiny diving board is a great place to meet local people.

16. Serra da Lousã Villages

Fast Facts

distance 11km	rating moderate
time 4 hours	map 252 (1:25,000)
centre map page 14	

Within easy reach of Lousã, these three mountain villages were abandoned en masse in the 1950s when local farmers finally gave up trying to make a living from the harsh terrain.

Tourism began regenerating these villages in the 1990s: Casal Novo has been lovingly and attractively restored, while Talasnal is an eerie combination of ruined and renovated buildings. Chiqueiro, though sparsely populated, was never truly abandoned, and is still very much a working village and farming community. This walk links all three places in a circular loop from Lousã, passing the lovely surroundings of the Castelo de Arouce along the way. Parts of the walk are steep and can be slippery in wet weather; good footwear is recommended.

Follow the Talasnal walk (p 95) to the castle, past the restaurant and up to the picnic area. As in the Talasnal walk, in the picnic area take the path off to the left marked Casal Novo, Talasnal, Vaqueirinho and Catarredor.

On reaching the junction in 200m, ignore the left-hand path marked with blue paint stripes and signposted Talasnal, and instead continue straight ahead, following the yellow equal sign (=). Ignore the steep path to the right almost immediately afterwards and keep going on this rocky path as it zig-zags up the mountain.

As you climb, there are fabulous views down into Lousã and across the rolling hills towards Coimbra. The area's frequent forest fires dramatically affect the landscape here; the unobstructed views are mainly the result of burnt vegetation, and plumes of smoke can usally be seen at various points in the distance.

Soon after the views open up, turn left at a T-junction with a wide forestry track. This particularly steep section follows a narrow spur uphill towards a small clump of trees; markers have largely been obscured here, but route-finding is easy if you keep to the broadest track and ignore minor offshoots built for forestry.

Near the top of this section of the climb, the track becomes noticeably stony, then in 100m, on reaching what looks like a T-junction, you need to go straight ahead. The first 10m are a bit of a scramble, but you'll soon find yourself on an old stone path edged with low walls, blackberry bushes and shaded by diverse trees; this lovely stretch gives some idea of what the route up from the castle was like in the old days.

Within about 100m, you arrive at the bottom of the village of Casal Novo; turn right at the T-junction here, following the blue dot (the left-hand junction is marked with a blue cross). In 1981, according to the census, Casal Novo was completely deserted, yet now it's being renovated at a faster pace than the other serra villages, and new houses for rent spring up annually; check at the turismo in Lousã for the latest list of properties.

The village rises steeply up stone steps, and the views across the plains to the north and west are stunning, particularly from a delightful picnic area about half way up. At the top of the flight of steps the village ends at a dirt road; turn right here to continue the walk, then left up a dirt track 20m later. Walk along this track through alternating wooded and scarred, burnt stretches, and follow the blue paint markings until you reach a dirt road in about 750m; turn left here. From this point you can see Talasnal in the valley to your left, the third of the trio of villages in this walk; in 200m you arrive at the village of Chiqueiro.

Chiqueiro has a more lived-in feel than Casal Novo as it's a working village, full of goats and dogs, noises and smells. It has yet to be caught up in the holiday cottage boom, and although Chiqueiro is described as an abandoned village the exodus to the valleys was less apparent here with many of the houses continuously occupied by local farmers. As the rest of the villages become a prettified reflection of the past, Chiqueiro lives in the present, yet it's probably the most accurate picture of what life must have been like 50 years ago in the Lousã villages. Chiqueiro is the highest point of the walk and among its attractions is a refreshingly welcome water fountain.

To continue the walk, head downhill through the village on the stone path marked with blue paint. As you leave Chiqueiro behind, the path flattens out and becomes grassy; from here, head steeply down the charred hillside to the dirt road below you, keeping an eye on Talasnal up ahead and watching out for infrequent blue paint stripes. (This is the trickiest part of the walk, and if the weather is bad you can double back to Casal Novo and turn left at the dirt road at the top of the village; it will lead you to Talasnal in about 2km.)

On reaching the dirt road, turn right, then cross the head of a small valley and you'll arrive at the top of Talasnal in just under a kilometre. Take the narrow track on your left that winds downhill through the village, and keep going until you leave the last of the houses and reach a T-junction. Turn right here and return to Lousã following the description in the Talasnal walk (p 95).

17. Penacova

Fast Facts

distance 10km		rating easye
time 3 hours		map 231 (1:25,000)
	centre map page 15	

The villages and hamlets across the Rio Mondego from Penacova are fascinating places to while away a few tranquil hours. The route between them winds along cobbled roads, old paths, or forestry tracks with views of the steep-sided Mondego valley.

It's a quiet, laid-back part of the country, and as most visitors to Penacova rarely leave the town or the campsites, you should have the walk to yourself.

The walk begins and ends at Penacova campsite, across the river from the town itself, and near the village of Carvoeira. Turn left out of the campsite to walk down the road, then turn right 100m later up a steep, narrow tarmac road, passing a small cemetery on your right. Follow this little-used road as it shadows the Ribeira de Sanguinho, walking through a large eucalyptus and pine forest. As you head further up, the rows of uniform trees are broken up by tiny fields, some crammed into the narrow valley bottom and others clinging to the valley sides; look out in summer for dazzling blocks of yellow sunflowers.

In 2km the road arrives at the village of Sanguinho; turn right here to walk up the cobbled road. It's a bit of an exaggeration to call this tiny place a village as there are no more than thirty houses clustered along the steep main street and they all seem deserted in the daytime; this is still largely a farming community and entire households decamp to spend the days in the fields.

At the top of the street, take the track off to the left just after the last house in the village. This track climbs sharply towards Penedo Redondo hill, then curves right and flattens out as it enters a forest. It's now a broad forestry track that stays just below the ridge, with lots of smaller, less distinct tracks leading off it. The forest here is recently planted with little wildlife to see, but there are good views of the Rio Mondego and the hills around the Lorvão monastery through occasional breaks in the trees.

Follow this track for 2km until you reach a definite fork in the track. Although there have been many smaller dead-end trails off the main route, this is the first time that both branches are of equal width and condition. Ignore the left-hand fork, leading downhill, and take the right-hand track going flat. About 100m later, turn right at a T-junction with a broader track, then take the right-hand fork 50m later, heading over the top of the hill. Amble gradually downhill on this broad track for about a kilometre, until after a steep descent you reach the hamlet of

Cume do Soito.

Cume do Soito is growing fast, sprawling across the countryside and merging with the nearby village of Sobreiro. It's not as pretty as Sanguinho, and there are more people around, but it still has the calm and easy atmosphere of the other local villages. The track reaches a tarmac road at the start of Cume do Soito; turn right here, then turn right immediately down a stony track so that you're almost doubling back on yourself. On reaching a road 200m later, turn right.

In 300m, the road bends sharply to the left; take the good forestry track off to the right 50m further on. Note that this track was tarmaced in places at the time of research, and this short section may be entirely paved in future years. Go straight ahead at a crossroads in 150m, passing a house with stone eagles perched on the gateposts—they're probably the only birds you'll see for a while, as this part of the walk heads into aggressively forested land.

In just 30m, the road curves around to the left; take the right hand track to continue walking straight ahead. There are acacia and eucalyptus trees all around you here, and the only gap in the monotony is when this over-harvesting has led to erosion and minor landslides. It's easy to see why the widespread planting of these invasive trees is one of the prime concerns of environmental groups in Portugal (see p 6).

It comes as a relief when, in a little over a kilometre, the track leaves the forest and emerges at the top of Sanguinho. Walk through the village, and turn left on to the road, but instead of following the road all the way back to the campsite, turn left in 150m down a broad track. You're now walking on the opposite side of the valley to the road, surrounded by trees and small fields, and it's one of the best parts of the walk to spot birds of prey. The track passes an old stone bridge after a few hundred metres, then narrows to a small path, more shaded and a little overgrown in places but still easy to follow. In 500m the path ends at the bottom of the valley, crosses the stream via a small concrete bridge and arrives at the village of Carvoeira.

It's hard to describe the sensation of coming into Carvoeira this way, sneaking around the back alongside fields and gardens then suddenly finding yourself in the heart of a beautifully old-fashioned village. Carvoeira is a wonderful medley of tiny cobbled streets hemmed in by simple houses, and there's an attractive and unusual stone arch bridging the road ahead. Once you've finished admiring the village's appealing architecture, you can turn to its more practical delights: there's a bar and a small shop selling bread here. You'll also find that this walk brought you to Carvoeira the long way round, and if you turn right at the tarmac road at the end of the village you'll reach the campsite in 200m.

Other walks

The countryside around Penacova is laced with walking trails, and the paths around the river valleys near the Lorvão monastery are particularly lovely. Just north of Penacova lies the Buçaco Palace Hotel, a strange neo-Manueline building set in vivid, green gardens. Shady paths wind endlessly among peaceful glades and fountains; there are some 700 species of trees, including a cedar planted in 1644.

Still further north, the Serra do Caramulo is an impressive range of rolling hills dotted with severe-looking boulders and enlivened by wildflowers in spring and summer. From the town of Caramulo, where there's a pension, a pousada and a wildly eclectic art museum, head southwest to Caramulinho, the high point of the range, or northwest through tiny farms to the village of Arca.

Just west of Coimbra, birdwatchers will enjoy the Reserva Natural do Paúl de Arzila. The freshwater marsh reserve is home to little bitterns and purple herons; spring and summer are the best times to see the birds.

Rainy Day Options

At the first sniff of rain, head to Coimbra, an appealing town dominated by the oldest and grandest university in Portugal. Loftily perched on a hill above the town, the university's squares and buildings are well worth a visit; the main attraction is the Biblioteca Joanina, a riot of floor-to-ceiling ornate gilt. Down the hill towards the river is the dense mass of the Sé Velha, built in the twelfth century and looking from the outside more like a fortress than a cathedral.

Southwest of Coimbra is Conimbriga, the largest Roman site in Portugal, and an important town in the second and third centuries. Excavated highlights include the substantial Casa de Cantaber and Casa das Fontes villas, both with beautiful mosaic floors and sophisticated baths. Conimbriga's inhabitants left in a hurry in the late fifth century, building a huge wall right through the middle of town in a vain attempt to stop the Suevi invaders; their swift exit did more than anything else to preserve Conimbriga in its Roman glory.

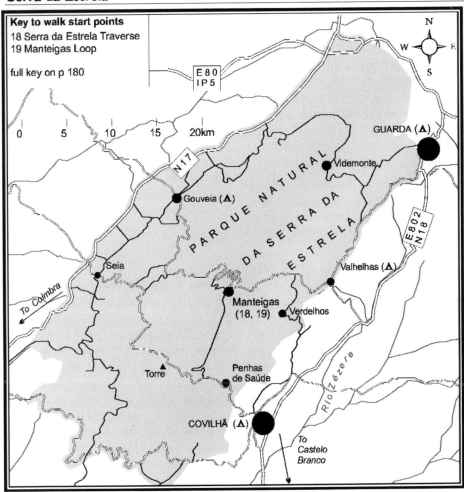

What's the weather like?

	Jan	April	July	Oct
Sun	4.5 hrs	7 hrs	8.5 hrs	6 hrs
Rainfall	187mm	100mm	40mm	100mm
Maximum Temp	7°	12°	20°	15°
Minimum Temp	-3°	2°	12°	7°

Average hours of sun, total average rainfall and average temperature in degrees celsius

Serra da Estrela

What's Inside

The Walks

Don't Miss . . .

A challenging, isolated, **five-day hike** around Portugal's wildest peaks, including the highest mountain in the land (p 109)

Pungent, robust, local **cheese** available everywhere (p 107)

A hike up the green, steep **Zezêre valley** (p 116)

The lovely **Casa de Sao Roque hotel** in Manteigas, one of the best small hotels in Portugal (p 107)

The Serra da Estrela is the backbone of Portugal, where among granite spires and mountain pastures the walker can find the highest peaks in the land. The alpine plateau and glacial valleys are riddled with an extensive network of footpaths that gives easy access to one of the best walking regions in Portugal. Small, tranquil market towns surround the serra and provide comfortable bases from which to explore the region.

Walking

Geography

The central part of the serra consists of the planalto superior or high plateau, rising up to Torre, which is, at 1993m, the highest mountain in Portugal. This unique subalpine plateau stretches southwest to northeast and is similar in character to the central mountains of Spain. Perfectly-formed hanging valleys, natural amphitheatres and large plateaus strewn with boulders are the scoured result of the last Ice Age. Small pockets of pastoral valleys enable shepherds to graze cattle, goats and sheep in the mild summers.

The rest of the year the upland is left to the elements, and this is one of the few areas in Portugal where skiing is possible. All areas above 1200m were designated protected countryside areas in 1990; you can't camp wild or light fires in these parts of the park.

The lower reaches of the mountain range have been farmed for centuries. Steep mountain faces have been terraced in order to grow crops, especially in the area around Loriga, to the south of the range, where granite and schist formations and a comparatively mild climate make this possible. Two of the largest rivers in Portugal, the Mondego and Zêzere, begin in the park, providing rare habitat and water for both irrigation and hydroelectric power.

Parks and Reserves

Founded in July 1976, the Parque Natural da Serra da Estrela is Portugal's largest protected area, covering 101,060 hectares, with a mandate to study, protect and develop traditional ways of life and the environment. The park has led the way in establishing and maintaining facilities for the walker. It was the first park in Portugal to establish a well-marked, thought-out network of trails with accompanying maps and route descriptions in both Portuguese and English. At the park offices the staff are friendly and knowledgeable, and if it's not too busy they'll happily help with planning an itinerary.

Sadly, destruction of the environment still goes on within the park, with developers having a stronger voice and deeper pockets than the conservationists. The construction of a hydroelectric pipeline down the upper Zêzere valley, one of the most beautiful areas of the park, is a case in point. The local governments and park authorities also have to address the inadequate access by public transport to the park and surrounding villages. Without a public transport system that works, the summer traffic jams and follies such as the car park on the top of Torre will continue to scar the park.

Trails

The trails are generally in superb condition, making navigation straightforward. It's sometimes a little too straightforward: to help fight forest fires some trails have been ploughed wide enough for a herd of wildebeest to get through.

There are three main trails in the park. T1, the hardest and most varied, travels along the spine of the park from Guarda to Vide. T2 hugs the western edge of the park, visiting small market towns on the way from Loriga to Vila Soeiro. T3, to the east, passes the Mondego and Zêzere rivers as it makes its way between Videmonte and Loriga.

All the routes are marked with yellow or red dashes depending on which part of the trail network you happen to be on. When trails where originally marked they appear to have been done from only one direction. The result is that sometimes the intrepid walker must look behind to see where the trail goes, especially in the high plateau near Torre.

Maps etc

Buying all the 1:25,000 maps to the park would break the bank — there are about 40 individual sheets. A much better option is the excellent *Carta Turística Parque Natural da Serra da Estrela*, a park-produced map adapted from 1:50,000 maps with the trail network superimposed. It's widely available throughout the park in tourist offices, park offices and in stores. The accompanying *Discovering the Region of the Serra da Estrela* booklet is an invaluable aid, describing all the trails in the park with times, distances and places of interest along the way. It's available in Portuguese and English.

For a more detailed look at wildlife and for a background to environmental issues in the park, pick up the multilingual *Estrela: A Natural Approach* from park offices.

Guided Walks

Park officials can arrange customised walks for groups through a program called Passeios a Pé no PNSE. Call one of the park offices (p 107) well in advance to arrange a walk. Rotas do Vento (p 4) runs a number of weekend trips to the park. Headwater Holidays, based in the UK (✆ (01606) 813333; www.headwater.com) organises week-long Serra da Estrela walking holidays each summer.

When to go

Whatever time of year you plan to go be prepared for sun, rain and everything in between. The summer months are the best time to visit the park. The days are long and usually clear providing perfect conditions for walking, although this is also the most popular time to come so be prepared for crowded accommodation.

Spring and autumn can also be wonderful, colourful times, but be ready for the rain that can come in off the Atlantic quickly and settle on the mountains for days on end. When this happens head for the rain shadow in the valley floors on the eastern edges of the park for some drier conditions. Leave the high plateau to the well-prepared and experienced in winter, as snow is common from December to May and visibility can be poor.

 # Flora & Fauna

The park has suffered from the effects of mismanaged forestry projects for generations. In the 1950s and 1960s huge swathes of natural Pyrenean oak and wild olive were

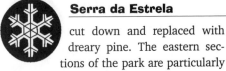

cut down and replaced with dreary pine. The eastern sections of the park are particularly ruined by this. Stands of non-native maritime pine, Douglas fir, Norway spruce and cluster pine are silent and devoid of animal life. In the few remaining **oak** and **wild olive** groves of the park, like the Moita do Conqueiro and remote sections of the Mondego watershed, the easiest animals to spot are the **rock sparrow, Bonelli's warbler** and **tawny owl**. The more interesting animals are also the best at concealing themselves; you'll be lucky to see the **beech marten, wild boar** and the elusive **genet**.

For the nature lover, the higher moorlands and Torre plateau are a real treat. The birds of prey are king here; **goshawk, booted eagles** and **red kites** dot the skies, and if you're really lucky you may see a golden eagle, even though there are no mating pairs left in the park. Other birds that enjoy the altitude are the **blue rock thrush** and **subalpine warbler**.

The subalpine meadows, with their expanses of mat grass and numerous brooks are home to the peculiar looking **fire salamander**. This bright-spotted amphibian is striking to look at but tends to only appear at night or in foul weather. **Natterjacks** and **European tree frogs** have been known to breed in some of the more remote ponds.

Along the lower slopes near Manteigas and Gouveia the noisy **great spotted cuckoo** can be seen looking for nests of other birds in which to lay its eggs. In the valley bottoms and farmlands look out for **Montagu's harrier, hoopoe** and **quail. Kingfishers** and **herons** are plentiful along the banks of the Mondego and Zêzere rivers.

People & Culture

People have sought out the solace of the mountains for thousands of years, and archaeological evidence of **prehistoric hillforts** and settlements is scattered across the park.

The mountains were the safe haven of Celtic tribes, acting as a natural fortress against the onslaught of the Roman invasion. The Lusitanian Che Guevara, **Viriatus**, fought a guerrilla-style war here against the Romans in the second century BC before he was betrayed and brutally murdered by three of his followers who had been bribed by the Romans.

Nowadays, the people of the Serra da Estrela are fighting a battle against the demise of its **population** as the young people leave seeking work in the cities. Although towns like Manteigas have maintained their population levels through the increase in summer tourism, the park as a whole has lost 5% of its population in the last 10 years alone.

The character of the land is reflected in the **Serra da Estrela dog**. These rugged beasts are huge and ferociously protective of their shepherds and sheep. Their deep-set eyes and loud bark scare even the bravest dog lover, and it's not hard to see traces of wolf blood in their lineage when seen up close. Once a common sight throughout the park, the dogs are now bred in kennels and pedigree puppies are sold to visitors rather than shepherds.

Food & Drink

The **Adega Cooperativa do Fundão** produces some of the best cheap wines around. Try the fruity, full-bodied **Cova da Beira**, which will wash just about anything down. More sophisticated palates should try the **Dão wines** from the western slopes of the Serra. The reds, soft and full of blackberry and blackcurrant flavours, are among the best in Portugal. Look out for wines from Bodega Cooperativa de Vila Nova de Tázem and Bodega Cooperativa de São Paio. You can also visit both these estates on a wine tour (p 119).

For once, the **cheese** is robust and full-flavoured, a pleasant change from the anaemic rounds of white curds in the rest of the country. Each local Bordaleira Serra da Estrela sheep produces more than 500 litres of milk a year, and the cheese is available at practically every shop in town. If you're around at the right time the cheese market at Celorico is worth a visit. It runs at the Municipal Market every other Friday from December to May; come early for the most atmosphere.

Tourist Information

Park offices

Head office, Rua 1 de Maio 2, Manteigas (✆ 275 982382, www.icn.pt/parques/pnse/pnse.htm), near GALP petrol station.

Information Centre, Rua dos Bombeiros Voluntários 8, Gouveia (✆ 238 42411).

Tourist Offices

Covilhã turismo, Avenida Frei Heitor Pinto (✆ 275 3101560), opposite the Jardim Público.

Gouveia turismo, Largo do Mercado (✆ 238 42185), across from the municipal market.

Manteigas turismo, Rua Dr Esteves de Carvalho (✆ 275 981129), near GALP petrol station.

Transport

Public transport around the park is very scarce. There are infrequent buses between Manteigas, Guarda and Covilhã, more during school terms. As always check with the turismo about times and frequency. Hitching is an easy way to get around but have patience and use your common sense about accepting lifts. If all else fails there are some taxis about, especially in Covilhã.

Money

There are cashpoints in Manteigas, Covilhã and Gouveia. Covilhã's the best place for more complex transactions.

Accommodation

Pião campsite, Covilhã (✆ 275 314312), 4km west of town up a steep hill, infrequent bus in August only; hitching fairly easy. Open year round.

Curral do Negro campsite, Gouveia (✆ 238 491008), 3km out of town on the way to Folgosinho. Open May to September.

Covão da Ametade campsite, basic and prone to flooding, but location more than makes up for natural hazards. On the N338

Serra da Estrela

out of Manteigas towards Penhas da Saúde.

Vale do Rossim campsite, basic campsite on T1 route between Torre and Gouveia; scheduled to reopen in summer 2000 after extensive renovations.

Valhelhas campsite (℘ 275 487160). Open May to September.

Camalhão rural campsite. Basic campsite with no facilities between Valhelhas and Verdelhos on north bank of Beijames river. Open summer only.

$ Pensão Residencial Central, Rua Nuno Álvares Pereira 14, Covilhã (℘ 275 322727).

$ Pensão Estrela do Parque, Rua da República 36, Gouveia (℘ 238 42171).

$$ Casa de São Roque, Rua de Santo António 67, Manteigas (℘ 275 981125). On a side road off Rua de 1 de Maio. Beautiful old house with friendly owner; don't consider staying anywhere else in Manteigas!

$$ Hotel de Gouveia, Avenida 1 de Maio, Gouveia (℘ 238 491010).

$$$ Estalagem Varandados Carquejais, Covilhã (℘ 275 3101120), on road to Penhas da Saúde, 5km outside Covilhã.

$$$$ Pousada de São Lourença, Manteigas (℘ 275 982450), 14km above Manteigas along a well-signposted road. Breathtaking views and excellent access to the Torre Plateau.

Shopping

The market in Covilhã is a great place to stock up on local produce and rub shoulders with the locals; it's about 500m along the left-hand road at the top of the square. On the lower slopes of Covilhã near the train station there's a giant hypermarket for those who want dried goods and backcountry cuisine favourites. The municipal market in Gouveia is excellent, and if you find it closed there's a general store next door that's crammed full of goodies.

The best bakery in all of Portugal can be found in Manteigas on Rua 1 de Maio and the town also has plenty of shops where you can pick up provisions. The pastelarias in Manteigas are a local institution, crammed full of elegant elderly women in for their mid-morning pastry.

Quick Quiz

8. How long is the Douro River?

(answer on p 184)

---

18. Serra da Estrela Traverse

Fast Facts

distance	111km	rating	difficult
time	5 days	map	Carta Turística PNSE (p 107) (1:50,000)
		centre map pages 16, 17, 18, 19, 20	

The best way to appreciate the wonders that make up the Serra da Estrela is to circumnavigate the mountain range. This route is made up from different segments of the park's established routes, showing a little bit of everything the park has to offer, from the windswept plains around Torre, Portugal's highest mountain, to the intricate traditional architecture around Verdelhos in the beautiful Beijames valley.

The five day suggested timeframe is only an outline, designed to separate the walk into manageable days with some sort of facilities at each day's end. The walk can be shortened or extended, and alternative routes and campsites are mentioned in the text. Prepare for rain and pray for sunshine is the mantra of safe travel in these mountains; waterproof and warm clothing is essential year-round, and even if you're only doing a day-long segment of the walk, be sure to bring emergency gear and spare food.

Day 1: Covão de Ametade to Vale do Rossim

Leave the campsite and turn right to walk up the main road, following the yellow markers. There are wonderful views down the Zêzere valley into the town of Manteigas. After 2km you arrive at Nave de Santo António where there's a souvenir stand on a large right-hand bend that in summer sells bread and refreshments. Soon afterwards a yellow arrow painted on a boulder on the left-hand side of the road indicates a right-hand turning, which you should take. This track leads to a vast, impressive grassland plain.

Despite the presence of a number of houses on the map, all bar one of them seem to have disappeared. Perhaps there's an extra-terrestrial explanation for this, as the Serra da Estrela is a notorious hotspot for UFO sightings and alien abductions. In 1997, a backpacker was reportedly abducted near Fundão, while in the same year a large flying saucer was spotted in the skies above Covilhã.

Back in the real world, keep this house on

your right and the large concrete cable car building on your left, always following the yellow markers. Ignore a path off to the left that leads back to the road; this track is part of the network of walking routes but heads towards Covilhã. As you see a road up ahead, the route curves round to the right, then moves left again before meeting the road. Cross over this road and head down a track towards a group of houses below a small reservoir. Ignore the turning to the left next to the houses—this leads down into Unhais da Serra.

The markers change colour here from yellow to red. The route leaves the track before it reaches the reservoir; a red arrow indicates the exact spot on the left. This is a tricky section; the path is difficult to find and very steep in parts. Always be sure that you see the next marker before climbing too far and look for piles of shepherd stones that are often easier to spot then the red paint. If you happen to lose the markers, head southwest, keeping the large, vertical, smooth rock face on your right. The path varies in quality from easy walking to occasional clambering over rocks.

The view, fantastic at the foot of the mountain, gets even better the higher you climb. As the path flattens out slightly, it curves round to the right next to a series of blue numbers painted on rocks, and emerges at a more level, grassy area. Markers are plainly visible here, even though the walking is over rough ground. After some time you'll be able to see the giant golf ball-like radar stations, decommissioned in the 1970s. Pass the top of the disused cable car and eventually reach the car park (yes, car park) at the top of Torre.

At 1993m, Torre is the highest peak in Portugal. Unsatisfied with its height, however, Dom João VI built a tower here in the early nineteenth century in order to extend the mountain to a more acceptable 2000m. João's tower has since been dwarfed by twentieth century follies, from the three storey shopping complex to the sprawling car park.

Despite the development, Torre's lofty vantage point is still impressive, offering a glorious 360 degree panorama on a clear day. The views to the east are the most alluring to the walker: the Serra da Malcata, the last stronghold of the Iberian lynx in Portugal, can be seen some 40km away, while in the distance you can make out the little-known Sierra de Gredos and Sierra de Gata in Spain.

Leaving the top of Torre, keep the road on your right and the two disused ski lifts on your left and you'll soon reach another road. Cross the road, looking out for the shepherd stones that mark the way every 50m or so. The path follows the line of the road for 100m before it veers off to the right. After 500m descend a little towards Lagoa da Salgadeiras. Here there are stunning bird's eye views down the Zêzere valley past Covão de Ametade 500m below. Walk along the edge of the plateau, remembering to be careful with your footing as there's usually a strong wind here.

Scramble down to a lake, then keep left as you pass a second dried-up lake bed. After a series of small ponds you emerge at a wide meadow. This meadow was once a lake too, but has slowly filled up with the remains of high altitude plants. The splendidly-named bogbean, a common aquatic plant on the plateau, can be seen in the ponds. Once through the meadow the path zigzags uphill. The trail seems to be better marked for travel in the opposite direction, so remember to turn around once in a while to check your bearings.

As you approach Cume mountain you pass a series of cairns, the first made of stone, the second and third of concrete; this last one is the true summit of Cume at 1858m. The trail goes straight on after the cairn. Be careful to take the correct path here and don't be fooled by the red dashed markers that lead down the T11 towards Curral dos Martins and beyond. Follow the solid red markers instead, straight past the third cairn and down over the ridge.

The path is harder to follow now. Descend for 150m as the path weaves around juniper bushes. Look for shepherd stones placed on top of boulders; they can be easily seen although it's not always obvious how to get to them. After the descent cross a large meadow, marked Charcos on the map. In the summer the alpine bloom is a treat as the plants struggle to attract insects so that they can reproduce quickly in the very short growing season.

On the other side of the Charcos meadow climb up until you come to a large cart track. This is the T13 coming to join up from Seia, 18km away to the west. Turn right and follow the track as it winds its way towards Vale do Conde, passing the small Covão dos Conchos dam on the way. Yellow markers begin to appear but luckily they lead in the same direction so don't be scared to follow them.

The large boulders that line the path at odd intervals start to disappear as you emerge at Vale do Conde, one of the most beautiful places in all of Portugal; the expanse of mat grass makes this a wonderful rest stop.

The most unusual inhabitant of this grassland valley is the fire salamander with its distinctive red spots. It's fairly docile and doesn't run away when you approach, but be careful not to touch its mildly poisonous skin. This high-altitude salamander is one of the longest-lived amphibians, thought to live for up to 42 years. If it's raining and you're not appreciating the walk so far, take heart: your best chance of seeing the fire salamander is either at night or in foul weather.

After walking through the valley for a few hundred metres look for the path to cross the stream. Once on the other side of the stream keep to the right-hand edge of the meadow. Soon the trail turns 90 degrees to the right, climbing up out of Vale do Conde and over the shoulder of Fraga das Penhas (1668m). The path isn't clear here so keep to the shepherd stones. Pass a concrete pillar and follow the ridge down the other side, then cross a stream and follow the path downhill.

The path winds down to the foot of the dam in a few kilometres, becoming wider and more pronounced before meeting a road. Follow the road and climb past an old shack, which acts as a bar in summer, and a little further, the dam watchman's house. There is a tap for water just past the house on the opposite side of the track; fill up here as this is the last water for 15km.

By the summer of 2000 the park should have completed the new campsite at Vale do Rossim with basic facilities for visitors. For those lured back to Manteigas by the thought of a hot bath and clean sheets, turn right at the first junction after the dam and follow the road down for 10km.

Day 2: Vale do Rossim to Gouveia

Starting at the dam, walk past the campsite then keep left at a junction along a tarmac road. Follow this road for 2km until the main road from Manteigas joins from the right. Turn left here and follow the road for another kilometre. Just past some power lines take the second gravel track on the right following the sign to Malhão, a small summit that you'll pass later in the walk. This broad and sandy gravel track is edged with pine plantations on the right and shrubs on the left.

After 4km you arrive at Nave da Cruz where there are the remains of an abandoned forestry building on your right, built in the 1970s. Although there's no water here the building does offer some shelter from the elements. Stop a moment to gaze to the right across the headwaters of the Mondego River. This is the humble beginnings of the longest river in Portugal, and in a day's time a refreshing swim in its cool waters awaits the dirty walker.

In 2km you'll pass the summit trig point for Malhão (1557m). Don't wilt yet as there's only one more summit to go before the descent to Gouveia. A solar-powered fire watchtower marks the summit of Santinha but don't hold out too much hope of seeking shelter here as the watchtower was firmly locked in both 1993 and 1999.

Now start to descend, winding your way past the church of São Tiago perched on a small peak to the right. After 2km pass a fountain on the right, the last water before Gouveia. Turn left at the T-junction to seek the pleasures of Gouveia and the campsite at Curral do Negro; right leads to Videmonte and the rest of the walk.

Descend a kilometre to another junction and turn left. Keep going until you come to an old abandoned forestry house on your right and a water reservoir on the left. There aren't many markers to reassure the indecisive walker. The track splits here so take the left-hand trail and follow the broad track for 2km through forest until you come to a concrete sign showing that it's only 6km until you reach Gouveia. A new dirt road has been ploughed making the trail obvious as it clings to the side of the valley.

After 2km you come to another concrete post with weathered-off writing; a yellow arrow directs the weary walker left along an old track. Keep left at a T-junction, then a few hundred metres later go straight on at a crossroads to begin the final descent into Gouveia. Follow the ridge around, ignoring a turning that leads back up the mountain. In 1km you arrive at the campsite, then in 3km more at the town of Gouveia.

Day 3: Gouveia to Videmonte

Climb back out of Gouveia, retracing your steps to the earlier junction with the T1 and the route back towards Torre. In 200m the track widens and there are a couple of park benches that make a good spot for a rest. Down the valley to the left the village of Folgosinho appears through the trees. There aren't many markers here but the track is wide and well-maintained. About 1km along the track, ignore a right-hand fork and curve down towards Portela de Folgosinho;

you'll soon pass a basic wooden sign for the park and large wooden arrows pointing to the left-hand path for Videmonte.

Then, 2km after Portela de Folgosinho, climb slowly up to the left of Galhardos (1323m), where you'll come to a junction. Turn left here, at the highest point of today's walk. Continue to head through the mix of silver birch and pine forest, following the ridge towards the rounded mountain called São Domingos.

The path curves to the right at the base of the mountain as the landscape slowly changes from open scrub to farmland where smallholdings cling to the landscape. At a crossroads a signpost indicates that you should go straight ahead to Videmonte. Take a break here to turn around and admire the fine views of the Torre Plateau and reminisce about your epic crossing earlier in the walk.

Come to a small junction and keep right. The terrain flattens out here, and there are tree plantations on either side of the trail. At a telephone pole a marker indicates a right-hand turn into the hamlet of Porto de Melo, which you should take. This group of buildings is reported to be the highest settlement in the park and it certainly feels like the most isolated.

Continue straight ahead, cross under some power lines and keep left at a junction, then keep straight when another track joins from the right. The imposing fortress town of Guarda is visible on the horizon in clear weather. Pass a typical mountain farm on the right then come to a crossroads where the path goes straight over. Ignore the sign pointing left to Linhares and Folgosinho.

At a junction just before a pine wood turn on to the left-hand track. Once on the other side of the wood curve around to the left, passing a football pitch that's seen better days but still boasts floodlights. You are now at the edge of Videmonte.

Follow the track into the centre of the village where shops and cafés provide a welcome opportunity to rest and replenish supplies. Be sure to pick up water in the village if you want to camp near here.

It can be confusing to leave the maze of cobbled lanes that make up Videmonte. Head for the small chapel of Senhora de Lurdes and its accompanying cemetrey, and if you get lost ask for the way to Quinta da Taberna.

Once out of town pass a small wood on the left, a quiet place to camp if you don't want to walk the extra 4km to the next camping spot. In 2km there's a junction where markers have been obscured by recent road repairs; the track to take is the second on the left that heads straight downhill. This track is a shortcut and meets up with the main track in 500m; upon meeting this main track turn right and follow it through farmers' fields dotted with large chestnut trees.

As the track descends to the Mondego river you pass a farm on the left then an abandoned building to your right. Just before the river is a small shrine to Senhora da Taberna, built by the people of Guarda in 1991, and across the bridge is a small field that makes an excellent campsite alongside the Mondego river.

Day 4: Videmonte to Valhelhas

Climb up the road from the river and turn left just before the Quinta da Taberna. A kilometre later at a crossroads, just on the edge of the forest, go straight across and into the woods. Although no centurion would recognise it today, this is part of the old Roman road that used to link Braga to Mérida. There are few markers for the rest of the day so try to stick to the main track ignoring the many smaller tracks that splinter off from time to time.

On the far side of the forest you come to a large ploughed junction; keep right here and follow the track as it curves down. Further to your right is the small valley of agricultural land that surrounds the Quinta do Fragusto. At the quinta, cross a small stream on a rickety metal bridge. The path climbs up the hill opposite; ignore the first right-hand turn and keep climbing. The path curves around the mountain and then reaches a T-junction, where you should turn right.

Yellow markers are nowhere to be seen but some trees are tagged with tape and these will lead you over the mountain. Keep climbing and cross under some power lines. This part of the walk is a little disheartening as you make your way through plantations of pine, climbing one false summit after another with no views.

Eventually at a bend in the track the forest clears. Across the valley you can see Belmonte and below you is Valhelhas. The route down has lost all its markers and tracks seem to come and go. The trick is to follow the ridge down, bearing right and aiming for Valhelhas. Emerge at the main track leading into the village, passing a small school on your left. Soon afterwards you reach the main road; turn left to go the village centre or right for the campsite.

Day 5: Valhelhas to Manteigas or Covão de Ametade

Walk through the village of Valhelhas, passing the turning for the road to Guarda and a fountain on your right, dated 1866. Just before you reach a new bridge, take the small lane off to the right down to the old bridge. Once over the old bridge, turn left and rejoin the main road, then turn right 30m later and start to climb up the forestry track. Keep going up until you reach a fork in the trail after about 500m of climbing; take the right-hand track and follow it along the side of the mountain. The track is in good condition and passes through groves of oak, chestnut and pine. This is a good birding area first thing in the morning and there are fine views across the Zêzere valley.

Almost 5km after the old bridge you reach a small patch of agricultural land and the track starts to climb; take the turning to the right here. After 100m you pass between two buildings, the right-hand one painted with a yellow marker. Follow the trail as it drops down to the meeting point of the Zêzere and Beijames rivers, and turn left just before the rivers. The next 4km are among the most beautiful of the whole walk.

Follow the track across a small tributary then just before you pass a farm on your left take the right-hand turning, looking out for a marker on a tree to the left of the turning. Pass a signpost for the rural campsite at Camalhão, open only in summer. Keep following the track past a hodge podge of stone barns until you emerge at the main road. Turn right at the road and cross the bridge into the village of Verdelhos, where there are a few small cafés and stores to pick up supplies.

Once across the bridge turn left and follow the now-orange markers up through the village. There is a signpost here for the Lamba da Cancelhas Footpath, a pleasant day circuit of the valley. Walk past a church, a fountain dated 1906 and a small shrine. Just after the shrine at a bend in the road turn left on to a smaller track. Follow this old cart track as it crosses a small stream and then climbs through fields. A new tree plantation has obliterated some of the trail; keep climbing up and try to stay left of the summit of Cabeço do Moreira (1197m) above you.

Cova is nestled in the saddle of the pass above you and can't be seen until you're almost on top of it. As you climb, look out for the power and telephone lines that give a clue to Cova's location.

As the track approaches Cova you have two choices. At an old chestnut tree a marker indicates a right-hand turn on to an old shepherds' path up through Cova. Although it sometimes vanishes as quickly as it appears, getting lost is a good way to explore this remote mountain hamlet. If you choose this path head past the small chapel to the saddle. The second way is less interesting but easier to follow; just stick to the main track as it climbs up to the pass.

At the saddle of the pass turn left at the junction and a little over a kilometre later you arrive at Poço do Inferno. After admiring the waterfall the walker is again faced with two choices.

The easy way home is to follow the track from Poço do Inferno down to Manteigas, 8km further on. There's no campsite in Manteigas so those wishing to camp will have to hitch up to Covão de Ametade or walk there following the Zêzere River. The other alternative is to follow the T3 to the main Manteigas-Covilhã road, then turn right and follow the road to the campsite at Covão de Ametade. For details of this route, see the Manteigas Loop walk on the next page.

Quick Quiz

9. In which year did the castle at Mirando do Douro explode?

(answer on p 184)

19. Manteigas Loop

Fast Facts

distance	31km	rating	moderate to difficult
time	1 or 2 days	map	Carta Turística PNSE (p 107) (1:50,000)
	centre map pages 21		

A long day or two shorter ones begin and end alongside the lovely glacial Zêzere valley. In between, the climb up to Alto da Portela rewards the effort needed to reach the top with stunning views of the Serra da Estrela. This is a good walk for those who want a taste of the Serra da Estrela but don't have the inclination for a longer outing.

From Manteigas, walk from Rua 1 do Maio towards the turismo, turning right down a cobbled road between the GALP petrol station and the turismo. After a few hundred metres follow the road as it curves around a large sewage works on the right.

Cross over a bridge, then turn left at a junction 30m later. A couple of hundred metres further turn right on to a forestry dirt road. Pass a heap of rusty old cars on the left-hand side of the track as the long climb to Poço do Inferno begins.

Almost a kilometre later, turn right at an orange spray-painted arrow, initially almost doubling back on yourself. The climbing gets tougher now, but pine and sweet chestnut trees provide shade for frequent rests. If you're lucky, one of the black redstarts that inhabit these slopes may show themselves; their distinctive, constantly-wiggling, red tail makes them easy to identify.

Turn left at a junction 300m later. Even though the trail looks straight on the 1:50,000 map, you in fact zigzag up the mountain. Yellow markers are not always visible as you climb up through more deciduous trees. There are great views through the trees down into the Zêzere Valley looking over the village of Carvalhais. Cross over a stream and 100m later take the right-hand fork going uphill.

Beautiful oak trees line the way as you pass a slowly crumbling white forestry building with Matas Nacionais written on its side. This building was built half a century ago to serve the workers who planted and maintained the trees of the surrounding hillside. Half a kilometre later, turn left at a junction down a well-defined, fairly level track with a yellow marker 50m along to reassure you that this is the correct route. The track crosses one of the many tributaries of the Zêzere by way of a concrete bridge. At a large bend not much further on, join a bigger track that turns right then soon doubles back on itself. Emerge on a well used dirt road and turn right.

The road becomes paved once you reach the waterfall at Poço do Inferno, 8km into the walk. The waterfall is more of a trickle in summer, needing autumn rains or spring snowmelt to look its surging best. Lots of picnic benches and tables make this a popular spot with picnickers, so if you want somewhere quiet to have lunch keep going up to the Alto da Portela.

Go around the bend here (and you may do so if you spend too long hunting for the right trail) past the waterfall and take the path leading off to the left opposite a large lay-by about 20m past the bend. The path is easy to lose as it climbs up beside the waterfall: the route has changed over time due to erosion.

There are now remnants of two trails marked with yellow stripes. The other obstacle to finding your way is the 1:50,000 map, which shows the path starting before you get to the waterfall when it really starts afterwards; this mistake was not corrected in the map's 1998 revision. The easiest way up is to keep well right of the river. Beware of the fact that the correct trail splits. The true right-hand path zigzags up the hillside while a false trail climbs up and over a small lump of rock then back down to the river. There are no yellow markers on the false trail but the path is well built and gets a lot of use by people making the same mistake.

Always keep heading up, aiming for the stone cairn above you. The trail slowly becomes more obvious as you near the top, where the track widens and flattens out. In 500m, join a wider track and turn right, then turn left on reaching a tarmac road a few hundred metres further on. Continue to climb gradually, looking out for green woodpeckers in the surrounding pine forest. This track will eventually lead all the way to the main Manteigas–Covilhã road 8km ahead.

Traverse along the Serra de Baixo passing by the Curral da Nave (1457m). Views open up northeast to the fortress town of Guarda and beyond it into Spain. The trees thin out, revealing a barren plateau heading up towards Malhada Alta, Curral do Vento (1656m) and Poios Brancos (1704m). The high winds and poor soil of the uplands prevent tree growth and only local shepherds farm here, using the moorland as summer pasture for cattle and sheep.

The Torre Massif appears to the west and is easily spotted by the radar stations on top. The huge granite walls present Torre at its most imposing and provide a pleasant backdrop to a picnic on one of the many lunar-like boulders that mark the landscape. The road becomes a gravel track after 2km with very few yellow markers. Eventually the stunning Zêzere valley reappears to the right. The track rises slightly and comes into a thin pine forest again. Finally, you reach the road next to a stand that sells cold drinks and tacky souvenirs in summer.

The standard route follows the road for 4km past Covão de Ametade where a beautiful if prone to flooding campsite is a clue to its origins as a glacial lake. If you can't say no to a shortcut, look out for a large sign labelled Cortadouro da Barroqueira about 500m after the souvenir stand on the right-hand side of the road. This narrow shortcut heads steeply downhill through silver birch and mountain ash and emerges back on the road a kilometre below the campsite.

Whichever way you decide to descend, be sure to stop at the Fonte de Paulo Martins, which provides the most unimaginably refreshing spring water; don't be surprised to see locals filling up with carloads of water, as the reputation of this spring is no secret.

On the left-hand side of the road 300m later the trail heads down to the valley floor. Initially narrow with loose rock, the path doubles back as you approach the bottom of the valley. The path curves round to the right following yellow arrows and soon broadens into an easy track.

As you approach Manteigas take time to admire the stone huts at Covões. These are in various states of repair: some have corrugated iron roofs, others are thatched with rye and broom. Still others have been modernised with solar panels, running hot water and all the comforts of home. Follow the valley, keeping the river on your left for about 2.5km, then cross over a concrete bridge and continue on the other side of the Zêzere river.

The track widens, passing a pine wood after 3.5km. Keep going down towards Caldas de Manteigas. The road becomes cobbled, then joins the road into Manteigas.

From here you can see a big, old water wheel in Caldas about 50m to the right of the trail, a relic from Manteigas' past when the textile industry, powered by the waters of the Zêzere, brought the first seeds of industrialization to this once remote valley. The wheel still turns, although the main textile plant further down the valley now uses more modern production methods. Turn left and walk along the road until in 1km you arrive back in Manteigas.

Quick Quiz

10. What, to the nearest half million , is the population of Portugal?

(answer on p 184)

Other Walks

There are enough walks in the park to keep hikers happy for weeks. The network of trails lends itself well to planning itineraries of various length and difficulty.

The T11, which links Manteigas with Torre, is a wonderful walk; those with their own transport can cheat by driving up the road to the pousada and starting there. This walk can be turned into a wonderful loop around the plateau by returning via the T1, visiting the Vale do Rossim on the way back.

The area around Seia and Loriga offers the curious walker the chance to marvel at the vanishing rural way of life. The climb up to Torre is a killer so those less willing to strain sinew may want to hitch up to the top first, then walk down the steep Garganta de Loriga. For those who know how to combine map and compass the rounded peaks of the Serra de Baixo to the southeast of Manteigas offer peace, isolation and the best panoramic views in the park.

The northern part of the park is less interesting and many of the trails are on road. Forestry plantations turn much of the scenery into monotonous blocks of dreary pine. The banks of the Mondego River are wonderful to amble alongside but the Zêzere River offers better access, especially near Valhelhas.

A forgotten corner of the park, which deserves to be explored, is around Verdelhos on the banks of the Beijames River. This beautiful watershed is lined with traditional stone and wood houses, built in a loosely common architectural style that melds perfectly with its surroundings. The rural campsite at Camalhão provides a suitable base and there's a circular walk around the valley, unmarked on the park map. Look for signs in Verdelhos for the Lamba da Cancelhas footpath. The route goes up to Poço do Inferno then to the peak of Azinheira (1035m) before returning to the valley floor at Camalhão.

Rainy Day Options

One of the best ways to beat the rain is to go on a wine tour. The two best cellars are near Gouveia in the villages of Vila Nova de Tázem and São Paio. You can visit both for free from Monday to Friday.

The Caldas de Manteigas Spa is a great way to get rid of those aches and pains. The refreshing Holy Spring is a cool 19 degrees while the other is a more reasonable 42 degrees. The spa is 2km south of Manteigas and is open May to September.

At first glance Covilhã looks rather charmless but the maze of back streets above the market make for wonderful exploring. Small alleys twist and turn revealing tiny shops and coffee bars tucked away from the standard tourist trail. Covilhã also has its fair share of pastry shops and restaurants.

Quick Quiz

11. What is the level of literacy in Portugal?

(answer on p 184)

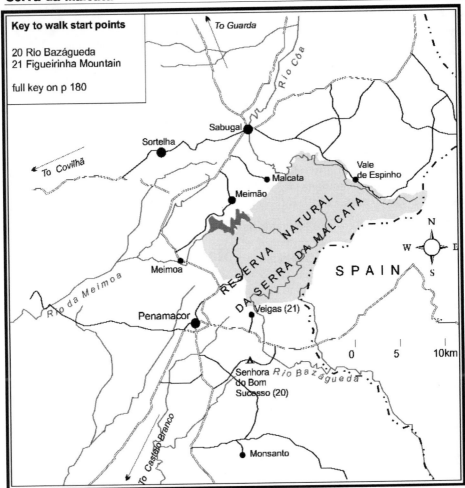

Key to walk start points

20 Rio Bazágueda
21 Figueirinha Mountain

full key on p 180

What's the weather like?

	Jan	April	July	Oct
Sun	5 hrs	8 hrs	10 hrs	7 hrs
Rainfall	96mm	57mm	10mm	62mm
Maximum Temp	12°	20°	32°	21°
Minimum Temp	6°	12°	16°	13°

Average hours of sun, total average rainfall and averag temperature in degrees celsius

Serra da Malcata

What's Inside

The Walks

Don't Miss . . .

Visit the last major Portuguese stronghold of the **Iberian lynx**, the most endangered wild cat in the world (p 126)

Wander amongst abandoned mills and bread ovens next to the **Rio Bazágueda** (p 125)

Spend a hot day by the pool at isolated but well-equipped **Freixial campsite** (p 124)

This forgotten mountain range on the border with Spain is one of the last refuges of the Iberian lynx, the most endangered species of wild cat in the world. Isolated pockets of Pyrenean oak and holm oak on the steep banks of the Côa, Bazágueda and Meimoa rivers provide the beautiful, feathery-eared lynx with undisturbed habitat. Although the chance of seeing one of these shy felines is slim, don't be put off visiting this remote region: the walking is easy and you're almost guaranteed solitude.

Walking

Geography

The Côa and Bazágueda rivers, along with the Spanish frontier, mark the boundaries of the rolling hills of the Serra da Malcata. The mountains run northeast to southwest with the twin peaks of Concelhos (1007m and 999m) the highest points in the reserve. Farming's tough here: the sandstone base rock doesn't hold water, so all the minerals leach out of the soil when it rains and most rivers dry up during the course of dry, sweltering summers.

Deep, steep valleys of deciduous woods in the eastern half of the reserve are the ecological survivors of decades of savage resource-stripping. Elsewhere, commercial plantations of foreign trees and damming of rivers have taken their toll and it's a small miracle that any wildlife remains at all, let alone thrives.

Parks & reserves

The 16,348 hectare Reserva Natural da Serra da Malcata was created in 1981 in response to local and environmental pressure to save the Iberian lynx and its remaining habitat. The reserve has done a remarkable job of halting the destruction of habitat and has even managed to reintroduce species that had vanished from the serra. There's still a way to go before the reserve can relax its efforts: poaching, chemical spraying and plans to dam more sections of the serra's rivers all threaten this ecological oasis.

The reserve offices are superbly organized even though resources are few. There's printed information in English and Portuguese about all aspects of the reserve and friendly staff go out of their way to help visitors. Unlike at other reserve offices in Portugal, rangers and biologists are also available to share their vast knowledge and expertise.

The reserve has established a series of trails on the northern fringe of the reserve away from the more ecologically sensitive areas. These walks vary in difficulty but most are designed to be done in an easy half-day. Outlines for two of these walks are available on the reserve's web site (www.icn.pt/reservas/rnsm/rnsm.html).

Trails

The walks covered in this book are on the southern fringe of the reserve away from the sensitive areas and accessible from Freixial campsite and from Penamacor. These trails are well-maintained dirt tracks, still used by farmers today. Reserve trails are marked with either red or yellow stripes.

Maps etc

The two most useful 1:25,000 maps are 237 and 248, but you'll also need 226, 227 and 238 to cover the whole reserve. The military

1:50,000 maps (21III, 21IV) are older and less useful, while the civilian 1:50,000 maps are almost prehistoric and no good for anything as they predate the Meimoa Dam.

The reserve produces the excellent *Serra da Malcata Nature Reserve* booklet, jammed full of information on flora and fauna as well as descriptions of three walks and one driving tour of the reserve. Although it's written in Portuguese, *Conhecer o Lince-Ibérico* has clear pictures and is a great introduction to the life of the reserve's mascot, the Iberian lynx. The section on identifying lynx droppings and footprints is worth the price alone.

When to go

Any time is the right time as far as the Serra da Malcata is concerned, though the heat of summer can be overbearing. Locals consider spring and autumn to be the most pleasant seasons, and the migration of birds at this time is an added attraction. The serra is too low to get snow, but a cool breeze can blow in from Spain during the months of December and January, bringing a wet, uncomfortable chill.

 # Flora

The **Iberian lynx** wasn't studied until it was almost too late. In 1976 the first scientific report shocked the Portuguese environmental movement into a desperate campaign to save the lynx and its vanishing habitat. Commercial forestry sustained by constant chemical spraying was replacing stands of **holm oak** and **Pyrenean oak** with imported eucalyptus and pine plantations. The Serra da Malcata was the last area with a substantial lynx population in Portugal.

It's hard to know exactly how many lynx now live in the reserve. Each solitary lynx can cover a territory of 10km^2 each night as it hunts mainly rabbits for food. It's believed that there are at least five lynx in the reserve with more in the surrounding area, especially in the Spanish Sierra de la Malvana.

The lynx can be confused with the smaller and more common **genet** and **wild cat** when seen from a distance, which have similar spotted coats. If you're ever lucky enough to see one up close, however, the lynx is immediately recognizable by the tufts of hair that sprout from the top of its ears and the jowl-like fur that hangs beneath its face.

Surprisingly for an area that has suffered so much environmental destruction, there's an abundance of wildlife, most of it easier to spot than the elusive lynx. **Red foxes** vie with the lynx at the top of the food chain, while the riverbanks within the reserve are home to **otters** and **Iberian frogs**.

The **black vulture** is the success story of the reserve. Spanish breeding pairs were slowly lured over the border by biologists who built nest platforms and left carcasses for the birds to eat. Eventually, temptation proved too much for the vultures and in 1996 some decided to stay and start breeding here. Appearing entirely black from a distance, the birds have a wingspan of up to 3m and a distinctive wedge-shaped tail.

 # People & Culture

Isolation and the threat of invasion run through the history of this region: Malcata has had Celts, Moors, dukes and dictators

123

fighting over its strategic location. None of the important characters from history stuck around much longer than it took for the dust to settle, though, leaving the locals to get on with daily life. That life has always been difficult, a battle for survival against the harsh climate and poor soils; migration in the 1950s and 1960s accounted for a decline of 40% in the area's population, and the exodus continues today.

Food & Drink

If you really want a taste of Malcata seek out **jeropiga**, the local plonk. This rough, unfermented wine won't exactly win prestigious awards, but it's considered essential to getting through the long winter months. Other local delicacies, which don't leave such a bad hangover, include spare ribs in bread and garlic and Penamacor **cheese**. The local smoked **sausages** are some of the best in the country: look out for chouriço de ossos, morcela, mioleira and bucho.

Tourist Information

Park offices

Head Office, Rua dos Bombeiros Voluntários, Penamacor (✆ 277 394467).

Branch Office, Largo de São Tiago, Sabugal (✆ 271 752825).

Tourist office

Penamacor turismo, Rua 25 de Abril (✆ 277 94316).

Transport

Without your own wheels you'll spend most of your time walking to your destination. Buses link Penamacor with the outside world via Covilhã, but there are no buses to the reserve or campsite. Even hitching can be tricky as most roads are deserted.

Money

Banks and cashpoints in Penamacor and Sabugal.

Accommodation

Freixial Municipal Campsite, 11km east of Penamacor off the N569 (✆ 277 394106). Basic café, swimming pool; open April to October.

$-$$ Rooms. Many places in Penamacor rent out cheap rooms; ask at the turismo.

$$$ Estalagem Vila Rica, Penamacor (✆ 277 34311).

Shopping

Penamacor's fortnightly market is a great place to see the hustle and bustle of the local population as they gossip and do their weekly shop; it's held on the first and third Wednesdays of each month. If you don't manage to catch the market there are plenty of small shops in the centre of town.

Events & Festivals

Feira de São Pedro (Sabugal, June 29); **Feira das Melancias** (Sabugal, first Thursday in September), the region's annual watermelon fair; **Senhora da Póvoa** (Vale Senhora da Póvoa, first Monday after Whitsun), annual religious pilgrimage.

20. Rio Bazágueda

Fast Facts

distance 7km	rating easy
time 3 hours	map 248 (1:25,000)
centre map page 22	

This gentle amble beside the Rio Bazágueda cries out for a picnic lunch. The walking is easy, so take time to relax in the shade of ruined mills or stretch out in sunny meadows.

The walk begins and ends at the Freixial campsite near Penamacor. With your back to the campsite gates turn right and then take the track almost immediately on your left. Walk past a couple of farm buildings off to the left. Cross over the Ribeira das Freixial via a concrete bridge and keep left 30m later as a track joins from the right. At a cross-roads 300m further on go straight ahead, passing olive groves and keeping the Rio Bazágueda on the left. In late summer, the river can dry up completely.

Cross over the Ribeira das Trutas (trout stream), a strange name for a stream that appears dry each summer with no fish in sight. Climb up a little as the trail continues along the banks of the Rio Bazágueda. Almost a kilometre later cross another stream. Soon afterwards the trail passes fields on the left and climbs to traverse along a terrace amidst an assortment of abandoned and still-used barns. This is a great place to have a picnic and poke around the skeletal remains of the old buildings; there's even an old bread oven here.

A further 500m along keep to the main track, avoiding paths off to the river. You'll soon approach Moinho do Fundeiro, a collection of buildings named for the now-ruined mill that stands amongst them. Keep the buildings on your left as you climb up a small ridge, then turn left at a T-junction once the buildings end. Follow the track down to the river. The views to Spain are superb from here and you get a good look at the higher peaks of the Serra da Malcata.

Cross the river near the remnants of an old footbridge. Once on the other bank turn right and veer towards the ruins of Monte das Eirinhas on the small knoll up ahead. Once you have the ruins on your right-hand side and a small stream between you and the ruins, turn left to follow the well-worn track up to the ridge. Climb the ridge, passing holm oaks and scrub before the trail flattens and meadows appear off to the left.

As you walk through the meadows looking for a place to digest lunch, listen for the scrambling of lizards as they scurry to find new hiding places. Easiest to spot are the sun-lovers: look for the hand-sized, brown sand lizard and the much bigger

green lizard, which opens its mouth and tries to bite when threatened. Jays and bee-eaters are common, and if you're lucky you may glimpse a red kite hunting for food.

After a kilometre, turn left at a crossroads. The path slowly descends towards the Rio Bazágueda; follow the track back to the main road. Once at the road turn left, cross the bridge and return to the campsite.

21. Figueirinha Mountain

Fast Facts

distance	12km	rating	moderate
time	4 hours	maps	237, 248 (1:25,000)
	centre map page 23		

This walk touches the fringe of the reserve giving close-up views of the Serra da Malcata's highest peaks.

It begins and ends alongside the Bazágueda river, passing through pleasant oak groves and less appealing pine plantations. To get to the trail, follow the N569 from Penamacor towards the campsite and church at Senhora do Bom Sucesso. After 7km turn left at the sign for Veigas, a hunting lodge for tourists who feel the urge to shoot something. Continue along this dirt road for 2km, then after the steep descent just before reaching Veigas take the left-hand track. This is a good place to park a car.

Amble along the dirt track for a little over a kilometre, then keep a lookout for two sets of ruined buildings down by the river. The first is called Moinho da Marmita and lies on the banks of the Rio Bazágueda. Casal do Rato, the second set of buildings, is about 500m further on, near the meeting place of the Ribeira de Bazáguedinha and the larger Rio Bazágueda. Once the Casal do Rato comes into view, take the small track off to the right that leads down to the river. Cross the Ribeira de Bazáguedinha and climb past the Casal do Rato along a well-worn track. The effects of eucalyptus plantations and logging have drastically altered the vegetation here, replacing the natural scrub with stands of monospecies.

As you climb towards Figueirnha, the views open out. Near the end of a 2km uphill stretch the track enters a pine forest and curves around to the left of the peak. Keep right at a junction just before the trail goes downhill and follow the track into the broad valley of the Ribeira de Valdedra. It's worth stopping to enjoy the views down the Ribeira da Queijeira to where it joins the Rio Meimoa, near the town of the same name.

Descend for a while, ignore the first right-hand turn and instead take the second right not far afterwards. Follow the valley up towards Monte do Salgueirinho, which lies at the base of the twinned peaks of Concelhos. Go straight on at a crossroads then turn left in 400m. The trail now follows one of the marked reserve paths and you'll see yellow and red stripes painted on rocks.

Cross the Ribeira do Salgueirinho then begin to climb up the ridge opposite. Take the second turning right (the first right dead ends at the ruined buildings of Poio). From this vantage point between the Mouca and Pojo valleys you can look left into the heart of the Serra da Malcata. The views are delicious, as are the place names. Avoid looking at the map if you're hungry, as it shows streams named after pork, bread and wine.

As you start the descent, the trail becomes more overgrown, and at the bottom of the ridge you meet the Ribeira de Pojo. Here, a steady supply of groundwater enables trees and dense bush to grow tall, making this perfect wildlife spotting territory. Follow the stream for 150m before turning right along the dirt track to Moinho do Pinheiro. Once you've passed this rustic farm, cross a stream and keep right at a junction soon afterwards.

The trail climbs slightly, then crosses a rock outcrop: it's a dramatic path, seemingly etched out of the cliff face. About 800m after the farm, arrive back at the ruins of Casal do Rato, and retrace your way back to Veigas.

Other walks

First things first. There are some trails and old logging roads that lead into the heart of the reserve. Try to resist the temptation to explore these sensitive areas so that the lynx can get it on and start reproducing.

The reserve has established a series of nature walks but you'll need your own set of wheels to get to the starting points. The Carvalhal Nature Trail, Cabeço do Pisão Nature Trail and the Espirito Santo Nature Trail all start near the village of Vale de Espinho and tend to follow the Côa river and its various tributaries. None of the trails are very long and all are an easy half day. The Sobreiral Nature Trail is a 5km circuit along the banks of the Meimoa reservoir (good for swimming), with some healthy climbs.

Rainy Day Options

Some of the strangest bullfights in Portugal hail from this region. Called the tourada raiana (bullfight of the frontier)

they go on throughout the summer. Young men link arms and carry huge oak poles to fend off the bull. They then take it in turns to run at the bull, the first gripping the horns, the second the neck until the last one there clings to the tail. The tourada continues until either the bull is worn out or there are no more brave (or stupid) young men left. Aldeia da Ponte is the closest permanent bullring, but many temporary ones are constructed in local villages: ask at the tourist office for dates and venues.

Wandering around the tiny lanes that make up Penamacor is a great way to spend a lazy day. As you stumble from one café to another, hunt around for the fine Gothic arches and Manueline touches that grace the town's buildings. The castle is still in good shape and is open to visitors, and the small town museum is worth a look. It's full of bits of stone and pottery from various archaeological sites, with pride of place going to a Roman incineration chamber, the only one of its kind found in the Iberian Peninsula.

Serra dos Candeeiros

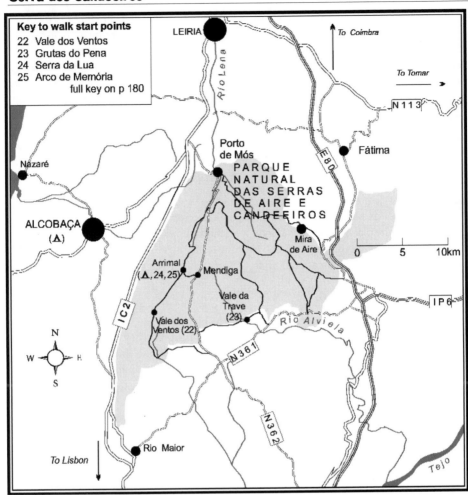

Key to walk start points
22 Vale dos Ventos
23 Grutas do Pena
24 Serra da Lua
25 Arco de Memória
   full key on p 180

What's the weather like?

	Jan	April	July	Oct
Sun	3 hrs	6 hrs	8.5 hrs	5 hrs
Rainfall	93mm	55mm	10mm	60mm
Maximum Temp	14°	17°	21°	18°
Minimum Temp	7°	12°	15°	12°

Average hours of sun, total average rainfall and average temperature in degrees celsius

Serra dos Candeeiros

What's Inside

The Walks

Don't Miss . . .

Limestone hills and underground **caverns** all around you, including the Algar do Pena, Portugal's largest cave (p135)

Twilight spectacle of the 11 species of **bats** in the serra (p 135)

A trio of fine day outings: the stunning monastery at **Alcobaça**, a pilgrimage to **Fátima** and the lovely town of **Tomar** (p 141)

L ocated half way between Lisbon and Coimbra, the Parque Natural das Serras de Aire e Candeeiros is a true step off the beaten path.

Walking

Geography

T he limestone bedrock of the Estremenho Massif dominates the physical and cultural landscape of the region. Broad glacial valleys divide the rolling hills of the serra, and in places deposits of clay form small natural lagoons such as the one at Arrimal. Elsewhere water seeps into the ground eroding the soluble rock and sculpting countless underground caverns.

The lime extracted from the stone is highly valued as an ingredient in pottery, tiles and the whitewash for which the region is famous. The cost to the environment of this extraction is immense, however, as extensive quarrying threatens to ruin delicate natural habitats.

Parks & Reserves

The 39,000 hectare Parque Natural das Serras de Aire e Candeeiros was founded in 1979 to protect and study this unique environment above and below ground. Although the park's disparate offices give the organization the appearance of a three-headed hydra, the park is generally well-run.

Of the three offices, the Information Centre in Porto de Mós is the most helpful. Here, eager staff will show you a short film about the park and let you see exhibits

geared towards school groups; this is also a good place to pick up leaflets and books about the park.

While the centres at Rio Maior and Mira de Aire also have some information, they're more focused on park administration.

There's a concerted effort to establish a network of walking routes in the park, funded by the government and EU and based largely on the French Grande Randonnée system. At the time of writing 14 circular walks have been established with more on the way, and staff aim to mark a long distance footpath around the park.

The park is also establishing a program of themed visits based on park geology, the underground world and cultural life of the park. This program will eventually include overnight stays and guided expeditions by park staff; although many will be geared towards school groups it is hoped that some will be open to the general public.

Trails

Routes are marked with an equals sign (=) on walls, trees and sometimes on posts driven into the ground; wrong turns are marked with a cross (X). Different walks are sometimes marked with different colour paint.

Generally the conditions of the paths are excellent as they tend to be well-used farm tracks of various sizes. Occasionally markers have been moved or vegetation has grown back but this is rare and navigation is on the whole easy.

Some paths have posts marked with numbers indicating points of interest. There's no other information at these posts, although the park is developing leaflets to accompany the walks, which include descriptions of these points of interest.

Maps etc

Most of the maps in the park are hopelessly dated: the 1:25,000 series (318, 328, 329) is from the late 1960s, while the civilian 1:50,000 maps (26B, 27A, 27C) were published in the 1970s. The military 1:50,000 maps (27III, 27IV) have been updated recently, with the exception of 26I.

The park produces a computer-generated map showing the vague location of its walks. Individual leaflets for each walk are being published; these include a rough sketch map and profile charts, and details about wildlife and local architecture.

Much of this information is also available on the park website (p 133). The *Guia de Aves PNSAC* is an excellent guide to local birdlife available from the park offices. Although it's written in Portuguese it has good illustrations and clear, easy-to-understand habitat diagrams.

Guided walks

Projecto Terra, Portela do Vale de Espinho, 2480 Arrimal (✆ 244 450655, e-mail projectoterra@mail.telepac.pt) runs group walks as well as mountain biking, climbing, caving and canyoning. You must book in advance and most activities require a minimum of five people.

When to Go

The mild climate makes the park an excellent year-round destination, although it can be hot in summer as there's little shade on the mountains. The campsite in Arrimal is only open in summer but most of the hotels offer

discounts in winter to make up for this inconvenience.

Flora & Fauna

The variety of habitat in the park results in a cornucopia of wildlife with more than 200 species of vertebrates alone, and the abundance of animals and the open terrain make for easy viewing.

The Parque Natural is best-known for its **bats** and the flying mammal has been adopted as the park symbol. There are 11 different species here, including the rare **large mouse-eared bat**. One of the easiest ways to catch a show is to wait for sunset and watch the bats emerge to hunt insects. Bats eat their own body weight in insects every night and use their large ears to navigate and hunt by echo location. The large numbers of caves provide places for the bats to hibernate in winter, while in summer most will live in tree hollows.

The park also provides important protection for the **chough**, a mid-sized black bird with a distinctive red curved beak. Although these birds generally nest on coastal or inland cliffs, in the park they build their nests exclusively in caves; look out for them in summer in low undergrowth or fields.

The best chance of spotting some of the park's other critters is to seek out the places where they like to congregate. Stone walls and rocky hollows are good places to spot **wall lizards** (also called ruin lizards) that scurry away into the undergrowth when approached. The two lagoons of Arrimal are well known for **European tree frogs** which have small suction cups on their feet that enable them to climb just about anything. Although the frogs are named for their habit of climbing to the tops of trees, they also live around ponds like these. In the evening the frogs gather to begin their chorus at the water's edge and are easily recognizable by their vivid green colour. Also common at the lagoons are **moorhens**.

The study of the plants in the park was an important reason for its establishment more than two decades ago. A quarter of all the plants in Portugal are found here, with more than 60 indigenous species. A highlight of any ramble is the chance to see some of the 25 species of orchids; look out in particular for the bright pink **woodcock orchid**.

The local people also make good use of seemingly ordinary plants. There's a long tradition of herbal country remedies here and research has been going on to find commercial uses for herbal and medicinal plants. If the park's plans are successful, the **heather** and **rosemary** that carpet and scent the hills around Arrimal may soon provide valuable income for the villagers.

People & Culture

Populated since prehistoric times, the people who live in the park have always taken advantage of local resources. Water and limestone are the common ingredients that have shaped and supported all aspects of life in the park, from agriculture to architecture.

The soft limestone has encouraged the craft of **stone masonry**; dry stone walls segment the landscape and support the construction of windmills and farms. Quarrying is the only industry of any real significance within the park's boundary, and there's a continual compromise between the harm that the industry is causing the environment and the need to protect local jobs. The park literature tends to portray stone extraction as a quiet, traditional activity, but in many areas huge modern operations have blasted out massive chunks of hillside and quarry lorries are a hazard on almost every country road.

The need to preserve **water** has meant that almost every house has a cistern. Across the park, these are no longer a mere practical tool, but have become an interesting and unusual feature of local architecture. The sheer variety of designs is a result of a combination of factors, from location and money to the creativity of the builder. Some cisterns collect roof runoff, while others are decorated with protective motifs, reflecting the Portuguese desire to call on a higher presence for help in preserving this life-giving substance.

Food & Drink

Make sure you're not driving if you order **Frango na Púcara**, an alcoholic chicken dish to die for. The true chef uses one cup of vinho verde, half a cup of port and two measures of brandy and then whacks the chicken in a clay jug to simmer for hours. Carnivores will enjoy the excellent Mira de Aire and Alqueidão da Serra blood and rice **sausages** (much more appealing than they sound). To wash all this down, try some of the wine from the Encostas d'Aire region. For something a little more healthy, the apples and pears grown by the Porto de Mós Co-op are delicious.

𝒊 Tourist Information

Park Offices

Park headquarters, Jardim Municipal, 2040 Rio Maior (✆ 243 994168; www.icn.pt/parques/pnsac/pnsac.html).

Information Centre, Jardim Público 2480, Porto de Mós (✆ 244 403555).

Exhibition Centre, Antiga Igreja Matriz, Mira de Aire (✆ 244 449700).

Tourist Office

Porto de Mós turismo, Jardim Público, (✆ 244 491323).

Transport

Public transport is very scarce around the park, and school holidays can dramatically reduce bus frequency; be sure to ask at the tourist information office about up-to-date timetables. There are three buses a day between Porto de Mós and Mira de Aire, and five buses a day between Porto de Mós and Alcobaça. Some buses go to Arrimal from Porto de Mós direct, while others drop you 2km away at Mendiga; there are about three buses a day in total.

Money

Banks and cashpoints can be found at Porto de Mós and Mira de Aire.

Accommodation

Arrimal Rural Campsite, 15km south of Porto de Mós just off the N362 at the Arrimal lagoon (✆ 244 450555). Showers, rarely staffed; open May to September.

$ Residential O Filipe, Largo do Rossio 41, Porto de Mós (✆ 244 401455).

$$ Quinta do Rio Alcaide, Porto de Mós, 1km out of town on the Mira de Aire road (✆ 244 402124). Fresh spring water swimming pool, rooms in converted mills; one apartment with kitchen facilities.

Shopping

Mira de Aire and Porto de Mós both have good supermarkets for picking up supplies. Mendiga has a fantastic little village shop which sells just about everything including kitchen sinks. Those camping in Arrimal must get up early to catch the bread van or else make do with the basic village store.

Events & Festivals

Festa de Arrimal (Arrimal, third weekend in May); **Festa de Lagoa d'Arrimal** (Lagoa d'Arrimal, June 23).

Quick Quiz

12. What % of Portuguese people work in agriculture?

(answer on p 184)

---

22. Vale dos Ventos

Fast Facts

distance 2.5km	rating easy
time 1 hour	map not needed
centre map page 24	

This short loop walk offers stunning panoramic views and a glimpse of life in the Serra dos Candeeiros.

The tiny village of Casal Valventos is located in a remote corner of the park, but it offers basic supplies. Bring binoculars for the views and the birds, but leave your map behind as this is an easy trail to follow.

The walk begins 800m south of the village of Casal Valventos; to get to the village from Arrimal, follow the road to Alcobertas. Look out for a sign marked Percurso Pedestre and a post marked with a Number 7, showing the start and end of the circular walk. Begin by walking towards the Centro de Acolhimento de Vale de Ventos, an old forestry building that has been converted to tourist accommodation; to stay here contact the park office in Mira de Aire (p 133).

At the Centre, turn right and walk down a good track passing a pine wood on the left and heading down into the valley. On a clear day there are great views across the patchwork of dry stone walls west towards Alcobaça and beyond. At a T-junction in 200m, turn right to head uphill. Look out for grouse and red-legged partridges in the surrounding fields. In another 200m, when the path comes to a fork in the trail, turn left. The trail flattens out and the village of Casal

Valventos can be seen straight ahead as you pass a radio antennae on the left. About 100m later, turn right at a T-junction, then turn left immediately afterwards on to a grassy track that leads into the village.

Once among the houses there's a maze of paths in all directions, but frequent yellow markers show the way. The village houses make good use of the region's plentiful limestone, and in summer you frequently see local stonemasons shaping the huge blocks that make up the homes' thick walls.

Go straight ahead at a crossroads, then turn right 50m later on to a dirt track; you'll arrive at the road in 30m. Go straight across the road on to a dirt track, then turn down a farm track 30m later passing some stone houses. There's a stone wall on your immediate left and beyond it you can see a quarry. In 300m, veer left towards the quarry rather than following the stone wall to the right. Most of the work in the quarry is done by hand, and it's common to see men balancing a rock on a rusty oil drum before splitting it with just a hammer and chisel.

The path crosses the head of a small valley at the top of the quarry, and you're soon heading gradually uphill on a wide rocky path flanked by dry stone walls. In 300m you come to a clearing; take the path straight ahead, ignoring the path on the right. Soo afterwards, walk down towards another stream and up a narrow, steep path bordered by a stone wall on the left and a hedge on the right. Aim straight ahead for a wooden post marked with two stripes. Head for another post higher up over more open moorland, cross a dirt track coming from the quarry and reach a stone wall about 20m later. The path now veers to the right, offering good views

behind the quarry down into the Arrimal valley. The moorland vegetation changes into limestone pavement, broken up by small patches of aromatic heather and rosemary.

The trail soon heads towards a stone wall that encloses a eucalyptus grove and follows the wall to the right, slowly becoming a dirt track. Ahead is a fire watchtower; ignore the path that leads straight to it and head right instead. The path becomes a rocky track once more and soon arrives at the road. Turn left and return in 200m to the starting point.

23. Grutas de Pena

Fast Facts

distance	10km	rating	easy to moderate
time	3 hours	map	27III (1:50,000)
	centre map page 24		

This is a wonderful walk in the southern tip of the park through olive groves and abandoned farms; limestone dominates the landscape wherever you look.

About halfway along is the Algar do Pena, the largest underground cavern in Portugal and a world away from the sound and light extravaganzas at the Grutas de Mira de Aire; you need to book a visit in advance through the park office in Mira de Aire (p 133). The trail is well-marked with red painted equal signs (=), but it can be overgrown in places so bring long trousers.

The walk begins at the village of Vale da Trave, 4km east of the main Porto de Mós to Santarém road. From the stone cross, leave

the village heading north along a broad dirt road. A sign for Grutas de Pena 250m later points left for cars; ignore this and turn right. Note that the Pena caves are alternately called Algar do Pena and Grutas de Pena on signposts and in park literature, but it's all the same place. In 500m, just past a farm house, there's a sign indicating the start of the Algar do Pena footpath. Take the right-hand turn here to follow the circular walk anti-clockwise along a shaded country lane. As you amble along watch out for short-toed treecreepers lurking among the olive trees.

Having walked roughly a kilometre along the undulating lane there's an olive tree on the right marked with a red trail marker. Turn sharp right at this easy-to-miss junction. In 20m the lane splits into three; choose the middle one. The trail is a little overgrown and may take a second to find: it bisects two more obvious tracks and there are markers on the stone walls. Watch out for spiky shrubs and thorny plants that can snag bare skin. The path twists and turns before it opens out at a small farmhouse on the right. Stick to the main trail as it levels out among the shade of olive groves and take a moment to soak in the fine views to the south.

At the next ramshackle farm building, veer sharply left uphill. Almost immediately there's another junction with a tree in the middle—go right here on to a short overgrown section. You emerge in the open once more after 50m; take the trail to the left then head across the field to go through the obvious gap in a stone wall. Go downhill for 100m until you reach a T-junction with a large dirt road. Turn left here, following the track uphill to a white building on the left and a quarry on the right. Pass behind the white building to where a group of crumpled barns heralds a change from farmland to the dense scrub that hides some of the 1500 caves that are thought to be in the park.

Arriving at the hamlet of Covao dos Porcos is a wonderful treat. The collection of abandoned farm buildings is its own outdoor museum. The decaying architecture allows you to see inside to the skeleton of the buildings to admire rural craftsmanship of the highest degree. In a field on the left there's an old covered stone cistern that's still filled with water for those who need a soaking on

a hot day. Be sure to replace the cover and leave everything as you found it, as water is precious here.

A post (Number 3) provides the opportunity to see first-hand the Herculean effort required to farm even a small plot of land up on the plateau. Look in the surrounding fields at the huge piles of stones carefully arranged one on top of each other in an attempt to get at the soil.

Continue to the post marked with a Number 4, then turn left at a T-junction. The old farm building on the right is a wonderful hodge podge of construction from different eras, slapped together through time. At the junction here take the main track to the right. Soon, the farmland clears and you're on a barren plain. Pass a couple of houses and then take the right-hand track. A signpost 300m later (Number 6) indicates an old stone cistern; turn right to join a bigger trail soon afterwards.

As you look to the left you'll see a number of small, private quarries. The Algar do Pena lay under a quarry just like this until it was discovered by accident, and maybe one of these other quarries hides yet more underground treasures. A series of posts signals the way for a few hundred metres, then on reaching a junction with a large stone, turn left. Eventually the trail begins to dip down, revealing the Subterranean Interpretation Centre of the Algar do Pena.

In June 1985, Senhor Pena, a 40-year-old quarry worker, set the fuse that blasted his name into spelunking history. The cavern he discovered is the largest in Portugal at 105,000m^3 and houses some of the best stalagmites and stalactites in the country. To protect the fragile nature of the cave, the

Algar do Pena is open only to prearranged groups; contact the park office in Mira de Aire in advance to arrange a visit (p 133).

Once you've had enough underground excitement, follow the track around to the back of the centre, where you'll find another sign for the Algar do Pena circuit. The track leads down into a small valley; keep going straight down the valley ignoring any uphill turnings. Keep left 300m further on when another track joins the main trail, then pass through the farm that gives its name to the Vale do Mar. Signposts indicate the way straight through a spaghetti junction.

Go past two more posts, and after about 500m there's another post next to a large boulder on the left-hand side of the track. Turn left here, down a smaller track, then turn right 20m later to arrive in 50m at a sign indicating the Algar da Aderneira. This large cavern looks unimpressive from a distance, but when you're directly overhead it appears to go straight down to the bowels of the earth. Unlike Ernest Fleury, the Swiss hydrologist who discovered the cave, today's amateur explorers must stay above ground, prevented from following Fleury by a large rusty grate. This is a wonderful place to sit quietly and see bats emerge for a night of hunting.

After poking around for a while, return to the trail and keep going downhill on the main path. After 400m you pass an old farm building and the path curves around to the right; keep right at a junction another 400m further on. The trail flattens out and meanders through fields then, 200m later, you emerge back at the farm near the start of the walk. Follow the country lane back to the village of Vale da Trave. Here, there's a unique experience waiting for you at the tavern nearest the stone cross. Not only can you cool down with an ice cold drink from the bar; in the blink of an eye, bartender becomes barber and you're whisked next door for a short-back-and-sides.

24. Serra da Lua

Fast Facts

distance 6km	rating easy to moderate
time 2 hours	map not needed
centre map page 25	

This short walk along a well-marked trail is a quick way to get spectacular views of the Serra dos Candeeiros and a close-up look at local farming methods. It's particularly good in the late afternoon, watching the sun set over the farmers threading their way home after a day in the fields.

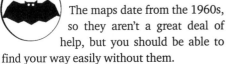

The maps date from the 1960s, so they aren't a great deal of help, but you should be able to find your way easily without them.

Begin the walk at the campsite by turning left off the road to the village on to the slightly overgrown trail next to a sign for the circuit. As you pass the Arrimal lagoon a post marked with a Number 1 signals the important role these lagoons play in the survival of both humans and wildlife.

The lake looks disturbingly green and lifeless from a distance, but close up you may see moorhens or the vivid green European tree frog. The tree frog mates in late spring, when the male croaks to attract the female; he's also particularly noisy after warm rain. On the far side, washhouses were recently built to discourage people from washing directly in the lake so as to preserve the fresh groundwater.

On reaching the main road turn right, then 30m later take a track to the left next to a house. The track is in good condition with a low stone wall on either side, built with boulders that must be laboriously cleared from the fields before planting can begin. The farmers work the land year-round, but autumn is the busy season. As crops ripen old men and women work through the day gathering the harvest. Even today, the narrow lines of corn, squash and vegetables are picked by hand.

Go straight ahead at a crossroads, climbing slightly uphill to reach a T-junction 200m later. Turn left here, but note that the right-hand turn will be the return route off the mountain. Keep low, ignoring the paint marks on the stone wall immediately to your right. The track narrows and broadens,

becomes shaded then open but climbs steadily out of the village. As the views to Arrimal open up it's not uncommon to see choughs near the ground and swifts and swallows zooming above the hawthorns and ivy.

After 500m more, there's a T-junction with a good track. Ignore the right-hand turning going uphill and instead take the left-hand route going slightly downhill. At this point you can see a line of abandoned windmills immediately ahead on top of the Cerro dos Casais ridge. It's an exposed hill, and the locals constructed the buildings so that the roofs of the windmills could be rotated, enabling the sails to catch the wind as it changed direction.

At the next junction, 200m later, ignore the left-hand track going downhill, and take the right-hand dirt track going uphill. At the first bend in the track take the left-hand narrow rocky path; this is a shortcut and you soon rejoin the main track. Turn left about 100m later on to a gravel track with a dry stone wall to the right. The views of Arrimal and the Serra dos Candeeiros open up the higher you climb.

As the path flattens out, take a stony path to the right, passing some abandoned buildings. About 100m later, join another track and take the path to the left going slightly uphill rather than the flatter right route, then in another 100m, join a good track turning slightly to the right. On passing a post marked with a Number 4, the landscape opens out into moorland and the mountain top flattens out. Odd, corralled eucalyptus groves dot the countryside, their stone walls a favourite hiding place for the Aesculapian snake. These shiny brown snakes were considered sacred to the legendary Greek physician after whom they are named. The

Romans kept them in their temples, believing them gifted with special healing powers, and today they decorate medical crests around the world.

There's a maze of paths now, but it's easy to find your way if you keep heading around the side of the mountain following the yellow markers. A post with a Number 5 marks a large dip in the ground that appears to be a sinkhole caused by the collapse of an underground cavern. The route slowly comes around to the Arrimal side of the mountain. Here you can see the another summit topped by a trig point on your left and a stone wall straight ahead of you.

Keep going towards the stone wall and turn left heading gradually downhill. As the stone wall curves around to the right, follow it across open land towards another wall

about 250m on. Turn right to follow this second wall, heading gradually downhill. The path becomes steeper and narrower here.

Below you, Arrimal is strung out along the valley floor, and from this viewpoint you can clearly see the pattern of the narrow crop strips that make up the communal fields. The strips ensure that both crops and villagers get an even share of the best soil at the bottom of the valley, an egalitarian system well-suited to the limited availability of fertile land in the surrounding countryside. As the path approaches some trees, turn right at a T-junction. In 300m, when the track starts going slightly uphil, take the left-hand fork, which is a little narrower and more overgrown. As the path opens up, you return to the junction at the start of the walk; turn left here to return to the campsite through the fields.

25. Arco de Memória

Fast Facts

distance	6km	rating	easy to moderate
time	2 hours	map	not needed
	centre map page 25		

This circular walk visits the Arco de Memória, an arch that marks the medieval hunting boundary of the monastery at Alcobaça. It's a pleasant route through orchards, woodland and open fields and there are great birdwatching opportunities along the way.

The return route crosses over the top of the Serra dos Candeeiros, passing the summit of Cabeço Gordo. The walk is marked with yellow equal signs (=); it's hot in summer so bring water.

Standing with your back to the campsite office turn left and walk towards the village of Arrimal. On your left is Lagoa Pequena, while on your right there's a modern church.

On reaching a cross built on top of a covered cistern in 100m, turn right. At the next junction turn left, where the strong-willed walker avoids refreshment at the rustic bar in the middle of the junction. Turn right 100m later on to the dirt road called Travessa Casal Frazão. The farm buildings here are fine examples of the local craftsmanship in masonry with their characteristic massive corner stones and grated chimneys designed to be big enough to smoke meat.

At the T-junction 200m later turn left, then 150m further on turn right up a wide stone path just after passing the rusting hulks of several abandoned 2CV cars. The trail is now rocky and uneven but is easy to follow as you climb steady uphill through olive groves. It's well worth taking frequent rests to enjoy the views across the glacial valley towards the hamlet of Portela do Pereiro.

Your route is clearly marked with yellow equal signs (=), but lots of trails branch off the main track so try not to get confused, especially if you visited the bar on the way out. The olive groves are ideal places to see the secretive golden oriole, easily spotted by its bright yellow body, black wings and tail.

Turn left at a T-junction, then follow the path as it levels out and heads around the side of the mountain until it reaches a field containing an unknown memorial with a weathered inscription dated 5/11/1925. Go past the memorial then walk between two abandoned huts; turn left at the next fork in the trail. Look up the mountain to see the ruins of several old windmills built to catch the prevailing winds. The path forks left, then levels out to follow the smaller valley away from the windmills, passing through eucalyptus groves that offer welcome shade.

Eventually the trail joins a wide dirt track; the Arco de Memória is clearly visible from here, a short detour to the left. The plump monks who built the arch gained their girth by having exclusive hunting rights over all the land between this spot and Alcobaça, 9km to the northwest.

To continue the walk, turn right at the junction; views open out here and there's a vast panorama of the surrounding Serra dos Candeeiros. After 150m take the left-hand trail by an old abandoned hut. Dry stone walls line this shortcut that quickly rejoins the main track. Now follow the track round to the right, ignoring a path leading downhill towards Termo de Évora. The track climbs as it enters a pine forest and the remains of a quarry can be seen among the trees; it's disused and overgrown, but large limestone monoliths still loom out of the vegetation.

At a T-junction a little further along turn sharp right and follow the ridge up towards Cabeço Gordo. The trees begin to thin out and you'll soon see a stone wall up ahead. If you want to detour to the summit, walk through the gap in the wall; otherwise, turn left to walk down the ridge following the line of the wall. There are yellow paint stripes about every 30m here. Looking down into the valley you can see Lagoa Grande in the Mendiga basin straight ahead.

Soon a small wooded valley opens up below you. The trail curves to the right at the head of the valley then zigzags down to the bottom. Enjoy the descent through glades of beautiful moss-covered holm oaks. The trail is steep in places but is easy to follow and this is a wonderful place for a picnic.

Continue down past a field on the left and a stone wall on the right. Soon afterwards the path curves out of the valley into an olive grove. Keep the wall on your left and you'll reach a farm building, in 100m, where you should take the dirt road towards the farmhouse on your left. Upon reaching a tarmac road, turn right and follow it for a while, admiring the mix of old and new houses that make up the hamlet of Arrabal.

Pass an old church that's unfortunately locked most of the time, then 100m later turn left down a stone track; if you see a lamp post with a yellow cross on it you've gone too far along the road. Hedgerows and stone walls alternately line the stone track; with luck and a keen eye this is a great place for spotting green woodpeckers and lizards. The path emerges at a tarmac road next to an old cistern; turn right at the road to return to the campsite in a few hundred metres.

Other Walks

There are 10 more marked trails in the park to explore. The Estrada Romana and the Serra Galega are close to Porto de Mós, while in the southern tip of the park the Chãos and Alcobertas circuit takes in more unknown park land. From the high ground of the Serra de Aire there are stunning views in all directions but there's no clear route, so take along a map and compass.

Further afield, the Pinhal de Leiria is a medieval pine forest about 30km northwest of Porto de Mós. Dotted with picnic areas and campsites, it's an ideal spot for some lovely walks near the coast.

Rainy Day Options

When it rains in a parque natural riddled with caves, head underground. The caves at Mira de Aire are the largest in Portugal, and the guided tour leads you through spectacular caverns made tacky with lights and noises and fountain displays. The caves are open daily. A few kilometres away are the smaller and quieter Grutas de Santo António and the Grutas de Alvados; neither is accessible via public transport.

Those wishing to literally step back in time should head to the Monumento Natural das Pegadas Dinossaurios de Serra de Aire to tread in footprints made by dinosaurs millions of years ago. The monument is open daily except Mondays, and is located just outside the eastern border of the park.

West of the park is Alcobaça, with everything a good market town needs: shops, restaurants and some of the best people-watching in Portugal. Dominating the middle of town is the huge Mosteiro de Santa Maria de Alcobaça, begun in 1178 and extended as the monks' income from their extensive land holdings increased. Inside, the abbey is stunningly simple: countless tall pillars stretch elegantly upwards and even at busy times there's a strikingly cool and calming atmosphere here.

At Fátima, a tacky souvenir town has sprung up on the strength of a vision of the Virgin Mary in 1917. Despite the awful 1950s basilica, some religious aura remains, and the devotion of pilgrims who approach the site on their knees is impressive.

Serra de São Mamede

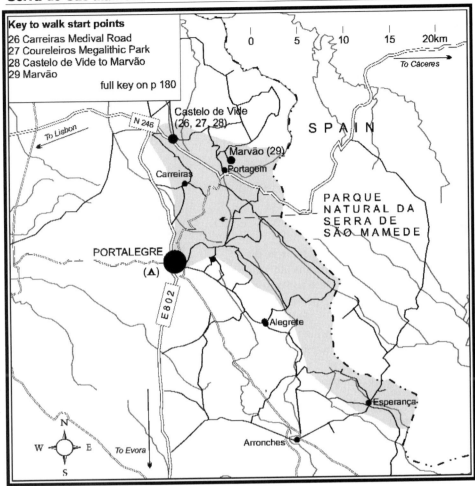

Key to walk start points

26 Carreiras Medival Road
27 Coureleiros Megalithic Park
28 Castelo de Vide to Marvão
29 Marvão

full key on p 180

What's the weather like?

	Jan	April	July	Oct
Sun	5 hrs	8.5 hrs	12 hrs	7 hrs
Rainfall	96mm	57mm	5mm	62mm
Maximum Temp	11°	19°	31°	21°
Minimum Temp	5°	10°	18°	12°

Average hours of sun, total average rainfall and average temperature in degrees celsius

Serra de São Mamede

What's Inside

The Walks

Don't Miss . . .

Spend some exploring the picturesque hilltop towns of **Castelo de Vide** and **Marvão** (p 151)

Follow a **medieval road** from the Serra de São Mamede to the vast plains of the Alentejo (p 148)

Amble along country lanes to gaze at **marvellous megaliths** close to Castelo de Vide (p 150)

Rising out of the vast Alentejo plain, the Serra de São Mamede's natural fortifications have been used throughout history to repel invaders. Rock outcrops and natural springs have offered shelter from the grinding monotony of the surrounding Alentejo plains since megalithic builders first decided to settle here more than 5000 years ago.

No longer Portugal's first defence against unwelcome guests, the region has opened its arms to visitors and its centres now boast excellent facilities for the tourist and the walker. A whole holiday could easily be spent exploring the maze of paths that link the region's beautiful whitewashed villages together.

 Walking

Geography

Throw limestone and granite together, add a pinch of Mediterranean and Atlantic climates into the mixing bowl of plate tectonics, bake for several hundred million years in the heat of the Alentejo and you get the Serra de São Mamede. Although the serra covers only a small area, it's rich in natural phenomena, and rock aficionados flock to the region to look at the Portalegre Tectonic Granite, made unique by the many geological faultlines that criss-cross the region.

Non-geologists may prefer to sit back and admire the views: from the serra's commanding position the vast, dry plains of Portugal and Spain stretch endlessly into the distance. What little rain falls on the Alentejo is largely due to the serra, as the mountains bar the path of rain clouds that zip across southern Portugal from the Atlantic.

Parks & reserves

The 31,750 hectare Parque Natural da Serra de São Mamede was created in 1989 with the aim of protecting wildlife and preserving local traditional life. The nagging problems found in the rest of Portugal are also present here: forest fires, poaching and pollution are causing major environmental damage.

The park is hailing tourism as the means of halting the park's declining population and allowing traditional ways of life to flourish. Incentives are available to promote local craftsmanship in wood, pottery and embroidery, and the handicrafts are then marketed across the region. Sustainable land use is widely encouraged as the park develops a network of pastoral walking routes.

But tourism is a double-edged sword. There's huge pressure on the infrastructure of tiny towns such as Marvão and Castelo de Vide in summer, while in winter these same towns are eerily empty and there's not enough tourist income to go around.

The park office and interpretation centre are well-run and there's always someone on hand to answer questions. They produce a number of leaflets in both Portuguese and English on the park in general; these are also available from the region's tourist offices. In the last few years the park has been busy creating a diverse series of walks in the area, one of the best-organized in the country. These are well-marked routes accompanied by English-language leaflets giving directions and a wealth of information on local flora, fauna and history.

Trails

Trails follow the extensive network of lanes and paths that have evolved since medieval times. Still used by farmers and villagers alike, these routes are generally in excellent condition. The park's leaflets detail some of the more interesting trails; many follow ancient Roman or medieval roads and all are marked with green and white painted posts.

Maps etc

Unlike Glam Rock, the maps of the Serra de São Mamede have outlasted the 1970s. Despite their age, routes are little-changed in many parts of the park, but once in a while don't be surprised to discover that a road or even a reservoir has obliterated a pleasant valley. Marvão and Castelo de Vide are inconveniently located at the corner of four separate 1:25,000 maps (335, 336, 347, 348), and you could forgo the expense and rely on the sketch maps in this book instead. The 1:50,000 maps (civilian 28D, 29C and military 28II, 29III) are equally out-of-date and less helpful.

Guided walks

Rotas do Vento (p 4) runs tours to the area as well as other places in the Alentejo; most last for two days. Sistemas de Ar Livre (SAL, p 4) run day walks all over the Alentejo.

When to go

Spring and autumn are the most pleasant times with hot days and cool evenings, and the spring floral display is an added bonus. Fewer tourists at this time also means a better selection of hotels, and even the most expensive places cut their prices. The summer is baking hot, making walking in the afternoon unpleasant; avoid the heat by starting early and taking an afternoon siesta.

Flora & Fauna

The natural forest of cork oaks, oaks, and olive trees still covers large swaths of the Serra, and pine and eucalyptus are less prevalent than in other parts of the country. **Sweet chestnut** trees provide shade and ample nuts for animal life, and the chestnuts are a warming addition to the region's winter stews. The banks of the Rio Sever are home to thirsty **poplar** and **ash** trees.

Wild boar still roam the park; look for traces of dug up roots and upturned stones and logs at the edge of clearings. Deer, rabbits and foxes can be glimpsed on the forest fringes. Reptiles and amphibians make their home in the serra's many watering holes: look out for **Iberian midwife toads**, **Iberian frogs** and **Bosca's newts** in soggy places. Of the birds of prey, the kestrel, Bonelli's eagle and the eagle owl are known to nest here, and you may see little owls and tawny owls. More easily spotted are white and black **storks** that build their huge, messy nests on buildings and tree tops. In the forest, listen for the drilling of the great spotted woodpecker and the distinctive call of the cuckoo, and keep an eye out for the ring ouzel, blue rock thrush and black wheatear.

People & Culture

In prehistoric times the peoples of the São Mamede were part of the wider Iberian advances in **megalith** building that may have been the origin of mega-lithic culture in Europe. Fertile river valleys such as the Ribeira de São João provided suitable farmland and encouraged settlement, and the fledgling architecture flourished.

By medieval times much of the artistic inspiration had dried up and the area had become a pawn to the whims of the invading Moors. The serra's strategic location and natural defences made it a prized possession, and when the Portuguese King Afonso Henriques conquered it in 1166 he set about fortifying his frontier. The stunningly beautiful **walled towns** of Marvão and Castelo de Vide are testament to the long struggle for this important border region.

Populating the border towns has always been problematic for the Portuguese authorities, and the isolated location that acts as a strong tourist magnet is also a major barrier to permanent settlement. There have been some boom times: the seventeenth and eighteenth centuries were very successful for the **textile** manufacturing industry in Portalegre, and the otherwise dour town is graced with some lovely mansions from that period. Less elegant, but more striking, is the twin-towered **cork** factory rising from Portalegre's skyline. Cork trees characterize the landscape throughout the Alentejo, and much of their bark ends up in the Portalegre factory en route to a new life as bottle stoppers: Portugal produces about 30 million corks a day, almost two-thirds of the world's supply.

Today, the fastest-growing sector of the economy is tourism, but despite its benefits the migration of young people to Portugal's larger towns continues and the region's pop-ulation fell by about 18% in the 1990s.

Food & Drink

The Moors left a spicy impression on the culinary traditions of the Alentejo. Pepper and hot piri-piri sauce are used more liberally then in other regions of Portugal, with garlic, almonds, oregano and fresh coriander also popular.

Alentejan dishes are justly seen as some of the best and most sophisticated in Portugal, and the region's food is served throughout the country. Try **sopa alentejana**, a bread-based soup laden with garlic and topped with a poached egg, or **porco à alente-jana**, a tastily inventive combination of pork and clams.

Those with cast iron stomachs can try **sopa de sarapatel**, a soup made with blood and offal, followed by **molhinos de coentrada** (tripe in a tomato sauce). Desserts are less cloying than in other parts of the country: try **Boleima bread cake**, made with apples or **bolo de castanha** (chestnut cake).

The region's **wine** is smooth and subtle, and the Alentejo is beginning to challenge the supremacy of the Dão as the producer of Portugal's most popular red table wines. Wine made by the local co-operativas of **Portalegre**, **Redondo** and **Reguengos de Monsaraz** is a great companion to any meal, but for something special, look out for the **Tinto Velho** wines from the **José de Sousa estate**, which are still made in clay amphoras and trodden by foot in stone tubs.

Tourist Information

Park offices

Head office, Rua General Conde Jorge de Avilez 22, Portalegre (✆ 245 207215).

Interpretation Centre, Rua Santa Amaro, Castelo de Vide.

Tourist offices

Castelo de Vide turismo, Rua Bartolomeu Álvares da Santa 81, main square (✆ 245 901361).

Marvão turismo, Rua Dr Matos Magalhães, (✆ 245 93104).

Transport

Portalegre is accessible from Lisbon (4 buses daily) and Évora (2 buses). There are less frequent buses to and from Castelo de Vide and Marvão; you may need to reserve in advance. Within the park, 5 buses a day link Portalegre to Castelo de Vide, while 3 a day make the trip between Portalegre and Marvão. There's only 1 bus a day between Marvão and Castelo de Vide; check for up-to-date times.

Money

Cashpoints and banks are available in Castelo de Vide, Marvão and Portalegre.

Accommodation

Portalegre Campsite, Quinta da Saúde, 3km above town on the EN18 (✆ 245 22848); open April to October.

$ Residencial Machado, Rua Luis de Camões, Castelo de Vide (✆ 245 901515).

$–$$ Rooms. Ask in the turismo or cafés in Marvão about rooms in private houses.

$$ Casa da Hóspedes Melanie, Largo do Paço Novo, Castelo de Vide (✆ 245 901635).

$$ Casa de Hóspedes Xinxel, Largo do Paço Novo, Castelo de Vide (✆ 245 901406).

$$$ Pensão Dom Dinis, Rua Dr Matos Magalhães, Marvão (✆ 245 93236).

$$$$ Pousada de Santa Maria, Rua 24 de Janeiro, Marvão (✆ 245 993201).

$$$$ Hotel Garcia d'Orta, Estrada de São Vicente, Castelo de Vide (✆ 245 901250).

Shopping

Castelo de Vide's Friday market in the Praça Dom Pedro V is a lively affair with all sorts of goodies among the stalls. The region is famous for its embroidery and patchwork, and the Parque Natural's policy of encouraging local craftsmanship means that these handiworks are widely available in shops and turismos. Some of the best examples can be found within the castle walls of Castelo de Vide, along with unique novelty items such as handmade cork dolls and toys. Stock up on food before heading for Marvão, as grocery stores in the village are sparsely stocked and sporadically open. Castelo de Vide is better for food, particularly at the tiny fruit and veg shops near the castle.

Events & Festival

Easter (region-wide, but particularly big in Castelo de Vide); **Festa de São Lourenço** (Castelo de Vide, 15 August), big folk dancing festival.

26. Carreiras Medieval Road

Fast Facts

distance	14km	rating	easy
time	5 hours	maps	335, 347 (1:25,000)
	centre map page 26		

Walk in the footsteps of the Crusaders as you follow the cobbled medieval road that once linked Castelo de Vide to the outside world. Stop for a rest in the hilltop village of Carreiras where a few small cafés provide the focus for daily life.

Traverse back along the shoulder of the Serra de Castelo de Vide admiring the panoramic views across the Alentejo plains. This walk is based on the park's *Walking in Carreiras* leaflet.

Leave Castelo de Vide via the EN 246-1. Before you reach the edge of town take the right-hand road that forks off opposite the Hotel Sol e Serra, signposted for the cemetério, zona desportiva, and Fonta da Mealhada. In about 100m pass a factory then turn right, taking the lower of two tracks.

The church and cemetery of Senhora dos Remédios are close by. Perhaps it was the sobering presence of the cemetery that inspired the creation of a zona desportiva along the route; your path for the next few hundred metres is lined with fitness posters and exercise stations for press-ups, sit-ups and a wide range of other contortions to prolong the life of the living.

In 300m, go straight across at a staggered crossroads. As you head uphill pass the imposing Quinta do Pasmar on the right. Although it has seen better days its battlements remain an outlandish touch.

The track narrows to a grassy path, but it's still broad and easy to follow. Soon afterwards, come to a T-junction with another broad dirt track and turn right. The track becomes cobbled as it passes a house on the right; once past the house turn left and climb uphill. The views over Castelo de Vide are worth frequent rests to admire, and on sunny days the town's whitewashed walls dazzlingly dominate the landscape.

At a T-junction with a tarmac road 150m on from the house, turn right. The road twists uphill to another T-junction in 250m, at a saddle over the Serra de Castelo de Vide. The right-hand road leads to the sanctuary of Senhora da Penha, while the left-hand way heads towards Carreiras and Portalegre and will be your return route. Ignore both these options and instead take the stony track straight ahead marked with the park's green and white post (Number 4); you're now on the route described in the *Walking in Carreiras* leaflet.

Follow the old medieval road, taking time to look at the intricate stonework used in its construction. The star-shaped pattern matches those around the castle in Castelo de Vide and in many of the streets and lanes surrounding the town. Form and function combine in an extremely durable construction technique; the variation of size and angle of each piece helps to anchor the stones to the slope and prevent erosion, and this stretch of road has lasted since the twelfth century.

Walk downhill admiring the workmanship as you pass through oak and cork oak forest. It's unusual to see both trees together, as corks tend to favour the Mediterranean climate of Southern Portugal while oaks prefer a more Atlantic climate generally found further north, but the mix is typical of the hodgepodge of plants and animals that characterize the Serra de São Mamede. This is good habitat for black-shouldered kites: watch for them as they hunt for rodents in the evening twilight.

After walking for some time you'll pass a building on the right. To the left here is a watering hole known as Água de Todo-o-Ano, and in another 50m on the other side of the path is a grain threshing floor enclosed in a walled field. Farmers have used the round, raised granite floor to dry, clean and separate cereals for centuries, and during harvest you can still see it in use.

At the bottom of the valley olive trees replace the oaks and the old cobbles disappear under tarmac. A few hundred metres later pass a park sign (Number 7) that indicates a left turning up a dirt track towards Monte Marujo. The path quickly becomes stony, climbing uphill then curving round to the right to cross a stream. Notice in the fields how generations of farmers have cleared the field of rocks and made strange-looking piles with the surplus stone.

Climb uphill past a couple of houses then arrive at a road a few hundred metres later. Cross over the road and walk up the cobbled path into Carreiras, just over 6km into the walk. There are a couple of café-bars among the maze of streets in Carreiras. The village's name comes from the word for cart track and it may have been the medieval version of a service station, situated as it is in the middle of network of roads. Walk through the village and come to a big open square with a road signposted for Marvão, Portalegre and Castelo de Vide. Take the left-hand road to Castelo de Vide following the park signs.

Although the walk follows a road here for 4km it's a very quiet country lane with barely any traffic. The views are superb and take your mind off the tarmac, particularly at Fonte de Carvoeiros about half way along, where there are picnic tables and a seasonal drinks stand. If you missed the threshing floor on the way down its round structure stands out in the fields below, and beyond it the empty-looking plains of the Alentejo stretch away towards Lisbon and the Atlantic. As you continue the walk, the silent stands of eucalyptus are in marked contrast to the vibrant, mature oak woods earlier in the walk.

A couple of kilometres after the viewpoint rejoin the road to Senhora da Penha. Turn right to follow the road signposted Castelo de Vide and head back into town.

27. Coureleiros Megalithic Park

Fast Facts

distance 10km	rating easy
time 3 hours	map 335 (1:25,000)
centre map page 27	

Amble back through time to the dawn of civilization on this easy stroll to the Coureleiros Megalithic Park below Castelo de Vide. Scratch your head and wonder at the purpose of these colossal granite slabs that have stood on the Alentejo plains for aeons.

Leave town between the Igreja de São João and the hospital in Praça Dom Pedro V. Walk past the Padaria Cucipaõ and carry on down to the small gardens at the Porta de São João. Turn left and walk around the gardens on to Rua dos Luis de Camões just in front of the Municipal Market, and keep following this road as it becomes cobbled and heads downhill.

This old medieval road has the same pattern as those around the castle in Castelo de Vide and in the walk to Carreiras (p 148). Pass a shrine on the right, then keep straight ahead at the next junction in 100m. Olive groves and stone walls line the lane as it winds its way out on to the Alentejo plains.

After passing a strange collection of large boulders and walking underneath a power line, you'll soon arrive at a tarmac road at a junction known as Peneda Torto (twisted rock). Cross straight over, taking the lane that runs behind the large anvil-shaped boulder to the left of the old gate. For the next 800m follow the walled lane through olive groves. At the gates of a large house keep straight ahead, ignoring a left-hand turning. Stick to the lane for a kilometre more until you emerge at a tarmac road. Turn right and cross over the train tracks, then take the first left-hand turning, following the sign for the Parque Megalítico dos Coureleiros.

All the megaliths in the park were constructed without metal tools and consist of a chamber and corridor that faces east towards the rising sun. They predate the Pyramids of Egypt by close to 2000 years and are some of the first examples of architecture in human history. Archaeologists have found evidence that point towards their use as communal burial sites over many generations. One recent theory suggests that the megaliths may have been designed to amplify and resonate noise much the same way a bottle does when you blow over the opening.

There are four main antas (megaliths) in the park, which you will soon reach. As you walk down the road the first megalith is on the left. Not many of the boulders that once formed this megalith remain but the outline is still easily seen. Move on quickly, as the next one on the right is a real treat. Huge slabs of stone remain and even the chamber is mostly intact. Not bad for 6000 years old! There's another megalith in the same field, but it's much smaller and only some of its stones are still visible. The fourth megalith is right next to a farm building in a field further down the lane on the left. It's amazing that this survived intact given that stone from the megalith would normally be incorporated into the building itself. Whoever constructed this building must have admired the megalith enough to preserve it.

After marvelling at the work of our ancestors, return to Castelo de Vide by the way you came. Cross back over the railway tracks, take the first left, follow this track for a kilometre, and keep straight on at the large gate. In another 800m, cross over the road and take the cobbled lane to Castelo de Vide.

28. Castelo de Vide to Marvão

Fast Facts

distance 11km	rating moderate
time 4 hours	maps 335, 336 (1:25,000)
centre map page 28	

This walk snakes along the wooded flank of Urra, a small hill that separates the fortified spa town of Castelo de Vide from the castle of Marvão, perched on a rocky crag above the Rio Sever.

On the way, pass through farmland screened by mature oak woods that ring with the sound of bird song. There are a few places to stay in Marvão (p 147), but if you want to catch the daily midday bus back to Castelo de Vide, get an early start to allow enough time to look around Marvão.

Take the Rua de Santa Amaro from the main square in Castelo de Vide and leave the town by the Porta de Santa Catarina gate. Once past the gate follow the tarmac road, passing olive groves and a large wall on the right-hand side, and walking beneath the imposing battlements of the Forte São Roque. Ignore the first left-hand turning and look out for views of Marvão ahead. At the second turning resist the temptation to turn left even though a signpost tries to lure you towards an ancient stone menhir a few kilometres north. Continue past an abandoned quinta on the left and keep straight ahead at the third left, then

150m later on at the fourth left turn down a small lane, passing the Casa de Vinha in 100m.

Continue past the casa as the lane becomes a dirt track, heading through olive groves and past farmland. You'll soon see an abandoned stone windmill on the left, marked on the maps as Moinho de Vento. This windmill once ground the grains from the local smallholdings, and although the mill is no longer in use many of the old farming techniques remain, as small-scale farms still dominate this part of the Alentejo. The rich landowners that farm the rest of the province have dismissed these pockets of land as unproductive; the result is low impact farming unchanged for decades.

The dirt track rises a little to a junction; turn right here, walking under the cork oak and chestnut trees that shade the trail as it returns to the main tarmac road. Turn left at the road and follow it for 700m until the road turns sharp left; once at the bend take the lane off to the right. Ignore the left-hand turning soon after joining the lane, and continue instead into a shallow valley dotted with more farms. Notice the medieval sarcophagus in one of the fields on the left.

Pass a fountain on your left, then take the right-hand fork on to a dirt track that slowly narrows as you enter an oak forest. Tucked away and forgotten, this wood has escaped the onslaught of both the axe and the encroaching pine that has been steadily planted since the turn of the century. The trail shows signs of its ancient origins as you walk over stone slabs up to a small ridge.

When the forest clears at Picoto, Marvão is visible up ahead, and behind you is your last view of Castelo de Vide. The trail is a bit overgrown here and some detective work is required. As you approach a large gap in the stone wall, cross through and keep the wall on your right for 150m, then jump back to the other side of the wall; this avoids fighting through thorn bushes that are successfully attempting to reclaim a section of the path.

Back on the trail the track is lined by two stone walls, and although still slightly overgrown the route's origin as a wide cart lane is obvious. Follow this path until you arrive at a well-used farm track. Turn left downhill where in 100m you pass farm buildings on the left with the usual collection of barking dogs and idle donkeys. Olive groves once more line the route as you stick to the main track. Keep a look out for a large white farmhouse on the left, and 100m after this at a junction turn right uphill, where the track becomes paved once more. Turn right when the track joins a larger road, heading uphill. At the top of the rise turn left, then in 200m turn left once more at a junction.

You're now on the modern road to Marvão; keep well to the side as it seems to be a badge of honour for Portuguese drivers to try to smash the sound barrier on blind corners. Walk up this road for a little over a kilometre, ignoring the left-hand turning to Santo António das Areias. About 200m after the Santo António junction, look out for a couple of houses on the left-hand side, and take the cobbled lane that goes uphill on the opposite side of the road. In 700m you'll reach a stone cross, where a power pylon marks the end of the cobbled track. Look out for a narrow path that zigzags off to the right up to the corner of the main road above. Once on the road turn right to walk through the formidable fortified gates into Marvão.

29. Marvão

Fast Facts

distance 9km

time 4 hours

rating easy to moderate

maps 335, 348 (1:25,000)

centre map page 29

Descend through an old oak wood to the Rio Sever to visit the medieval bridge and tower at nearby Portagem. The walk continues to rural Fonte Souto where two medieval tombs are cut into the rock, before it slowly climbs back up to Marvão, passing through the medieval hamlet of Abegoa on the way.

This walk is based on the park's Walking in Marvão leaflet and is marked with green and white painted posts.

Leave Marvão via the Porta de Rodão and walk down the road. Turn right after 200m next to the sign marked Centro da Saúde. Keep the buildings on your left and follow the path that begins at the back of a small car park on the edge of a cork oak wood. This evergreen crop has long been one of Portugal's most successful and famous exports.

The cork comes from the bark, which is harvested to about half way, leaving a gnarly, twisted top half and a deep, red earth-coloured bottom half. Once the tree has been harvested (and it can take up to 20 years for the cork to be ready) the bark is cut every 10 years or so. The painted numbers on many of the trees in the area indicate the last digit of the year they were last harvested.

Descend down the winding dirt track that soon reveals itself to be a cobbled medieval road with patterns similar to those found around Castelo de Vide (p 148). Keep on the cobbled road and ignore a dirt track off to the left after 500m. In a further 300m come to a left-hand junction where the path flattens out with olive groves on the left and cork oaks on the right. The left-hand trail leads to Fonte Souto, but first detour to Portagem by taking the right-hand track.

The kilometre-long route to Portagem continues to wind downhill, passing a communal washhouse not far from the village; turn right on reaching a tarmac road. Once in Portagem look out for the Roman bridge, rebuilt in the Middle Ages, on your left-hand side. Travellers in medieval times were charged a toll to cross the river, and the stone tower alongside the bridge is tall enough to ensure that no one could sneak across without paying.

The centre of the village is a little further downstream on the modern road; it has a few small shops, cafés and restaurants.

Retrace your steps back up to the junction and this time take the path that leads to Fonte Souto. Walk along the rough, stony track, heading slightly downhill between the stone walls that line the route. Cross a small stream then pass some farm buildings off to the right. A green and white post indicates the correct way straight ahead; ignore the farm track off to the right.

Ignore the Percurso Alternativo sign next to a green and yellow striped post at a right-hand track soon afterwards, and in a further 200m ignore another track to the right. Soon, the land becomes agricultural and you arrive at Quinta dos Conchinhas, where you turn right down a tarmac road.

Follow this road for 250m, then look out for a green and white post marked with a Number 7 just to the left of the road, beside a stone barn. This marks two tiny medieval rock tombs cut into a large, flat boulder on the other side of a stone wall. Not much is known about who was buried here or why, but they must have been extremely small to fit into the minute cavities.

After taking a look around, return back up the road to the Quinta dos Conchinhas, and walk up the path to the right of the quinta. This narrow stony path is initially flanked by stone walls but soon leaves the farm boundary and heads uphill. The huge granite slabs used to pave the path give way to cobble-stones, then as the path flattens out, Marvão becomes visible once more. To your right on a clear day you can see across the plains of the Alentejo to the majestic Serra da Estrela in the distance.

On arriving at a group of houses that comprise the hamlet of Abegoa keep straight on as the track becomes tarmac, ignoring two right-hand turnings in quick succession. Turn left next to a shrine to Santa Teresinha do Menino Jesus and walk uphill on a cobbled track that's shaded by huge chestnut trees and edged with moss-covered stone walls.

The hill is steep and the mossy cobbles can be slippery. Take your time on the slimy climb, especially if you're doing the walk in reverse, and have a good look across the walls at the large quintas that dot the route.

Stop for a rest from the climb when you come to a fountain. After a cool soak gather your strength for the last of the uphill stretches. Turn right at the fountain and carry on up to join the main road in a couple of hundred metres.

If you want to detour to visit the Igreja do Convento de Nossa Senhora da Estrela, much altered through the years and now an interesting mish-mash of styles, turn left here. The cross in the courtyard is made from Estremoz marble and is considered a national monument. Otherwise, cross over the road and follow a path that cuts off the bend in road. Turn right on rejoining the main road and return to Marvão.

Other walks

You could happily spend weeks exploring the Serra de São Mamede. The park has marked and published leaflets on three trails in some of the range's more remote corners, and the lack of public transport is the only hindrance to those with limited time.

Near to Marvão, the walk around Galegos on the Spanish frontier is a must for those who want to see more old piles of stone. Also worth a visit is the Iron Age hillfort of Castro da Crença, approached via a wonderful walk along a wooded section of the Rio Sever; take a packed lunch and siesta under a shady oak tree.

Closer to Portalegre, set off to walk under the shadow of São Mamede herself (1025m), which towers above a 10km circuit; head for the parish church in the village of Reguengo where the walk begins. It's also possible to walk from Marvão to Portalegre. The 20km route is mainly on quiet country roads, with a section through farmland past the Monte de Queijeira farm, and a short stretch on forestry track alongside the Barragem da Apartadura, which doesn't appear on the topographic maps.

To get a feel for the landscape of the rest of the Alentejo, head south to the village church in Esperança, where a visit to the pre-historic cave paintings at Lapa dos Gaivões is one of the many highlights of a day's walk.

For independently-minded readers the whole park is riddled with a maze of footpaths. Many of those marked on the map are still in use by local farmers, although others have been reclaimed by thorn bushes and bracken, and still others are now major roads. Pick up the relevant maps, pack your sense of humour, and good luck!

Rainy Day Options

If the unheard of happens and it's pouring in São Mamede, there are enough little gems tucked away in Portalegre, Marvão and Castelo de Vide to keep you occupied for a day or two. Castelo de Vide's narrow cobbled streets make for fascinating exploring; amongst them is the Jewish quarter, where the old synagogue is worth a visit. The castle rises above the Jewish quarter, and its walls and tiny houses hide a few trinket shops and local woodcarvers. The spa lower down in the town is open in summer.

Marvão's castle attracts hordes of tourists at peak times, but they soon disappear and the views from the walls are staggeringly vast. Although not as pretty, Portalegre offers more modern conveniences and the interesting Fábrica de Tapeçarias, the town's only remaining tapestry factory, which provides guided tours.

The turismo in Castelo de Vide sells a leaflet describing the local menhirs, antas and other megaliths; you'll need your own transport to see them. If the local ruins have whetted your appetite, head southwest to Évora, which on top of being one of the most enchanting towns in Portugal, is surrounded by more megalithic delights. Highlights include the Cromlech dos Almendres, a collection of almost 100 megaliths arranged on a gently sloping hill with magnificent views, and the massive Anta Grande do Zambujeiro, the largest dolmen in Europe.

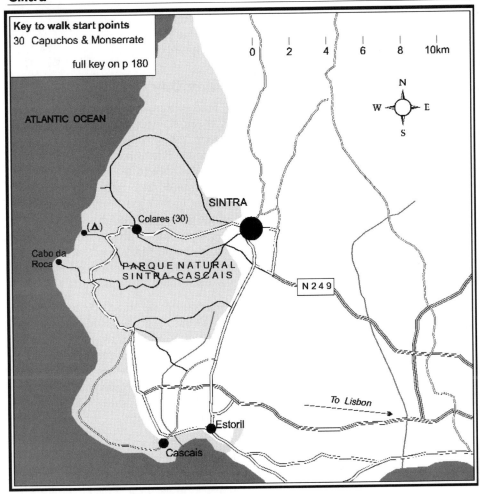

Key to walk start points
30 Capuchos & Monserrate

full key on p 180

ATLANTIC OCEAN

SINTRA

Colares (30)

(Λ)

Cabo da Roca

PARQUE NATURAL
SINTRA-CASCAIS

N 249

To Lisbon

Estoril

Cascais

What's the weather like?

	Jan	April	July	Oct
Sun	5 hrs	7.5 hrs	9 hrs	7 hrs
Rainfall	95mm	48mm	30mm	65mm
Maximum Temp	14°	20°	28°	23°
Minimum Temp	8°	12°	17°	14°

Average hours of sun, total average rainfall and average temperature in degrees celsius

Sintra

What's Inside

The Walks

Don't Miss . . .

Monserrate's vivid gardens, where you can lose yourself for an entire afternoon (p 162)

Convento dos Capuchos, a cork-lined monastery hidden amongst the woods of the Serra de Sintra (p 162)

Colares wine: rare, smooth and grown in sand (p 160)

Just an hour from Lisbon, the vibrant gardens and extravagant palaces around Sintra attract coachloads of tourists each summer, yet the gardens are so vast and varied that you can lose both yourself and the hordes in them without too much trouble. But the real delight of walking around here is following stone pathways that have linked the people to the land for centuries: only a short distance from tour bus hell you can easily go a whole afternoon without seeing a soul.

Walking

Geography

Serra da Sintra, the region's dominant granite outcrop, is the fruit of an ancient volcanic eruption. Its high point of Cruz Alta is contained within the tightly-controlled gardens of the Palácio da Pena, and the exotic trees planted here and in other gardens by waves of British visitors help to create the serra's misty microclimate by trapping moisture from sea breezes. The range becomes less cultivated on its western fringes then falls away towards the coast, where dramatic cliffs vie for attention with ugly hotel complexes. Elsewhere in the park, low-lying land is given over to an agricultural mix of small subsistence farms and vineyards.

Parks & reserves

The Parque Natural de Sintra-Cascais, a protected area since 1981, was upgraded to a natural park in 1994. Its main purpose is to preserve traditional rural life in the region, although its mandate also extends to environmental protection. In reality, much of this traditional life no longer exists, and the

park's efforts to fight inadequate building regulation and prolific expansion of eucalyptus and acacia trees are thwarted by the allure of short-term tourist development. The park office is hidden on a side street behind the Museu de Arte Moderna; it has a few leaflets and no information staff.

Trails

There's no official trail marking by the park office. Often, trails follow stone paths along well-worn routes adorned with azulejo (tile) signs; these are generally marked on the 1:25,000 maps. In forested areas tracks are less clear, and new development and planting have led to a vast number of unmarked, eroded paths. Throughout the park, trails have been marked by various visitors and the confusing plethora of different coloured arrows left by everyone from local scouts to tour groups is best ignored.

Maps etc

The 1:25,000 maps (415, 416) both date from the 1990s, and 1:50,000 maps (military 34IV and civilian 34A) are also up-to-date.

In theory at least, there's an official guide to walking routes in the natural park, but the *Guia de Percursos do Parque Natural de Sintra-Cascais* is rarely available in practice. Rough maps with all too brief summaries of these walks are posted on the park website (www.icn.pt/parques/pnsc/pnsc.html). More readily available is *Sintra: A Borough in the Wild*, a useful guide to the region's flora and fauna sold at the bookshop in the Museu do Brinquedo. Sunflower Guides publish a combination driving and walking guide to the area (*Landscapes of Portugal: Sintra, Cascais, Estoril*); it's good for ideas on where to go, but it was last updated in 1991.

Guided walks

The campsite at Praia Grande organizes twice-weekly walks in the Serra da Sintra; you need to book a day or so in advance (✆ 219 290581). Sintraventura (✆ 219 204037) offers excellent value walks run by the town council; book a few days ahead. HF Holidays (Imperial House, Edgware Road, London NW9 5AL, ✆ 020 8905 9558, www.hfholidays.co.uk) organize week-long-walking holidays around Sintra.

When to go

Summers are hot, although the region's famous mists cool the Serra da Sintra even in July and August. Most sites and beaches are crowded in summer, so if you're on a tight schedule, book accommodation in advance at this time of year, especially for the youth hostel. It's best to visit in spring or autumn, when the weather is pleasantly warm and most facilities are still open.

Flora & Fauna

The ancient forests of **oak** and **wild olive** that once covered this area have been cut down since pre-Roman times to provide land for farming. Dry stone walls enclosed fields at lower levels while some woods remained on higher, uneven ground more suitable for hunting than farming.

The last few hundred years have seen a move towards the replanting of much of the serra with domestic and foreign conifer trees. As the forest matures it creates its own microclimate. Water-laden sea breezes condense on meeting the cold surface of treetop needles, then the water drips slowly down to the soil below. The thick overhead canopy prevents the moisture from escaping and this leads to the frequent mists that cling to the serra even when the rest of the area is clear and sunny.

It's also an ideal climate for damp-loving plants and animals; there are 16 different species of fern, including the rare **woodwardia radicans**, and lots of frogs, toads and salamanders. Despite the preponderance of conifers, pockets of deciduous wood are reappearing as **jays** and other birds scatter acorns and berries in less dense parts of the forest. Listen out for the hammering of green and greater spotted **woodpeckers** here in spring. Elsewhere, invasive eucalyptus and acacia trees are rapidly taking hold, speeding up soil erosion and playing havoc with the area's biodiversity.

Further west, the scenery is more dramatic. Strong sea winds make it difficult for trees to flourish, and it's uneconomical for farming, so the region is mostly covered with gorse, heather, grasses and other hardy plants. Even here, humans have altered the landscape: barriers of **maritime pine**, which has wind-resistant elastic trunks and aerodynamic needles, have been planted allowing **olive trees** and **honeysuckle** to flourish sheltered from the harsh winds. Within the pine, you may see finches and birds of prey, including goldfinch, greenfinch and tawny owl.

People & Culture

Sintra's name probably came from the word Cynthia, personification of the moon in early local mythology; the Romans called their settlement here Mons Lunae (moon mountain), and there's evidence of an earlier, sacrificial moon-worshipping religion.

On a more mundane level, local people have relied for hundreds of years on subsistence farming, and tiny stone-walled fields cover the ground at lower altitudes. Higher up, as elsewhere in Estremadura, there are lots of **windmills**, particularly in the north of the park. You can arrange a visit to the Moinho de Vento São João das Lampas, a strikingly beautiful windmill, through the park office in Sintra (p 161).

Despite the park's attention to traditional rural life, **tourism** has long replaced agriculture as the region's economic mainstay. Tourists flock here for two reasons: to visit the spectacular coastal beaches, now choking under insensitive development, or to wander around some of the area's many **palaces**. These palaces are a legacy of the eighteenth and nineteenth centuries, when Sintra was full of aristocrats and rich merchants trying to outdo each other by designing ever more outrageous mansions with grand and exotic gardens to match. They dominate the skyline of the Serra da Sintra and have attracted the romantic traveller for centuries; however, the sites can be packed in summer, and it's pretty hard to sense the romance when you're squashed in on all sides by tour buses.

Food & Drink

Wine aficionados should seek out the scarce, smooth **Colares** red. Grown here since the thirteenth century, new vines have to be planted in the clay bed deep below the sandy topsoil, often up to five metres down, a strategy that protected the grapes from the phylloxera beetle that ravaged European vineyards in the nineteenth century. Digging the trenches is dangerous work as the sand is so unstable, and workers wear baskets on their heads to literally give themselves breathing space in case the walls of the trench collapse. Once the plants start to grow, sand is gradually piled up around them, and the vines are trailed close to the ground to protect against the strong Atlantic winds.

The wine is then aged in oak casks for at least 18 months until its velvety character is completely revealed. White Colares is available, although the red is acknowledged to be better; neither is widely available outside this tiny demarcated region. You can visit the Adega Regional de Colares and taste the end product if you call ahead (☎ 219 291210).

Other local wines are cheaper and extremely drinkable, although you'll need to buy these outside Sintra's old town as wine shops there stock little except port.

Queijadas de Sintra are famous all over Portugal and should satisfy any pastry addict's cravings. Sold in batches of six, they're tiny bite-sized tarts filled with sheep's milk cheese, egg yolks and enough sugar to keep the tooth fairy on overtime.

There's a clutch of good **restaurants** in São Pedro, just a few kilometres outside Sintra's old town. Carnivores should aim for the Toca do Javali (boar's burrow) at Rua 1 do Dezembro 12 (☎ 219 233503) for wild boar overkill; there's a separate game menu and boar skins underfoot as well as a number of ways to eat the restaurant's namesake.

Tourist Information

Park office

Head office, Rua General Alves Roçadas 10, Sintra, behind the Museu de Arte Moderna (℘ 219 235116).

Tourist offices

SIntra turismo, Praça da República 23, old town (℘ 219 231157); also small kiosk at the train station (℘ 219 241623).

Transport

Trains run from Lisbon's Rossio station to Sintra every 15 minutes. Bus 441 goes from Sintra to Colares and Praia Grande; trams also run for most of this route, but start a couple of kilometres outside Sintra. Catch the 435 bus to São Pedro from the train station or outside the turismo; 434 takes you to the Palácio Nacional da Pena.

Money

There are cashpoints and banks in Colares and Sintra.

Accommodation

Camping Praia Grande 12km west of Sintra (℘ 219 290581) bus 441 from Sintra, café-bar, shop, swimming pool.

$ Pousada de Juventude de Sintra, Santa Eufémia, about 4km out of Sintra, bus to São Pedro 2km away(℘ 219 241210).

$ Casa de Hóspedes Adelaide, Rua Guilherme Gomes Fernandes 11, Sintra (℘ 219 230873).

$$ Piela's, Rua João de Deus, 70–72, Sintra, on the road behind the train station (℘ 219 241691).

$$ Monte da Lua, Avenida Miguel Bombarda 51, Sintra, opposite the train station (℘ 219 241029).

$$$ Quinta do Conde, Colares, signposted from the village (℘ 219 291652).

$$$$ Estalagem de Colares, just outside Colares on the Monserrate road (℘ 219 282942).

$$$$ Quinta da Capela, Estrada de Monserrate, 1km beyond Monserrate palace on the road to Colares (℘ 219 290170).

Shopping

There's a great daily market (mornings only) in Estefânia, the more modern part of Sintra; mini-mercados are also better and cheaper in the new town. In São Pedro, there's a market on the second and fourth Sundays of the month; on the first and third Sundays there's a smaller market in Colares.

Events & Festivals

Festival de Música (Sintra, June and July), Sintra's internationally-renowned classical music festival; **Festa de São Pedro** (São Pedro de Sintra, June 29), religious festival with processions, music and dancing; **Noites de Bailado** (Sintra, end July to end August), international classical and modern dance; **Feira do Artesanato** (Sintra, first two weeks in August), large handicrafts fair with folk music and dancing in the evenings.

30. Capuchos & Monserrate

Fast Facts

distance	12km	rating	easy to moderate
time	5 hours	maps	415, 416 (1:25,000)
	centre map page 30		

Two of Sintra's most appealing sites lie within a short walk of each other in the woods of the Parque Natural. The Convento dos Capuchos is a fascinatingly weird monastery gradually being reclaimed by the surrounding woodland, while the mansion and gardens of Monserrate are a formal reminder of the time when Sintra was a playground for semi-idle and very rich Englishmen.

Neither site is accessible by public transport, so this walk begins and ends at Colares, a pretty village well-served by local buses and worth a visit if only to sample the robust local red wine (see p 160). The route follows old stone paths marked with pretty tiled (azulejo) signs for the much of the way, passing small villages and huge ornate quintas or mansions. Although there are no cafés along the route there are large picnic areas at both Capuchos and Monserrate. Restoration work on many of the buildings at Capuchos began in 1999 and may make some parts of the monastery off-limits until completed; check with the tourist office in Sintra.

The walk begins in Colares on the N247, the main road from Sintra to the coast. At the tight right-hand bend in the road, turn left following the signs to Colares up Rua José Costa. In 100m the road arrives at a small square bordered by a restaurant, art gallery, grocery store and cafés—an excellent spot to begin or end the day.

From the square, take the steep and narrow Rua da República uphill. Turn left after about 300m along Rua das Flores, a quiet street bounded by high whitewashed walls alive with cascading flowers in the summer months. The street becomes a narrow dirt path in 100m, and the route from here onwards is occasionally marked with a confusing array of coloured arrows. The path soon broadens and begins to climb steadily, and although this part of the trail is sometimes steep, overhanging branches provide welcome shade from the summer sun.

After 1km, turn left at a T-junction with a track marked with an azulejo sign as Caminha da Boca da Mata. Then 100m later, a fork off to the left is signposted Caminho do Rio Velho; ignore this track but note that this will be your return route from Monserrate. This section of the route is lined with cork oaks and eucalyptus and there are good views across farmland down into Colares; there's also a chance you might see foxes and rabbits here. Half a kilometre further on, ignore the track off to the right marked Estrada da Paiol and instead continue on the main track as it bends around to the left to cross the head of a small valley.

As you continue, the oak trees gradually give way to pine and the path becomes less sheltered; ongoing deforestation in this area makes route-finding a little tricky. At a T-junction 150m after crossing the valley, take the right-hand turn leading uphill so that you're almost doubling back on yourself, then turn left at another T-junction 50m later. At the end of a short steep section, go straight across at a crossroads of forestry tracks, and arrive at the Convento dos Capuchos 200m later.

The Convento dos Capuchos is a magical contrast to the more stylised parks and gardens of the rest of the Sintra region. Some buildings seem to have grown organically from the surrounding rocks, others are bizarrely lined with cork; all seem impossibly minute and unimaginably uncomfortable.

The monastery was founded in 1560 and its cells were home to monks for almost 300 years; the posthumously-famous Honorius, one of the original residents, lived here for 36 years before finally dying aged 95. A jumble of narrow, overgrown paths encircle the monastery and add to its charm, and a wooded picnic area lies just outside the entrance gates.

To continue towards Monserrate, stand with your back to the picnic area and take the wide forestry track going uphill straight ahead. The route from Capuchos to Monserrate is generally marked with white arrows painted on trees or rocks, but forestry practices and changing land ownership can obscure these arrows and alter rights of way. Although there are many junctions, the route is fairly obvious and follows the widest track except where it detours to avoid private land.

About 100m after Capuchos, take the right-hand track at a fork in the road, then ignore a left-hand turning 50m later. Turn left soon afterwards when you reach a T-junction at a large stone wall, and you soon pass a white building on your left as the track heads downhill. Take the right-hand track at a fork in the trail 150m after the building (the left-hand track is marked with a No Entry sign), then turn left in 100m down a more overgrown track signposted Caes Soltos. This section is eroded in places, and you'll occasionally have to navigate around logs and boulders placed across the trail to block vehicle access.

At a crossroads 200m later, turn left on to a better track going steeply downhill. When the track flattens out, keep straight ahead at a crossroads with two narrower tracks; 50m further on, ignore the wide track going downhill to your left and take the less distinct right-hand track. You soon come to a junction of five paths. Go straight ahead here, keeping two paths to your left and one to your right, then ignore the track off to your right in 50m. Pass a couple of ponds and keep straight ahead at a white building, then follow the track as it curves steeply downhill towards a green gate and a tarmac road. Turn right here and you'll arrive at Monserrate 50m later.

Monserrate is perhaps the most abiding memorial to the English love affair with Sintra. The gardens were created in the eighteenth century by an English merchant, Gerard de Visme, and enhanced by William

Beckford, a wealthy writer who stayed here in the 1790s while escaping a homosexual scandal in his native England.

Half a century later, Sir Francis Cook, another Englishman with money to burn, constructed a quinta in the grounds, much criticized for its neo-Moorish excesses. The future of the quinta and its possible renovation are still in dispute and the house is currently closed to the public. The Anglicizing of Monserrate was completed by the painter William Stockdale, who with the help of the head gardener at Kew transformed the quinta's extensive grounds with exotic species imported from around the world.

Today, the gardens are slowly being restored to their nineteenth century glory, but the untouched areas where Stockdale's exotica mix with native species are perhaps even more attractive. The gardens are open daily except public holidays from 10am to 5pm in winter; 10am to 6pm in summer.

To continue the walk, turn right out of the Monserrate gates to walk down the narrow tarmac road. After 750m, you pass a large house on the right called Quinta da Capela, which has been converted into a hotel and is a wonderful place to stay (p 161). Take the left-hand dirt track on the opposite side of the road, heading uphill. About 150m after leaving the road, a left-hand track is marked

Proprieda da Privado (private property); veer right here, then turn right at the end of a small water reservoir 100m later. Soon afterwards the path goes downhill and views open up west towards the sea.

At a wooden gate the track curves around to the right; follow this, ignoring the path uphill off to the left. The track changes to a rough-surfaced road and soon reaches a T-junction with a narrow tarmac road. Turn left here to enter the tiny village of Gigueirós, a quiet, pretty place with a large communal wash house and views down into Colares.

The road goes straight through Gigueirós and then narrows into a dirt track lined with cork oaks once the village houses end. The path passes a large gated house, the Quinta do Carmo, on the right and veers right to skirt around the quinta's walls, following the azulejo sign Caminho do Rio Velho. Colares becomes visible once more, and you can also see up to the village of Peneda and across to the Atlantic.

The path becomes cobbled, passes a few houses and crosses a stream before arriving at a junction with the Caminho da Boca da Mata 300m later. Turn right here to retrace your steps back to Colares, remembering to take the right-hand in 100m, then continue downhill until you reach the village.

Quick Quiz

13. On what date is Portugal day?

(answer on p 184)

Other walks

The best and most well-trodden short walk in Sintra is the route from the old town up to the Castelo dos Mouros and on to the Palácio da Pena. Start by following the main path through the Parque da Liberdade to Rua das Murtas, then turn right. Cross Rua Bernardim Ribeiro then take the steep, shady footpath signposted Castelo-peos from the church of Santa Maria.

This path takes you via spectacular views of Sintra up to the Castelo dos Mouros in about 20 minutes. The eighth century Moorish castle was captured by Afonso Henriques, Portugal's first King, in 1147. Its ramparts closely follow the ridge of the Serra da Sintra and seen from a distance seem integrated with the surrounding rocks. Standing among the ruins, it's easy to see why the Moors built a castle here: when Sintra's famous mists clear you can see south beyond Lisbon over to the Serra da Arrábida on the Setúbal peninsula, and west towards Cabo da Roca, the westernmost point of mainland Europe.

From the upper gate of the castle, cross the road and enter the maze of paths in Pena Park, a fabulous place to get lost among huge ferns and tranquil lakes. Even in misty conditions, you can get your bearings from the garish turrets of the Palácio da Pena, a shrine to tackiness and vivid colour with a nod to just about every architectural style ever conceived. The palace's fabulous over-the-top vulgarity continues inside, where it remains as it was when the last members of the Portuguese royal family fled from here before the 1910 Revolution, crammed to the brim with ostentatious furniture and eclectic knick-knacks.

For a more down-to-earth experience, walk to Nossa Senhora da Peninha, a ruined chapel perched on the eastern side of the Serra da Sintra and surrounded by low-lying heather and gorse. There are great views of the Atlantic from here, and more energetic walkers can continue towards the headland of Cabo da Roca.

Although the cape is a tour bus magnet, in between coach stops it can be desolate and dramatic. Elsewhere along the coast the beaches are often busy and commercialized, but the cliffs above them can still be a spectacular place for a walk, especially on a windy day when the sea is rough. Sunflower Guides describe a cliff walk from Praia das Maças towards Cabo da Roca, but ongoing building near the coast may make some areas difficult to access.

Rainy Day Options

Most of Sintra's tourist standards are outside the centre of town and are best enjoyed in the sunshine; see the earlier parts of this chapter for suggestions.

Sintra itself is dominated by the massive kitchen chimneys of the Palácio Nacional, a largely fourteenth century palace where Moorish influences blend easily with traditional Portuguese azulejo panels. While you're at the tourist office, visit the Museu Regional, which is housed in the same building; its archaeological collection has recently been revamped and it's now an excellent reflection of the region's early beginnings. Down in Estefânia, the modern art museum houses a collection of works by international post-war artists including Hockney, Pollock, Lichstenstein and Warhol.

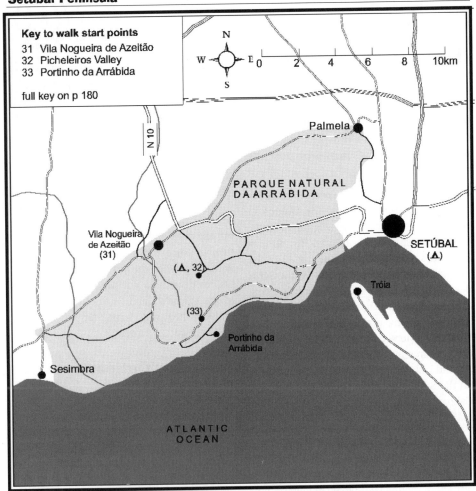

Key to walk start points
31 Vila Nogueira de Azeitão
32 Picheleiros Valley
33 Portinho da Arrábida

full key on p 180

What's the weather like?

	Jan	April	July	Oct
Sun	4 hrs	8 hrs	10 hrs	7 hrs
Rainfall	95mm	52mm	12mm	74mm
Maximum Temp	14°	20°	28°	23°
Minimum Temp	9°	12°	17°	14°

Average hours of sun, total average rainfall and average temperature in degrees celsius

Setúbal Peninsula

Don't Miss . . .

Hike down the steep slopes of the **Serra da Arrábida** to a great seafood lunch at Portinho da Arrábida (p 175)

Take a guided tour of the José Maria da Fonseca **winery** (p 172)

Picnic on creamy-soft Azeitão **cheese** washed down with **Moscatel de Setúbal**, the region's famous dessert wine (p 170)

Hidden just across the Tejo estuary south of Lisbon lies the enchanting Serra da Arrábida. Stroll beside centuries-old vineyards and Renaissance mansions, or begin a walk at a former monastery perched high above the ocean and end up gorging on fantastic fish stew at a seaside restaurant.

Walking

Geography

Visually, the Setúbal peninsula is dominated by the limestone ridge of the Serra da Arrábida, which rises from the sea to a height of 500m. The influence of limestone is also seen in the dramatic and hard-edged profile of the peninsula's southern cliffs and in the proliferation of caves in the area. Away from the serra and the cliffs, the peninsula's softer inland hills have been shaped by generations of farmers. Large estates now dominate the peninsula with only a few pockets of natural deciduous woodland remaining.

Parks & reserves

The Parque Natural da Arrábida was created in 1976, principally to protect the region's flora and vegetation. Of the park's 10,820 hectares, the most ecologically important areas are the integral natural reserves located around the Serra da Arrábida. These areas are of special scientific interest and public access is restricted. The park also works to preserve the cultural heritage of the region, with programs in place to encourage small-scale production of local cheese and honey, to the restoration of windmills and other traditional farming methods.

The park's headquarters are in Setúbal, where a range of publications is sold. It's a busy office with no separate information division, and although the efficient receptionist elevates multi-tasking into an art form, there's no one to talk to about walking routes or conditions. Over the last decade more emphasis has been placed on improving pedestrian access and there are now around 10 marked trails, all well-described in the park's literature.

Trails

Trails are signposted with red and yellow equal signs (=) painted on posts or trees. Wrong turnings are marked by a red and yellow cross (X), and left and right turns are marked by a hard-to-decipher variation on the equal sign. In some places markers are placed too far apart to be useful, and in others they've been obscured by bushes or knocked down by track widening. Large-scale planting of pine and eucalyptus has led to problems with trail erosion and the popularity of the area with local mountain bikers is speeding up the destruction.

Maps, etc

1:25,000 maps of the area (454, 464, 465) are up-to-date, although many smaller farming or forestry tracks are not included. The 1:50,000 military map (38I) shows even fewer tracks but is also up-to-date, while the civilian 1:50,000 map (38D) dates from the early 1970s and is pretty useless.

The park office publishes *Caminhos: Parque Natural da Arrábida*, which details nine walks and includes 1:25,000 map reproductions. It's a useful Portuguese-language guide, although junction directions are complex and the map reproductions are too small to be of much use. The office also sells an illustrated map of the park with good wildlife symbols but without the detail needed for walking.

Guided walks

SAL (Sistemas de Ar Livre), a walking club based in Setúbal, organizes Sunday walks as far afield as Évora in the Alentejo, but focuses mainly on the Setúbal region. The regional tourist office (p 171) has details of upcoming walks, or you can call (℘ 265 227685) or check the SAL website (www.sal.jgc.pt). There's no need to book; just show up at the designated time and place.

When to go

The Setúbal peninsula can be very hot in summer, particularly away from the sea in the sheltered valleys. Spring and autumn are pleasantly warm with some rain; beaches are quieter at this time although some coastal restaurants close down. The campsite at Picheleiros is open year round.

 Flora & Fauna

The protected natural reserves around the Serra da Arrábida are rich in biodiversity, and the natural life here reflects the region's original ecological make-up. Among the trees that make up the pockets of ancient forest around the Serra da Arrábida, the most significant is the **Portuguese oak**, which lives only on the Iberian Peninsula and in North Africa.

Closer to the ground, keep a look out in spring for the tiny **narcissus calcicola**, a bright yellow daffodil native to this part of western Portugal. The Serra da Arrábida's inaccessible heights are an important nesting site for a number of birds of prey, including **peregrine falcon, eagle owl** and **kestrel**.

Outside the protected areas, centuries of human influence have completely transformed the landscape. Much of the land that was farmed or forested has since been left to revert to scrubland, and heather, gorse and rosemary scent and cover the hills. The thick-trunked **olive** trees typical of the region were introduced in the eighth century by Arab settlers and are said to be amongst the oldest varieties in Portugal.

For many years, the Arrábida region was an important royal hunting ground and by the beginning of the twentieth century wild boar, wolves and deer had been hunted to extinction. Most of the mammals that remain, which include **genet, fox, wild cat** and **badger**, are both nocturnal and timid; the best time to glimpse them is at dusk.

Also at dusk, head for the area's limestone caves as they begin to disgorge thousands of **bats**; watch for the Mediterranean horseshoe bat and Schreibers' bat early on in the evening and stay up later to spot the greater horseshoe bat. In the open bushy country north of the Serra da Arrábida look out for hoopoes and bee-eaters.

 People & Culture

The sea has guided people to the Setúbal peninsula since Palaeolithic times. Evidence of prehistoric occupation has been found at the Lapa da Santa Margarida (p 175), and remains of Roman fish-salting works dot the coast, although these early visitors made little permanent impact on the landscape.

By the fifteenth century, the Setúbal Peninsula was becoming one of the places to be for the Portuguese wealthy, and ever since that time the human landscape of the Arrábida has been dominated by the aristocracy's grand houses, ornate gardens and large vineyards. The building boom reached a height in the seventeenth and eighteenth centuries, and the region around Azeitão is thick with **baroque palaces**. On a smaller scale, the local producers of Azeitão cheese and honey have lived for centuries in small, one-storey houses with minimal openings to keep cool in the summer and warm in winter.

The surrounding countryside is dotted with **windmills**, especially in the Serra do Louro in the north east of the park. Many of the windmills were in use well into the twentieth century, and although most are now ruined, the parque natural is busy restoring two of the windmills as part of its mandate to preserve traditional activities in the region.

Food & Drink

Picnics just cry out for the region's soft, pungent **Azeitão cheese**. The cheese-making process is begun by leaving ewe's milk to curdle in a large clay pot next to the fire, then the curds are scooped into cylindrical metal moulds. The result is a creamy, pale yellow or white cheese so soft that aficionados recommend scooping the cheese from the rind with a spoon.

Another self-catering treat is the fantastic local **honey**, aromatic with the diverse flora of the Serra da Arrábida and still made in the gardens of the old Convento da Arrábida. Sweeten up your mid-morning coffee with a **torta de Azeitão**, a Swiss roll with sweet egg filling.

Restaurant main courses are dominated by **fish** & **seafood**, and the restaurants at the harbour village of Portinho da Arrábida are some of the best places to sample the local bounty. Try caldeirada, a fish stew with tomatoes and potatoes, or arroz de marisco, the Portuguese version of paella; both are made to share, so take a friend.

Moscatel de Setúbal is the peninsula's favourite tipple, and a glass of the sweet, fortified dessert wine is a perfect end to a meal. The muscat grape has grown in the region for more than 2000 years, having been first imported from North Africa by the Phoenicians.

Making moscatel has since evolved into a unique process; once the right balance of sugar and alcohol is achieved, the fermentation process is halted by the addition of brandy, then the muscat grape skins are returned to the wine and left until the following spring. Younger wines are fresh and heavily scented, but as the wine ages, more subtle flavours emerge and the wine deepens to a dark amber colour—Moscatel can be aged as much as 80 years.

Red wines are less famous but still excellent; those made with the Periquita grape have a silky texture tempered by a robust body and perfectly complement Azeitão cheese.

Tourist Information

Park Office

Head office, Praça da República, Setúbal (𝄢 265 524032), Monday to Friday only; www.icn.pt/parques/pna/pna.html.

Tourist Offices

Regional tourist office, Travessa Frei Gaspar 10, Setúbal, just off Avenida Luisa Todi (𝄢 265 539120).

Municipal tourist office Praça do Quebedo, Setúbal, near the local train station (𝄢 265 534222).

Transport

Public transport within the park is limited to the service from Sétubal to Sesimbra, which stops at Vila Nogueira de Azeitão; about 20 buses daily. From Lisbon, take the ferry to Cacilhas from Cais do Sodré station, then catch a local bus to Azeitão. Information about public transport in Azeitão is limited, so pick up a timetable in Setúbal or Cacilhas.

Money

Cashpoints in Setúbal and Azeitão; larger banks in Setúbal.

Accommodation

Picheleiros, 3km from Vila Nogueira do Azeitão, signposted from the N10 (𝄢 212 181322). Shop, café-bar; open year round.

$ Pensão Bom Regresso, Praça de Bocage, Setúbal (𝄢 265 29812).

$ Residencial Todi, Avenida Luísa Todi 244, Setúbal (𝄢 265 20592).

$$ Residencial Bocage, Rua de São Cristóvão 14, Setúbal (tel 265 21598).

$$ Residencial Setúbalense, Rua do Major Afonso Pala 17, Setúbal (𝄢 265 525790).

$$$ Albergaria Solaris, Praça Marquês de Pombal 12, Setúbal (𝄢 265 522189).

$$$$ Quinta das Torres, Vila Fresca de Azeitão, opposite the modern José Maria de Fonseca winery just east of Vila Nogueira de Azeitão on the N10 (𝄢 212 180001).

$$$$ Pousada da Palmela, Palmela (𝄢 212 351226).

Shopping

There are a number of well-stocked mini mercados in Azeitão, but head for the Pingo Doce on Avenida Luisa Todi in Setúbal if you need anything out of the ordinary. The small market on the main street in Azeitão is the best place to find fruit and vegetables, and on the first Sunday of each month there is a huge produce and craft market in town.

Events & Festivals

Feira da Santiago (Setúbal, last week of July & first week of August), the biggest agricultural and industrial fair in the region, includes craft markets, traditional folklore and bullfights; **Festas das Vindimas** (Palmela, first week in September), annual wine festival complete with fireworks and barefoot wine stomping; **Festas da Semana Sadina** (Setúbal, week around 15th September); **Festa do Espírito Santo** (Azeitão, 1 November), Azeitão's big annual event, in honour of Nossa Senhora da Arrábida.

31. Vila Nogueira de Azeitão

Fast Facts

distance 9km	rating easy
time 3 hours	map 454 (1:25,000)
centre map page 30	

Vila Nogueira de Azeitão is an attractive town dominated by the local wine industry, in particular the cellars of José Maria da Fonseca, which are open to the public and well worth a visit. The surrounding land to the sheltered north of the Serra da Arrábida is wine-growing country, and although many of the old quintas are no longer used for growing grapes their grand and imposing houses often remain.

Elsewhere, the land is dramatically barren with a haphazard network of red dirt roads favoured by local mountain bikers. The route is well-marked with red and yellow equal signs (=); wrong turns are marked by a cross (X). The walk passes near the campsite at Picheleiros and can start and finish there, but the description below begins and ends in Azeitão.

The walk begins at Rua Helena da Conceicão dos Santos é Silva, the road that climbs steeply uphill between the José Maria da Fonseca cellars and the police station. Save the wine visit for the end of the walk in summer, as this initial climb is steep, hot and lacks shade. The road changes to a track shortly after you pass a wooden map announcing that you're now within the boundaries of the Parque Natural da Arrábida; keep to this track as it climbs up and over the Alto da Madalena ridge. The

views behind you across the Rio Tejo to Lisbon are stunning and the huge Rio-like statue of Cristo Rei towering above the Ponte 25 de Abril is impressive even from 30km away. The bright red bridge opened in 1966 as the Ponte Salazar but was swiftly renamed to commemorate the revolution that deposed his regime. The track goes downhill past the Quinta da Alto da Madalena and arrives at a narrow tarmac road in 2.5km.

Turn right at this road, then take the dirt road off to the right 100m later. (Campers should continue along this road, which leads to the Picheleiros campsite in 300m.) The badly eroded dirt road climbs steeply uphill through pine and eucalyptus. At the top of the climb, take the right hand fork, following the red and yellow markers. The route here follows a ridge along a wide dirt track popular with lycra-clad mountain bikers and there are good views along the Ribeira da Ajuda valley. After following the ridge for a while you emerge into a hollow. Look out for the red and yellow markers on the trees here; the trail out of the hollow is the first one on your right. At a T-junction 200m later, turn right, then turn sharp right again at a crossroads a little further ahead. Forestry and farm tracks criss-cross this part of the walk, and although most of them aren't marked on the 1:25,000 map each junction is clearly marked with a red and yellow sign. Turn right at a junction 300m after the crossroads, then turn left in another 50m.

The Serra da Arrábida behind you is an impressive backdrop while ahead you can see the rocky outcrop at the western edge of the Alto da Madalena, topped by some impressively enormous quintas. Just 50m later, turn right to follow a narrow path through patches of broom and heather. When this emerges at a wide track lined with cork oaks, turn left and follow the track for 300m, then turn right to head across a clearing towards the bottom of the rocky outcrop.

The trail climbs steeply up this outcrop for about 50m, then meets a gravel road; turn right here. Views of the Serra da Arrábida are excellent from this vantage point, and there's a chance of seeing peregrine falcons and other birds of prey over the mountain range. Turn left 50m after joining the gravel road to continue uphill, ignoring the turning to the right at the Quinta do Santo António a little further on. Once you reach the top of the ridge there are more fabulous views over to Lisbon. Slowly, the track becomes more developed with street lights and houses until you eventually emerge at the road to Vila Nogueira de Azeitão. Turn right here, and follow the road for 1.5km into Azeitão, passing some ornate quintas along the way.

The town is a good place to stock up on food, in particular at the tiny, colourful produce market on the main street; there are also some great cafés and a few good restaurants. Most visitors, however, come here for the wine. The José Maria da Fonseca wine cellars are an ideal place to sample the region's famous Moscatel dessert wine, although if its sweetness is not to your taste, the town's wine shops also stock a range of local reds and whites.

Quick Quiz

What are Portugal's renowned tiles called?

(answer on p 184)

---

32. Picheleiros

Fast Facts

distance 3km	rating easy to moderate
time 1 hour	maps 454, 465 (1:25,000)
centre map page 31	

This walk provides a sedate way to appreciate the hulking massif of the Serra da Arrábida, by far the most spectacular and recognizable feature in the Parque Natural da Arrábida.

Its higher reaches are designated a special botanical reserve, and walkers must get permission from the park office in Setúbal to tackle its challenging scree slopes.

Begin the walk by turning right out of the campsite at Picheleiros (to get here from Vila Nogueira de Azeitão, see p 172). Walk along this narrow, undulating road for about a kilometre, passing old quintas and vineyards, until you reach a crossroads. Turn right here to follow a dirt road heading steeply uphill. Pass a couple more quintas and turn right after 200m, then take the left-hand junction 200m further on at the Quinta do Aloendro, climbing steeply all the time.

The track begins to go downhill but soon flattens out, revealing spectacular views of the Serra da Arrábida. Genets and badgers live in this area of the park, although both these nocturnal animals are notoriously difficult to spot. You're more likely to see bird life; look out for the boldly colourful bee-eater perching on bushes and Bonelli's eagles flying above the Serra. The trail heads downhill once more, then curves around to cross a small stream. Soon afterwards look out for a post marked with red and yellow paint on

your right, and take the small, left-hand dirt track going steeply uphill here; if you reach a white house, retrace your steps as you've gone too far.

This track reaches a clearing in 50m then curves around to the right. The track here is narrower and can sometimes be overgrown, although it is easy to find and occasionally marked with red and yellow paint. The short, dense scrub here carpets most of the Serra da Arrábida and provides good cover for small mammals and birds. Continue along this track for a few hundred metres until you round a right-hand bend and come to a fork; take the left hand fork on to a smaller, narrower path (a red arrow painted on a tree points the way). The track soon widens as it passes a corrugated iron hut and crosses a small valley floor.

This is another excellent place to see songbirds, especially if you wander off on to one of the many narrow paths that climb the mountain range. In 200m you reach a T-junction with a dirt road. Turn right here, and stay on the main road following the red and yellow markers; they will lead you back to the campsite in about 600m.

33. Portinho da Arrábida

Fast Facts

distance 7km	rating moderate
time 3 hours	map 465 (1:25,000)
centre map page 31	

Portinho da Arrábida is a pretty fishing village complete with restaurants serving fantastic seafood dishes, and with excellent beaches nearby. High above it, the Convento da Arrábida hugs the slopes of the Serra da Arrábida with panoramic sea views.

Although the former Franciscan monastery is now private property, visits can be booked at the tourist office in Setúbal. Between the monastery and the village lies the prehistoric cave of Lapa da Santa Margarida, a bizarre sea-lapped grotto complete with a huge modern shrine inside.

The walk begins at a dirt track about 50m west of the entrance to the Convento da Arrábida. There is some parking available here at the side of the road; those without their own transport might want to consider renting bicycles in Setúbal for the sometimes steep but stunning ride to the monastery, as public transport doesn't come this way. Even if you miss out the monastery, it's worth taking a look at the tiny chapels that stretch in a line towards the ridge of the Serra da Arrábida. The chapels' double purpose was to represent the stations of the cross and, on a more mundane level, to provide shelter for meditating monks. Construction, which began in the mid-seventeenth century, was both haphazard and half-hearted; of the

strange mix of circular, octagonal and square buildings, only one was ever completed.

Follow the dirt track downhill for just 40m, then take the steep dirt path to your right at the second bend, signposted Caminho da Praia. This is the most tricky part of the walk as the path here is extremely steep. After 150m the path emerges on to an old cart track overhanging with branches and stone paving still visible in places. This turning can be hard to find on the way back, so it's a good idea to mark the junction with twigs or leaves. Views open up here, down to the fishing boats at Portinho da Arrábida, out towards the narrow, overdeveloped Tróia peninsula, and beyond densely wooded slopes to the sea.

After about 750m, the track emerges at a tarmac road. Turn left here, then turn right about 20m later down the side road signposted Portinho da Arrábida. Follow this quiet road for 500m until you see a huge white house on your left. Turn down the lane on the opposite side of the road to the house,

175

then take the path off to the left 20m further on just before a set of iron gates. Follow the concrete steps down to the breathtakingly clear water where caves await the brave explorer. The largest of these is the Lapa da Santa Margarida, a damp, vast cavern where traces of human occupation dating back to the Palaeolithic era have been found. On one side the cave is open to the sea, while at the back, stalactites jostle for attention with an incongruous shrine to Santa Margarida.

Retrace your steps back to the road, and turn right to continue to the beach. At the edge of Portinho da Arrábida the old fort has been converted into an oceanography museum (closed Mondays). At Portinho da Arrábida there is a small harbour lined with identikit restaurants serving excellent seafood—try the caldeirada (fish stew), a local speciality. You can turn around here or keep walking through the village, following the lane along to the Praia da Anixa. The beach can get fairly crowded with summer tourists, although it's much more pleasant here than at the ugly over-developed beach just across the water on the Tróia Peninsula.

Follow the road that leads uphill at the far end of the beach, looking out for the Roman fish salting works about halfway up. The salt works are a good turnaround point, although those in search of a decent beach should continue to the main road, then turn right to go to Praia da Galapos, a beautiful spot for swimming or sunbathing.

On the way back, it can be hard to find the path up to the monastery—it's about 20m to the left of the junction and difficult to notice until you're almost on top of it. Be careful, too, near the top of the climb. When the path becomes closed in above you by trees and bushes, look out for the sharp left-hand turning leading steeply uphill; this is the well-worn but very steep section that began the walk, and will soon lead you back to the Convento da Arrábida.

Other walks

There are a number of marked trails in the Parque Natural da Arrábida area. Shorter walks include a stroll along the Roman road west of Setúbal, beginning at the Pousada de São Filipe in town. The *Caminhos* book (p 168) also describes the Grande Rota, a 25km hike across the length of the park, from Santana in the northwest to Palmela in the northeast. This walk passes through the campsite at Picheleiros, making a relaxed two-day hike feasible, although it misses out the interesting town of Azeitão and the coastal edges of the park.

You need permission from the park office to visit the heights of the Serra da Arrábida, a special biological reserve with stunning views all around. Alternatively, avoid dealing with the park bureaucracy yourself by visiting the steep and challenging scree slopes on a guided walk with SAL (p 169).

The park office in Setúbal also acts as the headquarters for the Reserva Natural do Estuário do Sado, and a similar *Caminhos* book is produced for this area. The reserve was created to protect the wetlands around the Sado estuary and river, and stretches from Setúbal as far south as Alcácer do Sal (see p 177). It's hard to see much evidence of wildlife protection along a coastline dominated by industrial monstrosities and insensitive tourist development projects, and walking in the area is limited to brief strolls between factories and hotel complexes. Despite all this the area boasts a rich and varied wildlife and is an important habitat for migratory birds—flamingos are a common sight in autumn and winter and white storks stay for the spring and summer.

Resident species include the bottlenose dolphin, ubiquitous on posters for the reserve and for estuary tour groups but in reality down to less than 50 animals as industrial and agricultural development increases. Many of the short walks in the *Caminhos* book meander along old salt pans, an economic mainstay of the area since Roman times.

Further west, take a blustery walk at Cabo Espichel, the southernmost point of the Setúbal peninsula. Here, the rugged cliffs drop suddenly and dramatically hundreds of feet to the choppy waters below. Stroll from the ruined Santuário de Nossa Senhora do Cabo, a 17th century church with an azulejo-panelled chapel, down to the Praia dos Lagosteiros where dinosaur footprints are fossilized into the rock.

Rainy day options

The Setúbal peninsula only appears on tourist itineraries as a stop en route from Lisbon to the beaches of the Algarve, although it attracts a lot of day-trippers from the capital.

In Vila Fresca de Azeitão, visit the gardens of the Quinta da Bacalhao, a sumptuous early example of Renaissance architecture. The formal box-hedged grounds were begun in the 16th century when the quinta was bought by the well-travelled Brás de Albuquerque, son of the first viceroy of India, and have been sympathetically restored in the last few decades after many years of neglect.

Alburquerque's itchy feet and classical education are reflected in the designs of the azulejo-lined formal garden paths, which show scenes from Africa and the Middle East, biblical stories and Greek mythology. The quinta's main tourist magnet is the oldest dated azulejo panel in Portugal (1565), housed in a pavilion in the grounds. It depicts the biblical story of Susannah and the Elders, in which the married Susannah was falsely accused of promiscuity by two elders whose advances she had spurned; the truth of the matter was uncovered by Daniel when the elders, interviewed separately, told conflicting stories.

Towns in the region are generally low on tourist sites. Setúbal has a smattering of churches, including the Igreja de Jesus, one of the earliest examples of Manueline architecture in Portugal. A more interesting and less crowded choice is the splendidly faded estuary town of Alcácer do Sal, which climbs in narrow cobbled alleyways from the sea to the magnificent vantage point of its modest castle. The castle itself is built on 5000-year old foundations, and the town's salt industry has been run at various times by Greeks, Phoenicians and Romans. Despite its long history, Alcácer is a quiet place where nothing much happens except for three days around the first Saturday in October, when the annual agricultural and industrial fair takes over the town and everyone dances, watches bullfights and generally overindulges.

❓ Quick Reference

Reading

This is a selection of our favourite books about Portugal. Visit your local independent bookshop for other suggestions, or contact one of the following (most of which have given Ben a job at some point in his life):

Stanfords, 12–14 Long Acre, London WC2E 9LP; ✆ 020 7836 1321;www.stanfords.co.uk

The Travel Bookshop, 13–15 Blenheim Cres, W11 2EE; ✆ 020 7229 5260

Wanderlust, 1929 West 4th Ave, Vancouver, BC, V6J 1M7, Canada; ✆ 604 739 2182

Traveler's Bookstore, 22 W 52nd St, NY 10019, USA; ✆ 212 664 0995

Wildlife

Laurence Rose, *Where to Watch Birds in Spain and Portugal* (Hamlyn).

Oleg Polunin and B E Smythies, *Flowers of South-West Europe*(Oxford University Press).

Travel

Take your pick. Rough Guides are best for the north and out of the way places, Lonely Planet is good for Lisbon and the south. Eyewitness Guides includes lots of detail on tourist sights, and the Blue Guide has solid, detailed information on Portugal's history.

Food & Drink

Jean Anderson, *The Food of Portugal* (Hearst Books).

Richard Mayson, *Port and the Douro* (Faber and Faber).

Jan Read, *The Wines of Spain and Portugal* (Faber & Faber). Out of print.

Edite Vieira, *The Taste of Portugal* (Grub Street, USA).

Literature

Carcanet Press (4th Floor, Conavon Court, Blackfriars Street. Manchester M3 5BQ; ✆ 0161 834 8730; www.carcanet.co.uk) is a prolific publisher of Portuguese literature. Contact them for their latest catalogue.

Eça de Queiroz, *The Mandarin and other Stories* (Dedalus); *The Illustrious House of Ramires* (Quartet).

Fernando Pessoa, *The Book of Disquietude*; *A Centenary Pessoa* (Carcanet).

José Saramogo, *The Year of the Death of Ricardo Reis*; *The History of the Siege of Lisbon* (Harvill Press).

Miguel Torga, *The Creation of the World*; *Tales from the Mountain* (Carcanet).

Language

The Berlitz phrasebook is well worth taking, even if you only use it to decipher menus.

Maps

Michelin's *Portugal*, at a scale of 1:400,000, is a good road map of the country.

For Portugal on the Internet, see our website at www.pilipalapress.com

Language

In this brief vocabulary section, we've included English to **Portuguese** translations, together with a *phonetic* rendition of the word.

Basics

yes	**sim**	*seem*	no	**não**	*nawm*
hello	**olá**	*o-lah*	goodbye	**adeus**	*er-day-oosh*

please	**se faz favor**	*ser fazh fer-voar*
thank you	**obrigado/a**	*ob-ree-gard-oo/ah* (men say oo, women say ah)
good morning	**bom dia**	*bawm dee-er*

Do you speak English?	**Fala inglês?**	*Fa-ler eeng-layzh*
I don't speak Portuguese	**Não fala portugês**	*Nawm fer-ler poor-too-gayzh*
I (don't) understand	**(Não) compreendo**	*(Nawm) Kawm-pree-ayn-doo*
How much?	**Cuanto custa?**	*Kwan-too koosh-ter*
Where is ... ?	**Onde está?**	*Ond-er ish-tah*
I'd like ...	**Queria ...**	*Ker-ree-er*
Do you have any rooms?	**Tem quartos vagos?**	*Taym kwar-toosh vag-oosh*

Useful Walking Phrases

What's the weather forecast?	**Quais são as previsões do tempo?**	*Kighsh sawm ash prer-veez-oysh der taym-poo*
How do I get to?	**Como se vai para?**	*Ko-mo ser vay per-er*
What village is this?	**Que aldeia é esta?**	*Ker al-day-er ay ish-tah*
How far is the next village?	**A que distância fica a próxima aldeia?**	*A ker dist-an-cia fee-ker ah prox-eem-a al-day-er*
Where does this road/path lead?	**Para onde vai esta estrada/este caminho?**	*Per-er ond-er vigh ish-tar estr-ah-der/ish-ter cam-een-yoo*
Is it near here?	**É perto dáqui?**	*Ay per-too dah-kee*
I'm lost	**Perdi-me**	*Perdee mer*

right	**direita**	*dee-ray-ter*	left	**esquerda**	*ish-ker-der*
near	**perto de**	*per-too der*	far	**longe de**	*lon-ghe der*
cold	**frio**	*free-oo*	hot	**quente**	*kaynt*
rain	**chover**	*shoo-ver*	snow	**nevar**	*ner-var*
cloudy	**nublado**	*noo-bla-doo*	windy	**vento**	*ven-too*
thunder	**trovão**	*tro-vawm*	sun	**sol**	*sol*

Quick Reference

Days, Months & Numbers

today	hoje
tommorrow	amanhã
yesterday	ontem
Monday	segunda-feira
Tuesday	terça-feira
Wednesday	quarta-feira
Thursday	quinta-feira
Friday	sexta-feira
Saturday	sábado
Sunday	domingo

1	um (a)
2	dois (duas)
3	três
4	quatro
5	cinco
6	seis
7	sete
8	oito
9	nove
10	dez
20	vinte
30	trinta

40	quarenta
50	cinquenta
60	sessenta
70	setenta
80	oitenta
90	noventa
100	cem
200	duzentos
300	trezentos
1000	mil

January	Janeiro
February	Fevreiro
March	Março
April	Abril
May	Maio
June	Junho
July	Julho
August	Agosto
September	Setembro
November	Novembro
December	Dezembro

Glossary

Some unfamiliar or Portuguese words used in our walk descriptions or found on maps

shepherd stones	pile of stones used to mark a route
quinta	country estate, vineyard or large house
azulejo	glazed, painted tile (p 11)
casa abrigo	mountain shelter
espigueiro	stilted grain storage structure

caminho	path	estrada	road	montanha	mountain
rio	river	ribeira	stream	lago	lake
albufeira	reservoir	ponte	bridge	cume	summit

Key to area maps

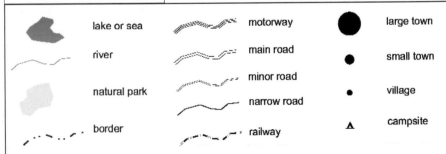

- lake or sea
- river
- natural park
- border
- motorway
- main road
- minor road
- narrow road
- railway
- large town
- small town
- village
- campsite

180

Index

Quick Quiz Answers

1. None. He never left Portugal.
2. 1993m (Torre)
3. 1755
4. 1974
5. 1935
6. 1911
7. Vintage port years
8. 12 strings (6 double strings)
9. 927km
10. 1762
11. 10.5 million
12. 85%
13. 20%
14. June 10th
15. azulejos

Oops! #5-15 should read #4-14 there are two question #4's.